Rooted in Place

Rooted in Place

Family and Belonging in a Southern Black Community

William W. Falk

Rutgers University Press

New Brunswick, New Jersey, and London

Library of Congress Cataloging-in-Publication Data

Falk, William W.
   Rooted in place : family and belonging in a southern black community /
William W. Falk.
      p. cm.
Includes bibliographical references and index.
   ISBN 0–8135–3464–X (hardcover : alk. paper) — ISBN 0–8135–3465–8
(pbk. : alk. paper)
   1. African Americans—South Carolina—Social life and customs. 2. African
Americans—Georgia—Social life and customs. 3. African American families—
South Carolina. 4. African American families—Georgia. 5. Home—South
Carolina. 6. Home—Georgia. 7. Family—South Carolina. 8. Family—Georgia.
9. South Carolina—Social life and customs. 10. Georgia—Social life and
customs. I. Title.

E185.93.S7F35 2004
975.7'0049607301734—dc22

                                  2004000302

A British Cataloging-in-Publication record for this book is available from the
British Library.

Manufactured in the United States of America

Contents

Acknowledgments   *vii*

Introduction A Brief Autobiographical Note   *1*

One A Region, a Place, a Man   *11*

Two The World of Work—as Experienced and Interpreted
by Older Men   *27*

Three Strong Women   *51*

Four What Did You Learn in School Today?   *73*

Five In the Lord's House   *100*

Six Race and Everyday Life   *118*

Seven Home Is Where the Heart Is   *144*

Eight The Power of Place   *172*

Appendix   Some Notes on Methods, the Study Site,
and Emergent Theory   *191*

Notes   *201*
Index   *217*

Acknowledgments

All books reflect the work of far more persons than the author. I was helped early in my career, and for a long time during it, by support from the U.S. Department of Agriculture. As I began the initial fieldwork for this book, I received support from the American Sociological Association's Fund for the Advancement of the Discipline. I also received support from the University of Maryland's General Research Board program. I have always felt fortunate to be a faculty member at the University of Maryland, especially its College of Behavioral and Social Sciences and its Department of Sociology. Here I benefited from support of one kind or another rendered by the dean's office—especially by Irv Goldstein, Stew Edelstein, and Cindi Hale—and by the faculty, students, and staff in sociology, where my colleague Stanley Presser read an early draft of some of the book and pushed me hard for a major revision. I was assisted in a variety of ways by graduate students, including David Cotter, Liana Sayer, Gwyn Weathers, and especially Tony Hatch. And my administrative assistant, Wanda Towles, helped with numerous revisions.

The greatest influence on the book came from colleagues away from the university. Mil Duncan, Peggy Hargis, Gene Summers, and Susan Webb read earlier versions of the manuscript. My longtime pal, Tom Lyson, not only read an earlier version of the manuscript but also prodded me, over a number of years, to not give up and to "get it finished!" Sonya Salamon pushed me to rethink, reconceptualize, reorganize, and quite simply overhaul the manuscript. Her lengthy written comments were immensely important. But even with this kind of critical reading, I still had much to do—and consequently more people to thank, three in particular. First, David Myers was the social science editor at Rutgers University Press when I began to shop my manuscript. His initial enthusiasm and offer of a contract precluded my considering any other publisher. Second, an anonymous reviewer's critical reading was of significant help, not only in shaping a better story but in making it more sociological. Third, and most important, after Kristi Long replaced David Myers at Rutgers, she in effect made me redo my manuscript from start to finish. I went from anger to grudging acceptance to full-blown appreciation for this; Kristi's interest in the project and criticism of it made for a much better book. Carol Stack was the last person to read the manuscript before I returned the final revised version. She helped me clarify some things, and her enthusiasm led to our working together on a new title. Paula Friedman copyedited the manuscript; her outsider's view and writer's eye improved the book immensely and buoyed my hope for its success. Richard Weedman's help was crucial in getting permission to use Jonathan Green's beautiful art on the book's cover.

I must also make some more personal acknowledgments. No one cares more and prods me more unmercifully than my wife, Geraldine. As she has with other books of mine, she would often say, "Are you working on the book?" The librarians in Coastal City were always helpful with whatever requests I made as were those at the library in Colonial County. I am especially indebted to the people I spent time with in Colonial County, none more so than AC and his family. With or without their help, my research would have proceeded, but my time with them definitely made me reconsider my intellectual objectives.

I have chosen to dedicate this book to two people. First, AC never tired of my pestering him with questions, or of assisting me in ways large and small. My friendship with him evolves and continues. It is a great pleasure to dedicate this book to him, even if he must remain anonymous. I want also to dedicate this book to my former neighbor and Lowcountry friend, Robert Poetzman. Meeting as Maryland neighbors on a small island and discovering our joint passion for a particular Lowcountry place was one of life's little mysteries—so, too, was his unexpected and tragic death. To AC and Bob, two men unknown to each other but with much in common: having known you has enriched me immeasurably.

College Park, Maryland
March 2004

Rooted in Place

Introduction

A Brief Autobiographical Note

This book grew out of years of research on the American South, especially the rural South. It was the site of my doctoral dissertation nearly thirty years ago and it remains my primary interest today. Given my formative years, landing in the rural South and having a thirty-plus-year fascination with race may seem hard to explain.

I was raised in Michigan and graduated from a consolidated, rural high school. There was, to the best of my memory, only one black student, the daughter of a couple who ran the dump outside our small town. Although she was one of the best students in the school, I knew her only slightly and have no recollection of her at any social functions. Our athletic teams (of which I was often a member) competed against schools demographically carbon copies of ours—white. This, of course, was true for most white people of my generation.

All that my friends and I knew of people different from us, especially blacks and Jews, was that locally they lived in their own areas outside Detroit: Jews in Oak Park; blacks in River Rouge, Livonia, and the city proper. "Civil rights" was a term unknown to us at that time. We had our world, they had theirs. There were virtually no opportunities to meet on common ground. My first large-scale exposures to black people came from attending a Ray Charles concert at the old Ford Theater in Detroit and from joining the military. For me, the military was crucial. The base where I lived was racially integrated; this provided an everyday experience that was unique for me, and I played basketball for the army on a team that was racially integrated. Many of the other teams we played were also integrated. Because we traveled and spent so much time together, all assumptions about what I "knew" were readily challenged.

When I returned to the United States after serving in the military, I came home with a somewhat different outlook on our country and with a new British wife. I also came "home" to a new place, Texas, where my parents had moved while I was away. I had grown up hearing every racial and ethnic epithet one could imagine, but my wife hadn't. She thought Americans were very crude on the race issue and, not having grown up in fear of my father, she was willing to challenge him on his stereotypes. In time, so was I—not only because of my time out of the United States or because of my wife, but also because, when I began my undergraduate studies, I took a course in sociology. There, I was introduced to a much more complex way of thinking about the social world. Among the terms I learned that heavily influenced me was "ethnocentrism." This is the tendency to judge everything by the values we hold and to conclude that ours are right and everyone else's are wrong, that other cultures are backward, that our way is best. There is a dogmatism to this that makes individuals (and groups) block out, or be unwilling to consider, the world in its full complexity. This is particularly true for some religious groups, especially any to which the term "fundamentalist" is attached—be they Christians, Jews, or Muslims.

At the same time that I was wrestling with ethnocentrism, I was also learning about Charles Horton Cooley's concept "the looking-glass self."[1] This model posits that our selves are formed in large part in light of what others think of us; in time, we are what others want us to be. We try to meet their expectations. I was my father's and my culture's child, prejudices (which I still had), other preconceived notions, and all.

By the time I graduated from college (1969), I had lived through a revolution of sorts—the civil rights movement and the fledgling antiwar movement. Both were vivid demonstrations of the need to challenge prevailing norms and the values associated with them. For a young sociologist, it was all about power—who had it and how they used it. This background drew me to two things that have stuck ever since. First was an interest in race. This was clearest in my master's thesis on the Ku Klux Klan but also emerged in my first job as a research sociologist for the Dallas Independent School District, and eventually when I wrote my doctoral dissertation on school desegregation. Second was a strong belief in the power of C. Wright Mills's "sociological imagination,"[2] the closest I come to having a professional mantra or profession of faith. Mills, writing in the 1950s, felt that people needed a quality of mind to understand what was going on *outside* of them (in the larger society) so that they could understand what was going on *inside* (as they tried to make sense of these sometimes discrepant worlds). This mindset also required that individuals grapple with the intersection of their biography with history; phrased differently, you see the world in a certain way because of the circumstances into which you are born and the historical era in which you live. I was living through revolutionary movements, not the least inside my own head as I wrestled with the values I learned as a child and the values to which I was increasingly drawn, values that challenged those older ones.

Discovering the South

I had lived in Texas for ten years. There is an expression in Texas, "The South stops in Dallas and the West starts in Fort Worth." I was well aware of the South because I was living in it and because I was reading about it nearly daily in the newspaper (especially during the height of the civil rights activity). I also read a considerable amount of southern fiction. But when I began my doctoral dissertation on rural school desegregation and traveled extensively throughout rural East Texas, the South became a more real and raw thing. The sophistication (if I can call it that) of race in Dallas in the early 1970s was replaced by truly stark racial differences in the areas I visited. And I was lucky to have a wonderful tour guide of sorts, a native southerner who served as my dissertation advisor, Art Cosby. Especially through his sponsorship, I got to work on a regional research project that focused on the South. This work continued when I joined the faculty at Louisiana State University as a young assistant professor.

As a direct result of this project, I met my longtime friend and collaborator, Tom Lyson. Together, we decided to write a book about the changes we were witnessing in the South during the 1970s and 1980s.[3] It was a time during which the media gave considerable coverage to the "New South." This was widely thought of as an economically dynamic, demographically changing, more socially progressive South. But Tom and I wondered: How widespread was this "New South"? Our experience and sociologically informed sense was that there were really two Souths—the new one, which got so much fanfare in the media, and the old one, where (in nearly all ways) things were pretty much what they had been all along. When we wrote our book, we tried to geographically capture this with a series of regional distinctions. Besides the obvious rural and urban areas, we knew, one area was truly unique to the South: the Black Belt. This consisted of counties with either majority African American populations or racial proportions that are markedly different from what one would expect. (For example, in 2000, Jefferson County, Mississippi, was 87 percent black.) This demographic reality was bound to be related to other social forces, to include economic inequalities. And when we ran our analyses, the Black Belt and its residents fared the poorest in a region (the rural South) that nearly everyone thought decidedly poor.

After we completed our book, I continued to write about historically black counties, but my new job (as chair of the Sociology Department at the University of Maryland) slowed my research. When I stepped down as chair in 1996, I was determined to write a book specifically about historically black counties. My time as an administrator had dulled but not killed my passion for the subject!

Some Notes on Methodology and Serendipity

I had lived in and written about the South for nearly all my adult life. So when I set out to write a book about historically black counties, I knew quite a bit about them. The book I had in mind was a social history using census data back into the 1800s. Considerable time and energy was spent (especially by my graduate students) on organizing the data and I was confident that an important book would result. But I also knew, from my earlier work with Tom Lyson, that I did not want to write a book that would be read only by academicians. Instead, I wanted to write a book that would be accessible to a general readership, in part because "the story," as I came to call it, would intrigue them. But what would this story focus on? I knew much about the scholarly literature on the "great migration" of African Americans who left the South in hopes of better lives elsewhere. There is a huge literature on this in the social sciences.[4] Much to my surprise, there was far less known or written about the question I decided to pose: why didn't all African Americans leave the South? As historian Jimmie Franklin[5] has said, "The problem in studying the black migration is that few scholars have examined systematically why many of the blacks best equipped to leave the South often did not. . . . The point is that cultural issues related to non-racial features of the American South and to regional attachment had a direct bearing on black southerners' decision to remain at home" (220). So, who stayed and what were their lives like in a place that so many people, including social scientists, assumed was so bad?

My plan was to pursue this question with census data. But because I also wanted to write a readable book, I thought it would be helpful to visit some historically black counties and collect people's stories about their lives there. I envisioned, initially, visiting three counties—one in the Mississippi Delta (the most widely catalogued and written about part of the Black Belt), one in the central South (running across the middle of Georgia, Alabama, and Mississippi), and one in the Lowcountry (the coastal marshy area of South Carolina and Georgia). I had access to these places through academic colleagues at regional universities.

Much to my surprise, my trip started and ended in one place, Colonial County (a fictitious name) in the Lowcountry. It was an odd choice in some ways, mostly because it is not a cotton county or replete with plantations (although, to be sure, there were some) that so neatly fit the stereotype of the rural South in which many black people still live. Indeed, nearly five million African Americans live in the rural South and many, not too surprisingly, live in what were cotton counties, cotton being a crop that went out of production in many places only to return more recently. The Lowcountry, however, is not cotton country, and it has its own unique history of African American settlements.

Aside from wanting to visit this area because of its geography and economic uniqueness (falling outside the more well known and written-about cotton and plantation areas), I was (fortuitously) influenced by two books, anthropologist Carol Stack's *Call to Home*[6] and writer Melissa Faye Green's *Praying for Sheetrock*.[7] Each tells a story about African Americans in the Lowcountry. Stack's book focuses on African Americans returning "home" (to the rural South) from migration to other places. Green's book focuses on the conflict between a powerful white sheriff and a local black man, a man who eventually decides to run for public office and confront the sheriff and all that the sheriff stands for—historical racism and a dominant white power structure in a county that was majority black.

Like Stack and Green, I was curious about race and everyday life in a historically black place. I had no sense of antagonists and protagonists (as one finds in Green's book) or of the role played by return migrants (as in Stack's book). Instead, I simply wanted to spend a little time chatting with local people to find out what their lives had been like in this historically black place, and why, more specifically, they had never left, as so many others did.

My single greatest stroke of luck in this entire journey was being introduced to someone from Colonial County, an African American student at a regional university. She expressed a willingness to assist me, at first by introducing me to her grandparents. After several meandering conversations with them, it was clear that her grandfather, a man I call AC, was very knowledgeable about the county and willing to help me. He represented the age group in which I was interested (people over sixty years old) and could introduce me to other older people, the generation who had made a choice to stay rather than leave when leaving was a very common thing to do.

Initially, I spent three months in Colonial County. Subsequently, I returned at least once a year for several years. By now, I have traveled every road, paved and unpaved; visited in people's homes; gone into many of the stores, the library, city hall, and other similar places. I read every publication I could find about the county and the region, all made available to me at the local public library. I also read the local newspaper, mostly on microfiche, back to its beginning, over one hundred years ago.

My "sample" of local people was definitely not random but, rather, purposive. AC introduced me to many of his relatives, including his siblings, children, and former wife. Through AC, I also got access to elected officials and others in the county. And, of course, I spoke in passing with other people—black and white, young and old—as I made my way around the county and in neighboring counties. The impressions I formed were based on all these, but mostly from time with AC's family and especially AC. His voice, reported or not, is heavy in this book.[8]

In that way, this volume is akin to Theodore Rosengarten's *All God's Dangers*.[9] Rosengarten went to Alabama to interview some older African Americans about their lives in the South. Instead, he wound up writing a book based on lengthy interviews—much of the book's text—with one person. Like myself, he started out with one aim and shifted his focus somewhat, given the opportunity. This is precisely what happens to many who do "field research," who actually go out and talk to people. One can never know ahead of time what people might say or where it might lead. This uncharted territory makes the work spontaneous, exciting, and, to be candid, a little worrisome since the researcher has less than full control.

In some larger presociological sense, I was guided by Studs Terkel's approach to dealing with people—just let them talk long enough and they almost always say some really interesting things. It was well into my time in Colonial County before I realized how little time I had ever previously spent simply talking with people as research subjects. My career was much like that of most sociologists, using secondary data and computerized statistical programs. For once, I thought, I will actually talk to the people in whom I have been interested from afar. I will visit them in their own places, trying to discover what their lives are like. And I did.

A Methodological Caveat

Like most sociologists of my generation, I was neither trained in nor a practitioner of ethnography. However, I had read about it as a student, taught about it in my courses, and read ethnographic accounts on a wide range of sociological topics; indeed, some of the most widely read and, not coincidentally, readable books in sociology are ethnographies.[10] In short, the basic principles and practices common to ethnographic fieldwork were known to me, and, to be sure, ethnography is, like playing the piano, something learned by doing.

Given my general sense of ethnographic accounts (at the time, two in particular: Carol Stack's *Call to Home* and Mitchell Duneier's *Slim's Table*),[11] I felt that I could comfortably discuss with strangers their lives and experiences. I was assisted in my self-confidence by conversations with several friends and colleagues, key among them my good friend, anthropologist/ rural sociologist Sonya Salamon; her good friend (to whom she referred me), Carol Stack, who spoke with me about fieldwork in general but also, more particularly, about being a white researcher in an historically black place; sociologist, southern native, writer about the South, and longtime southern resident Peggy Hargis; my colleague, ethnographer Lory Dance;

and writer Melissa Faye Greene, another white outsider who had also spent time in the Lowcountry. From these people, I was told that I would be well accepted if I simply acted like "myself." This was especially reassuring to hear from Lory Dance, an African American, who told me that being "genuine" would go a long way toward winning people's confidence and trust.

There is well-known concern expressed in the social science literature about white researchers in black communities. Do people really tell them what is on their minds or not? During my time in Colonial County, I never felt that people were telling me things I might want to hear rather than the truth. People always seemed very open and honest in their stories. I never probed into personal things (e.g., someone's divorce or legal problems). In fact, I deflected them or tried to sidestep them if they arose. I did as my tutors had suggested: I asked local people what kinds of questions they would ask if they were me. I listened carefully. I took good notes. I did all of my own transcribing and reviewed my notes at the end of each day. I noted the most significant things learned, and then asked, in subsequent meetings, about those things.

But, I am an older, white man. Although I am confident that people were very candid in what they told me, it is certainly the case that other researchers—African Americans or members of other nonwhite racial/ethnic groups or women—would ask questions different from mine and, no doubt, learn things I did not. My initial questions were almost exclusively about residential history. Inevitably, though, other issues arose—issues about work, school, religion, family life, and the myriad of seemingly mundane things that make up everyday life.

There is no doubt that much of what I asked, observed, and interpreted was influenced by who I am: not just a white, middle-aged man but someone who for years has had a passion for all things southern, from *bar-b-que* in Texas to *barbecue* in North Carolina; from buttermilk biscuits in Alabama to beaten biscuits in Maryland; from redfish and oysters in Mississippi to rockfish and "ersters" in Virginia; from the Blue Ridge Mountains to the barrier island beaches; from the jazz and blues music in the Delta to "good ole Rocky Top" in Tennessee; from the "Texas two-step" and "Fais Do-Do" in one part of the South to clogging in another part; from the dialects of white people in Appalachia to radically different voices on the Outer Banks; from the dialects of black people, speaking "gullah" or "geechee" or "flat" or "country" on the East Coast to those of other blacks speaking "Cajun" or "Creole" in Louisiana; from the literature of such North Carolinians as Reynolds Price and Kate Gibbons, such Mississippians as Eudora Welty and Barry Hannah, or such Georgians as Alice Walker or the younger Tina Ansa to, going back in time, the writings of Joel Chandler Harris, who authored the "Uncle Remus" and "Brer Rabbit" stories, based on slave narratives. To be sure, all of these things influenced me, *as me,* in what I set out to do and how I did it, in what I asked and of whom I asked it.

I have continued to read anything remotely related to African Americans and migration, settlement patterns, religion, family, and so on. Collectively, my time in Colonial County and my reading have made me even more comfortable about what I did and the story I have told. The story is heavily dependent upon, and told in, the voices of local people. It is also told, as much as possible, exactly as it was told to me. This is crucial, and requires a brief explanation.

A Note on Language

Many African Americans in the Lowcountry have a pronounced dialect, called sometimes "gullah," sometimes "geechee." The former refers most often to the dialect of South Carolina, the latter to that of Georgia. In either case, it is a local patois that takes some getting used to, a patois most common among older, longtime residents, least common among young people and new residents. Certain words are pronounced, and certain grammar is used, in ways that may seem technically incorrect from the vantage point of formal, standard English. I have tried hard to render this in a way that allows the reader to hear what I heard; I believe strongly that this is an important part of the story being told. The tale is told in the *actor's* words, not ones I might substitute to make them sound, by some measures, better. None of us sound in everyday speech as we would if we were to write what we wished to say. On the other hand, I have not quoted "uhs" and other pauses, except where these seemed to reflect truly pensive moments. In reading other ethnographic accounts of African Americans in the Lowcountry, a similar rendering is found.[12]

And So . . .

In this book I have tried to paint a picture that depicts life in a generally overlooked place (a historically black county); a place (representative of all historically black counties) that has given birth to a large part of the American population; a place inhabited by Native Americans before the Pilgrims, America's other "founders," arrived; a place so unique and so much a part of American history that it is hard to believe that it is nearly undiscovered, and little understood, by most social scientists and the general public; a place that begs for our attention even while remaining overlooked; a place (like most rural places) off the interstate and so mostly off the map, figuratively and literally, for most of us.

Although I am not a native southerner, I have lived all my adult life in the South. I am *from* there at the same time that I am, to some immeasurable degree, *of* the place. For better or worse, it is part of me. It continues to fascinate me. I have lived "in" it for upwards of forty years, hence I am "of" it, even if by my own choosing. John Shelton Reed, surely sociology's most well known Southerner and scholar on the South, has said, "I suspect sociology needs more Southerners, real ones or spiritual ones, . . . to tell sociological stories about particular people, particular groups, particular societies. And interesting stories they could be."[13] Whether "real" or "spiritual," my sense of myself is primarily "southern." I can only hope that mine is an "interesting" story. It is a "story," I felt, entrusted to me. My experience was much like John Egerton's, when he spent time with a similar (albeit white) family: "gradually over those weeks and months, a bond formed between us. . . . They were the narrators, the historians, the deliverers of an ancient and contemporary human record; I was the conduit, the vessel for their story's survival and safekeeping."[14]

Mine is a story emphasizing the African American population as represented by one family in one community, in one rural county. Despite having what might seem a very limited study site and number of participants, inevitably I drift into issues that transcend these limits, issues that one finds in nearly all human communities in developed countries. Much like William Least Heat Moon,[15] I traveled the back roads. And paralleling his experience, not only what I was in search of captured my attention, but also those things that were unexpected.

And so, my story begins.

One

A Region, a Place, a Man

No region of the United States has been more written about and analyzed than the South. It is a place of great mystique and mystery, rough-edged and roguish on the one hand, magnolia-scented and charming on the other; a place of severe poverty and enormous wealth. It is a geography with everything from coastal oceans to mountain lakes; marsh grass and live oaks in one place, bluegrass and piney forests in another; oysters and shrimp on the coast, cotton and catfish inland; sophisticated urban cities, and rural areas constituting the greatest concentration of poverty in the United States.

Crisscrossing the region is a system of interstate highways. On the easternmost border is Interstate 95, one of America's busiest highways. It starts in Houlton, Maine, at the Canadian (New Brunswick) border, and runs the entire length of the East Coast, ending in Miami Beach. Along the way, it takes the traveler from the bucolic countryside of New England to the urban density and gridlock of Boston, New York, and Washington, D.C. As it enters Maryland, it crosses the Mason-Dixon line and, according to some people, enters the American South. But for many, a truer sense of having entered a new region of the country begins once "outside the Beltway" of Washington. The further into Virginia the traveler goes, the more southern things feel—from the ways people talk and interact to the stores one finds.[1]

Signs for "historic Williamsburg" (which used slaves imported at Jamestown) and for the Museum of the Confederacy in Richmond are further reminders. Once one crosses into North Carolina, cotton bolls start appearing in fields adjacent to the highway, and South Carolina brings signs for Charleston and for Georgia's coastal and equally southern-feeling counterpart, Savannah. Even nearly fifty miles inland from the coast, live oaks festooned with Spanish moss and occasional scenes of marsh grass are reminders of this gothic area that locals call "the Lowcountry."[2]

Given that the South's geography is so expansive, it is possible to find oneself in tremendously diverse circumstances. Places in the hills or mountains of Kentucky, Tennessee, or Georgia look different, and their people in fact sound different, than do those in other parts of the South. One of the most striking differences is that the northern parts of the region are also the whitest, with many counties having no African Americans or other minorities among their populations. One of the South's most unique subregions is largely unvisited and unknown to most southerners and those traveling through the region; this is an area called "the Black Belt."

The Black Belt

The Black Belt is the quintessential South. It has what is stereotypically the South's defining characteristic—plantations, with their slavery histories. Not coincidentally, the Black Belt still has a disproportionate number and percentage of the South's African American population. The Black Belt actually forms a crescent, beginning on Maryland's Eastern Shore and going down the Atlantic coast through the Tidewater of Virginia, the coastal (except the Outer Banks) and central areas of North Carolina, and the marshy Lowcountry of South Carolina and Georgia; it then heads west through the red clay hills of south-central Georgia (where farming replaces fishing), and on through the central parts of Alabama and Mississippi, before ending in the Mississippi Delta, with the Mississippi River's adjacent states (with contiguous counties), including the largest expanses of the Delta in Mississippi and Louisiana and lesser parts of Arkansas and Tennessee.

Sociologist Arthur Raper described the region well in the 1930s: "In the heart of the South, there are approximately 200 counties in which over half the population is Negro. These counties are like a crescent from Virginia to Texas and constitute the Black Belt. . . . The Black Belt includes the most fertile soil of the South, and contains a disproportionate number of its poorest people. The ownership of the best land is in the hands of a comparatively small group of white families; landlessness and chronic dependence is the lot of over half the white families and nearly nine-tenths of the colored."[3]

Over a half century later, little had changed. In the mid–1980s, Jim Auchmutey and Priscilla Painton, reporters for the *Atlanta Journal and Constitution*, put it this way: "Beyond the swelling suburbs of the modern South lies a land of rich soil and poor people, a crescent-shaped region stretching from the tobacco fields of Virginia to the cotton flats of the Mississippi Delta. This was slave country, sharecropper country, the wellspring of the great black exodus to the North and to cities such as Atlanta. Today the Black Belt is an abandoned land, avoided by industry, failed by agriculture, left behind by the rising black political class it spawned. By almost every measure—industry, income, infant mortality, education, poverty, housing—the Black Belt badly trails the rest of the rural South."[4] In other words, it is the poorest place in a region that has more than its fair share of poverty, and its poverty is as well-rooted as the oldest trees there. It is heavily characterized by what economist Robert Hoppe has called "persistent poverty"— that is, places in which poverty is embedded so deeply that it replaces itself from one generation to the next.[5]

If one drives across the Black Belt, through many of these persistently poor places, one journeys through time. It is as though the hands on a clock were wound backward and the old and the new collide. Although this kind of experience often occurs when one travels through rural areas, it is especially pronounced in the rural South in general and the Black Belt in particular. One can still find Mail Pouch ads on the sides of barns; huge, weathered Coca-Cola signs made of aluminum (not the newer plastic models); crossroads communities; small towns with "the quarters" or what were at one time called "Niggertowns" or, more politely, "nigra neighborhoods"; town squares with casual workers waiting early in the morning for whatever work might be available for the day; old, slow-moving men in coveralls (sometimes pronounced "coverhauls"); domino parlors, sometimes in strikingly ramshackle buildings without air conditioning; Nehi cola or RC Cola signs; women walking with umbrellas opened like parasols against the sun; children riding bikes alongside the road or shooting baskets at a makeshift basketball goal; wooden houses along the road with up-ended tires buried in the yards to hold flowers; bottles with colored water at the windows; trucks hauling trees to a mill; vegetable stands; melons and other fruits for sale alongside the road; pickup trucks (that staple of rural America), many with beaten-up aluminum fishing boats in the back (but some pulling the latest in high-tech bass fishing rigs); trailers that look like anything but "mobile" homes; the occasional public school but at least as often a Christian academy (another term for "segregation academy"); roadsides frequently littered with Kentucky Fried Chicken boxes, beer cans, and other signs of contemporary America; unusable trucks, cars, and similar refuse in yards and alongside houses; a hot dusty feel in summer, a cool sometimes frigid feel in a winter accompanied by the expectancy that winter won't last long; red mud on roads during rainy times; dead animals on and alongside the highways; mangy-looking dogs in yards; and everywhere, winding in, among, and through everything near the road, mile after mile of kudzu vines. Indeed, kudzu appears to have a plan of its own for what the rural South should look like—and to have decided that it should be everywhere.

No matter how dense the kudzu grows, however, it cannot hide the weathered appearance of so much that is there, so much that constitutes, collectively, what we think of as the rural South. And no part of the rural South is more weathered, more beaten-looking than the Black Belt. The scenic hills of Appalachia provide "hollers" that help to hide the abject poverty of many of the residents (nearly all of whom are white); such scenery is mostly absent in the Black Belt. Even in the coastal Tidewater (of Virginia and North Carolina) and Lowçountry areas, where kudzu has recently started to appear, the presence of poverty is more apparent than hidden. It is found most often right alongside the road in a patchwork quilt of "communities," a term that refers to any collection of several small houses and, occasionally, a neighborhood store.

Geographically and economically, the Black Belt is characterized heavily by plantations as well as by farms. Planters, as a class, were unlike farmers; they were more involved with running a business than with tilling the soil themselves.[6] Indeed, it was former slaves and poor whites who, after the Civil War, constituted the bulk of a plantation's population, and they were the ones who did the actual field work. In a British model of gentility, the planter had a fiefdom, on which the serfs (poor whites and blacks) were, in effect, indentured servants. But eventually this land-based economy faltered, the industrial revolution occurred, world wars took men off the land, and people exposed to the idea of a better life began to seek it outside the region.

The Promised Land?

Beginning in the immediate post–Civil War period, the first large-scale, nonforced migration of blacks in the South began. The movement was initially limited and concentrated mostly in moving close to one's previous home. It was only toward the end of the nineteenth century that the rate of migration picked up and that the destinations came to be farther away. Eventually, what started out as a trickle grew to a flood. Reinforced and celebrated with spirituals and hymns, some sung before the Civil War, the movement increased of African Americans leaving the South in search of a better life in the North. As an old Negro spiritual says,

> We'll soon be free.
> We'll soon be free.
> We'll soon be free.
> When da Lord will call us home.

The "home" this song refers to has a double meaning—both Heaven and heaven on this earth, the North. A more contemporary song is cited by historian Pete Daniels: "Like Muddy Waters, a lot of southerners got the 'Walking Blues.'"[7] Or as sociologist Carole Marks rightly puts it (citing Ray Stanndard Baker),[8] capturing the magnitude of this movement, "The Great Migration is the most noteworthy event, next to emancipation, which has happened to the Negro in America."

There can be little doubt that what writer Clifton Taulbert says in his personal memoir rang true for many rural African Americans: "It was July . . . the month our relatives and friends came home to visit from up North. Oh, how I remember those well-told Marco Polo stories of a life too good for me to even imagine! Deep within most of our hearts, we harbored the desire to be part of that good life that waited for us all just North of the Mason-Dixon line."[9]

Some Left, Some Stayed

What is crucial to understand about these migration processes— no matter when they occurred and no matter how many people were caught up in them—is this: although millions of blacks moved out of the South, millions stayed put. Some left briefly, only to return later; others never left. Although not specifically referring to those who stayed, the title of a 1981 presidential commission captures this population well: "the people left behind." Whoever read the book or saw the movie *The Color Purple* received some insight into these migration processes—African Americans venturing out into the larger world only to return "home" at some later date.[10] Anthropologist Carol Stack beautifully captures this in *The Call to Home*, a book driven in part by Stack's analysis (with geographer John Cromartie) documenting the magnitude of the return migration of African Americans to the rural South.[11]

But given what life was like in the rural South a hundred years earlier (during the late 1800s) and on into the early 1900s—and, for that matter, right up into the 1960s—if a black person had an opportunity to leave, who wouldn't? Phrased differently, why would any black person choose to stay? Yet millions did—why? Were they lazy? Indecisive? Had they good jobs and homes that they didn't want to leave? Did they see little opportunity outside the South?

What was true during the late 1800s, in the early 1900s, and on into the 1960s, is also true today: a majority (54 percent) of all African Americans live in the South, many in rural areas. Thirteen percent of *all African Americans* live in the rural South; 23 percent of *all blacks in the South* live in rural areas; 93 percent of *all rural blacks in America* live there. How can we explain this?

What is known about outmigrants is this: they are younger, better educated, better trained, with comparatively fewer ties to the local community and more willingness to take risks, which they are betting will be rewarded by better opportunities.[12] But, knowing this, the questions about who does not move seem answered. Or are other factors more important, but largely unknown because no one has really asked?

Demographic findings suggest the possibility of certain generational differences among black folk (or all folk, for that matter): Do younger people reject local norms and seek alternatives that they presume will be more to their liking? Do older people, for whom the norms have been in place longer, simply acquiesce and accept things as they are—in fact, value them in a "goes along and gets along" way? Or, conversely, is the older persons' seeming acceptance also an act of empowerment, since one can influence most that which one knows best?

Race and Place

In much of the rural South, one thing is axiomatic: race and everyday life are intermingled to such an extent that sorting one from the other is nearly impossible. Race influences where people live and who their neighbors are, where people go to school, where people go to church, where people go for recreation, even where people go for a bite to eat. And nothing is more confusing, and at times generative of conflict, than trying to sort out the "truth" about shared family histories. Anyone with even a passing knowledge of the Thomas Jefferson–Sally Hemmings relationship and what has ensued two hundred years later can recognize the significance of addressing honestly and accurately historic interracial relationships, especially the progeny they produced.

W.E.B. Du Bois said that the twentieth century would be characterized by "the race question." He has turned out remarkably prophetic; indeed, at times the century seems to have been dominated by the race question, almost consumed by it. Race is so much a part of the American experience that it seems impossible to understand what America and Americans are without considering race. And nowhere is this more true than the American South. With its history of slavery and its well-known legal, political, economic, and social oppression of generations of black people even after their so-called "emancipation," the South is clearly an important stage on which the race drama has been played out.

Race enters our consciousness when we are little children. It comes in quietly and with little fanfare, in ways mostly subtle but sometimes not. And, as with Humpty Dumpty, despite all the king's horses and all the king's men, no one can ever fully alter what happens afterward. We are who we are, when we are, where we are, in part because of race.

To experience the world as a social thing is to experience it through a set of lenses. These lenses are a composite of the social, historical, and cultural experience of an individual—*but* always, always grounded in a place and a sense of it. This composite is a social structure, a "thing," just as surely as any physical object. It is what the sociologist Emile Durkheim called a "social fact," something external to and coercive upon the individual.[13] Thus the individual's sense of the social world, experience of social facts, is what shapes "the world" as the individual comes to know it. As the sociologists Peter Berger and Thomas Luckmann say, this sense "cannot be wished away."[14] This is precisely how race presents itself to us.

Nowhere is this clearer than in where people live, both in urban and in rural areas—especially for those urban areas that have been increasingly and disproportionately characterized by growing minority populations (African Americans in particular) and declining majority populations. At the same time, many cities (especially inner cities) have become poorer and poorer—so much so that some of their neighborhoods are persistently poor, with the poverty experienced in one generation repeated in the next.

Whereas we typically think of urban areas as disproportionately minority and poor, rural areas, regardless of where they are located, are thought of less often and with little consideration, generally, given to minorities. Rural areas contain roughly one-fifth of the total U.S. population; thus, although the country has become decidedly urban, much of its population still remains in the countryside. It is likely that many people think of rural areas as virtually all white—and, indeed, for vast parts of the United States, that would be an accurate picture.[15] There are only three large expanses where the picture is wrong: much of rural California, with a large Hispanic presence; much of the Southwest, with a large Hispanic and somewhat smaller Native American presence; and the Black Belt in the South. This latter area must be understood in some historical context to fully appreciate its prominence and (for both whites and blacks) possible power to affect a people's consciousness of themselves.[16]

As the United States exited the nineteenth century and entered the twentieth, two states, Mississippi and South Carolina, still had majority black populations and a few (Alabama, Georgia, and Louisiana) had percentages nearly as large (over 40 percent black). This is one of those historical facts that seems lost on nearly everyone, even most social scientists. In those states, there are counties that, until the present time, always had greatly disproportionate black populations. Indeed, some were over 90 percent black. Even today, Jefferson County, Mississippi, is 87 percent black.

In such places, race and place became truly defining: The place could only be understood in light of race, since race, and all it portends, was such a prevalent, dominant trait. This same kind of long-lasting effect is, one would assume, present in all places where race has historically been so decidedly prevalent, even if the absolute number of majority black counties has decreased.[17] The larger fact remains: these are places where black people either were the numerical majority or were a very large proportion of the total population. One would expect blacks to have had, in such cases, a disproportionate effect on the place. Again, they had been a defining part of what the place was, perhaps *the* defining part.

Some of the majority black rural areas have identities that were, from the outset, meant to distinguish them from their white neighbors. These places range from the northernmost parts of the South to the Mississippi Delta. Copperville, Maryland, for example, was begun as a place apart from its immediately adjacent white neighbor, Tunis Mills.[18] Located on Maryland's Eastern Shore, Copperville was one of many such all-black enclaves. Tiny in population and in geographic size, this place was and still is home to many African Americans. Located about one thousand miles away, about as far as one can go and still be in the Black Belt, is another such place, Mound Bayou, Mississippi. This has always been a majority black locale with its own elected officials.[19] Copperville, Maryland, and Mound Bayou, Mississippi, provide convenient geographic markers for the two ends of the Black Belt, Copperville sitting in an area not widely known for its plantation heritage but having one nonetheless (the Wye Plantation is nearby), Mound Bayou residing in Bolivar County, truly a "cotton county" and equally truly one of the poorest places in the country. Almost exactly halfway between these two diverse, historically black places, and in a location equally flat, is another historically black place, Yvonne,[20] a small crossroads community in the marshy Lowcountry of Colonial County.

Colonial County

Colonial County's history reflects the presence of Native Americans, the Spanish, African Americans, and eventually the British, from whom the county got its name. Today there are about ten thousand residents. African Americans constituted a majority of the county's population for nearly two hundred years, until the late 1980s. At that time, whites became the majority group and, with development of the land near the water, in only one decade they have become about 60 percent of the county's total population.

The land in Colonial County is typical of the Lowcountry of South Carolina and Georgia. It is mostly flat and wet, with a vast amount of acreage consisting of water and marsh grass or, in drier places, pine trees, live oaks, and palmettoes. The term "hill" is reserved for nearly any place that is a foot or two above sea level, hence less prone to the continual swampy wetness of nearly everything else.

Most people enter the county from U.S. 17. When coming from the north, one has a sense of floating along through a sea of marsh grass, miles of it. Herons, gulls, and pelicans in flight are commonly sighted. The occasional dead otter by the side of the road is a reminder of the species' presence.

An alternative way to enter the county is by water. Indeed, the entire eastern boundary of the county is water, as are much of the southern and northern boundaries. In fact, one of the county's most notable areas is an island, where residents and dozens of local commercial fishermen enter and exit the county by water on an everyday basis. Nowhere is the lushness and beauty of the locale greater than from their viewpoint; the sun shining off the water reflected against a backdrop of golden marsh grass and mature live oaks and pine trees on shore yields a gorgeous sight. As one woman told me, she likes to lie down on her dock and stare out across the marsh, where boats underway appear to be "floating on air."

One of the commercial fishing boats in Colonial County is called *Amber Waves* and that is exactly what one sees while driving along parts of U.S. 17. Further, on a clear winter's day with a little northerly breeze, those amber waves are viewed under an immense canopy of blue. With no trees to obscure the horizon, the sky is like a tightly stretched canvas, shaded darker overhead, lighter (almost white) on the horizon—crystal clear and almost overwhelming in either case. There is a sense of one's smallness against this landscape, not unlike being in the desert or the Big Sky country of Montana, or in another spacious, open, and historically black place, the Mississippi Delta, which one writer said "looks ironed flat."[21]

After crossing over the Conaty River Bridge, suddenly one arrives in Conaty, the county's largest town, with around two thousand people. Upon entering the town, the beauty of the marsh and all that surrounds it is left behind, replaced by the unevenness one often finds in rural towns, more beaten up than bucolic but holding spots of grandeur if one looks hard enough.

Entering the county from the south is another waterborne experience, with several miles of marshy scenery broken up by the occasional river. After you cross the Winding River, large live oaks draped with Spanish moss form a kind of tunnel, wrapping themselves around you as you make your way. Signs for a national wildlife refuge and new and expensive housing developments are the first indicators of places where people might live or visit. Houses along Highway 17 are few in number until you arrive in Yvonne, the largest "town" at the southern end of the county.

Worlds Apart

U.S. 17 is the main artery through the county, at least for county residents. It is the county's "Main Street." It is paralleled by Interstate 95, only a few miles away but representing a far greater gap, one that cannot be measured in distance alone. For most Colonial County residents, the interstate has brought little but a flow of cars across their geography. To be sure, it has created some service sector jobs at the interstate exits, but, beyond that, the interstate is rarely used by most local people. For them, Highway 17 is the principal road into and out of the county. There is a mini–mass exodus in the morning, with people heading to work in the neighboring county's largest city and its islands. And in the evening, back they come.

One county administrator described Colonial County as in an era of transition, especially with the extensive development of expensive houses along the waterfront. The only obvious sign of this effect is when visiting Bauman's, the grocery store nearest the priciest part of the new waterfront development, a development that locals refer to as the "fly-in" community, since one segment has its own runway and residents all seem to have hangars for their private planes. At Bauman's, a typical Saturday will find an odd mix of expensive cars and the more representative Colonial County vehicles—pickup trucks and older cars, both American and Japanese. The potholed parking lot outside and the absence of exotic bottled waters inside are reminders that the local culture has not yet been replaced by the newcomers (in sharp contrast to the upscale Harris Teeters grocery store found on the nearby islands).

Most Colonial County residents rarely see or hear from their new neighbors on the waterfront. Whether flying or driving in, whether weekenders or more permanent residents, the newcomers find that most of the services they need and use fall outside the county. Colonial County has no upscale restaurants, furniture stores, gift shops, galleries, or hair salons, and the clothing stores once found downtown are long gone, replaced by the ones at the new discount mall along the interstate.

There, one can find many of the major designers. However, Ralph Lauren Polo shirts, Tommy Hilfiger pants, Bass shoes, and Coach handbags are displayed by few Colonial County residents, disproportionately young people, some of whom work at the mall. Nor is Mikasa china likely to be found on their dinner tables. It is also the case that relatively few paychecks ever come from the upscale mall for Colonial County workers. On a typical weekday morning, few cars at the mall with Lowcountry plates bear the Colonial County name and the total number of such Lowcountry cars does not exceed about twenty-five. The larger neighboring counties seem to furnish about as many employees as Colonial County. Most of the cars in the enormous parking lot are from out of state and, as Colonial County has found, early financial success for the mall has been difficult to sustain; now, as many storefronts are empty as are occupied. Nearby gas stations and fast food restaurants, however, seem to have a more sustainable clientele and future.

One of these establishments has caused considerable embarrassment for county officials and residents—it is the Café Risque, which some locals might call the "Slut Hut." Its main attraction is nude young dancing women, some of whom, according to the owner, are college students. A series of articles in the local paper laments this sorry state of affairs, and the question of how the place got permission to be built is hot on many people's minds. What is the appropriate zoning for such a place in a rural county? The "café's" marketing strategy is clear: adult entertainment. Several signs along the interstate, well in advance of the correct exit, promote the establishment. None offer the more commonly seen AARP discounts or free meals for the children. The side of the building nearest the highway is covered with nearly billboard-size pictures of smiling young women, precisely the kind of women that certain adults (viz., men) would like to see. An enormous sign helps to bring things into even sharper image: "Truckers Welcome." And, in what seems a planned touch of comedy, directly adjacent to the café's parking lot is a large, well-lettered sign, "Truck Tires." Sure enough, there is an actual tire store behind the café. Places like the Café Risque used to be found in large numbers along Highway 17 as it went through Colonial County, but the interstate helped to kill those businesses, since tourists and others moved from one highway to another.

The larger lesson here is this: like much else along the interstate, what may catch the eye of tourists and other travelers has little direct bearing on most Colonial County residents. For them, nearly all of what happens on and around the interstate is of little interest. Equally uninterested are most noncounty people driving along the interstate; they are driving *through* this place, not *to* it.

Yvonne

Yvonne is essentially the county's southern anchor. Some historically black places give a clear sense of what established them: Peace, Alabama, or Africa, Ohio (and Africa, Indiana), or Promise Land, South Carolina. This is not true for Yvonne. Even local history books cannot explain the name.

This is a place that has always been a mix of black and white families, but it became virtually all black by the late 1950s. Bauman's Grocery Store, a small mom-and-pop restaurant, a gas station, and a convenience store are clustered around the intersection of U.S. 17 and Route 33. Less than a mile away, where Route 33 intersects the interstate, there are a no-frills motel and a couple of fast food restaurants.

The bulk of Yvonne's residents live along U.S. 17. Folks are stretched out for a mile or so, living in "block" (cement block) houses, frame houses, house trailers, and a few double-wides (two trailer segments designed to fit together to form one larger house). Houses can also be found down some dirt lanes, which meander through pine trees before ending at one house or a cluster of houses, usually occupied by people related to one another and living on land that has been in their families for generations. Indeed, in Yvonne, a very few names account for a disproportionate percentage of the population. As one would expect in such a place, nearly everyone seems related to everyone else.

In general, the gorgeous scenery around much of the county is like expensive wrapping on an otherwise flawed gift (something that could be said about nearly all poor rural places, places that have a sharp divide between form [geographic beauty] and content [nearly inescapable poverty]). The drive along U.S. 17 for the unsuspecting tourist is probably sprinkled with comments such as "How can people live like that?" or "Can you imagine living here?" At times, it seems that as many houses as not have abandoned cars or boats or refrigerators or car engines in their front or side yards. And the depth of this impression is multiplied several-fold if one ventures down Route 33.

Route 33 forms a meandering crescent as it wends its way around the county's eastern area, following a river (and the water in general). Most of the drive is through the blackest part of the county, the "Homewood District" (named after a local plantation). The highway passes through the communities of Homewood, Randolph, Smithville, and Pineland before ending in Conaty. It is not unusual to make this sixteen-mile trip and see no white faces the entire time. A small "park" (really a large tree and a small shaded area with a picnic table) in Homewood almost always seems populated by people leaning on or sitting in cars, just hanging out. The park is where people congregate when they are not working. This particular place has become a source of local pride since it was reclaimed from drug dealers who, in the late 1980s, were openly plying their trade there. An odd-looking urban influence is apparent in the county in the number of hand-lettered signs that say "Say No to Drugs, Say Yes to Life" or similar admonitions. At this particular park, a large hand-lettered sign says "No Drugs Aloed" (exact spelling).

Drugs, as it turns out, are an important if embarrassing part of the county's history. They came in initially on the boats of commercial fishermen. At that time, the main crop being imported was marijuana and most of the people involved, including some prominent politicians, were white. Most black people believe that the "big shots" involved in county drug activity are still white, in part because no blacks own shrimp fishing boats, the vessels on which the drugs most likely enter the county. With Colonial County's hundreds of miles of coastline, the county was, and to some degree still is, a smugglers paradise. There are an almost uncountable number of little creeks coupled with a large number of dirt or secondary roads leading back to the water; with the interstate close by, drugs were easy to get into and out of the county.

By the late 1980s, both the drug of choice and the race of those most heavily involved changed; crack cocaine replaced marijuana and blacks replaced whites as the ones most likely to be involved and caught with some regularity. The local paper often lists the names of those caught for "possession" or the more serious "possession with intent to distribute." In virtually all cases, the names listed are of people from the Homewood district or Conaty, and in either case the persons are nearly always black. As it turns out, drugs have had an effect on many black families, even the best.

AC's World

Not far from where Route 33 and U.S. 17 intersect, set back from the road a hundred yards or so, lives a sixty-six-year-old black man, AC. He has lived in Yvonne all his life. His present home is only one-quarter mile from where he, like his mother's family before him, was born. His father's parents had come from "Carolina" (meaning South Carolina), his mother's from Georgia (or, as AC says, "Joja"). His family's entire history, whether in Georgia or Carolina, is grounded in the Lowcountry.

He had been raised locally and, other than on occasional trips out of the county, had never left the place. He had time to spend with me partly because he had lost his job of almost thirty years when he was injured and a lung disabled. The steel mill where he worked had closed, displacing several hundred workers, many only a year or so away from being able to draw retirement. Since then, AC had worked at odd jobs, mostly doing small construction projects but also doing some much larger ones, including building block houses. (In fact, during his life, he has built about forty of these for friends and relatives.)

AC's physical stature belies his disability. He looks like a football linebacker or lineman, with a powerful upper body and immense arms. As he tells me, he must "weigh 'bout 265." Eventually, his weight became a running joke between us, with me telling him that I need to put some sandbags on my side of the car to even out the load. AC's weight is almost all muscle; he is simply a big man.

AC lives today with his wife of thirty years. This is a second marriage for both of them. AC's former wife, the mother of his five children, lives down the road in a house built on land inherited from her family. Her brother lives across the street, and other relatives live in adjacent houses. Similarly, AC's aunt lives next door to him, and he is "renting" (on those occasions when the rent is paid) another house to a niece. He built the latter, small house for his mother when she grew aged.

AC's remaining brothers and sisters (of whom there were originally twelve) all live in the county, except two sisters who moved to New York; two brothers and a sister are dead. The siblings' ages range from fifty-three to eighty-three, reflecting the fact that AC's father had some children by his first wife, who died, and then the rest by AC's mother.

AC's three daughters all live within five minutes of him. His two sons live in the next county. All his children have children of their own and, for the daughters and one son, all the children were born when the parents were not married. The daughters each have three children, and one son fathered four children before getting married, almost twenty years ago, and subsequently having no more children. The other son has one child, and will have no more.

Although AC only finished the fourth grade, each of his children either graduated from high school or obtained a G.E.D. And all have always managed to stand on their own financially, with three (both sons and one daughter) having had military careers. One daughter has become a very successful nurse, and another, in her late thirties, has gone back to school to work on a degree in business.

This is a family that has weathered some very difficult times: a painful divorce between AC and his first wife; two family members killed on the highway near their home; one of AC's brothers drowned, and one shot to death by his wife; one family member going from being the most prominent black politician in the county to being sent to prison for allegedly facilitating the sale of drugs. Despite these difficulties, this family has survived—not only survived, but prospered in its own way.

Some family members moved away, but most did not. And, if they left at all, they left only for a short time or a time (via military service) largely out of their control. Always they returned, returned to a place that many outsiders would see as grim, a place offering little, on the surface, to make people want to live there. But AC's family did want to live there. Why? Why did they never leave this place—or leave briefly, returning at the first chance? What was it about this place that made them so committed to it?

Two

The World of Work—as Experienced and Interpreted by Older Men

For older black folk in Colonial County, the world has always been a place of work, usually from a very early age. School was something that black people often attended, but just as often they quit before graduating, and there was a gendered side to this: boys usually quit very early, often while still in elementary school and the girls continued awhile longer. Why? Because, following the traditional agricultural family model around which much of the United States was developed, the boys were needed in the fields and the girls' work at home could be postponed a bit longer or more easily built around the school day. To be sure, the girls worked; it was just that their tasks and hours were different than the boys.

In my very first meeting with AC, we talked about his introduction to the world of work. Like many rural people, AC had known work and everyday life so interwoven that it was hard to tell where one started and the other stopped. For AC, work *was* everyday life, a very natural part of it. This was, and is still, the common experience for millions of people who grow up on farms or in rural areas. Doing "chores" may sound quaint to many who live in urban areas, but if you were among the rural folk these daily tasks integrated you into the family unit differently than did blood alone; they made you a contributor; every task you did was one less for others to do. You learned early on that others depended on you just as you depended on them. *The* key aspect of this for AC was that it led inevitably to having a

sense of responsibility—a sense that others (whether people or farm animals or whatever else) depended on you and, in turn, you simply *had* to do
certain things.

For sociologists, this involved, in the most Durkheimian way, a kind of
"precontractual solidarity." The assumption that you would do what others
expected was what provided the basis for a moral order in which your word
was your bond. You did not need written contracts and legal threats to know
that you were expected to do certain things. To be sure, you might not have
wanted to do them but hard work and working hard were the normal events
in everyday life.

Timber Cutting and Pulpwooding

Now, at age sixty-six, AC has nearly six decades of work experience. "Girls didn't have to do the work of the boys, no cuttin' firewood. My
father made sure they went to school but the boys had to work or be in the
field, helpin' out. I musta' been about eight when I helped my mother gather
crops on the islands. That was mostly women and children working there,
not the mens. My father and older brother was in the woods dippin' turpentine or rakin' or doin' somethin'. I was about ten years old when I got
my first public job [i.e., for wages], doin' pulpwood.

"We had quite a few men comin' in from Alabama and Mississippi. Had
a great demand 'cuz this big timber company took over this area down here
[pointing down the road to an area still used for timber cutting]. They could
boss them [the outsiders] more than they could these local people [laugh-
ing at the memory]. So they had quarters for them to live; built these little
ole houses for them. Had them dippin' boxes, not cuttin' timber. Dippin' gum,
you know, turpentine? There were fo' [four] big camps. Timber was played
out by the early or last part of the sixties. I went with my father a few times,
dipped gum when the pulp ran. Dipped boxes."

AC and all of his brothers learned much about the world of work when
the turpentine industry was still very active in Colonial County. For many
black men, this industry provided jobs working in the woods, "dippin' gum
and rakin' boxes."[1] "Dippin' gum" was done with pails placed by trees that
had been slashed to encourage the gum (resin) to run from them. "Rakin'
boxes" was a necessity because some of the gum that was drained from the
trees inevitably spilled on the ground. This made it a fire hazard, since one

live cigarette butt or match could start a fire that, enhanced by the ground resin, could race up a tree and spread to others. Thus "rakin' boxes" involved raking around the trees to keep them free of ground resin, reducing a major fire hazard.

Also, like all his brothers, AC eventually worked in the pulpwood industry. This industry continues to provide many jobs today. It is hard, dirty work, mostly cutting and hauling pine trees but also, in some places, removing large stumps. But today the industry has become much more technologically sophisticated, and most trees (harvested commercially) are cut down by a large piece of equipment that looks like something from the movie *Edward Scissorhands*. A huge pair of mechanical scissors makes a cut and the tree is down. This simplicity is explained, in part, by the fact that the bulk of trees harvested are of a similar size, about fifteen inches in diameter. The standardization makes possible the routinization of the harvesting process and, in turn, the need for comparatively few workers.

The trees are hauled to a pulpwood processing plant, which in Colonial County means they go to Coastal City. There, facing the scenic marsh and intracoastal waterway, sits the area's largest pulpwood processing plant. It gives off a horrible odor, usually pushed along by the prevailing southern or southwestern breeze. The odor is unmistakable whether one is eating at a donut shop practically next door to the plant, at any of the fastfood or barbeque joints, or in the area's most popular Chinese restaurant. Even playing golf at the largest municipal course is affected by what the British would call the "pong" of the pulpwood processing smoke.

"Pulpwoodin'" was something that AC had in common with his brothers. It offered more than just a job; it offered both liberty (working on one's own) and enslavement (having a sense that your family needed your financial contribution, no matter how meager). So, at once, young men were both given independence from, and tethered to, their families. Eventually, as happened with each of his brothers, this forced a separation between AC and his father. And, also like most of his brothers, he found the separation coupled with discovering that a local girl was pregnant and he had to get married.

Life after Pulpwoodin'

When AC and his brothers first started working in the pulpwood and turpentine industries, much of the work was outside Colonial County—

not a huge distance away, but far enough to require living there in camps during the week.[2] This often led to fathers and sons working together but also, somewhat inevitably, it led to the sons' rising sense of independence and resentment that, often, they gave a disproportionate share of their wages to their fathers.

AC's brother Terrence, now in his late fifties, remembers this best. When he was fifteen, "I went turpentinin' but it was more like bein' a slave. You makin' money for the man what own the turpentine camp but you ain't makin' no money for your family back home. They were in the same situation. I work there 'bout three weeks, and when we got ready to leave, Daddy got paid but I didn't know how much 'cuz he never let you know that. So he gave me ten dollars [and he laughs at the memory of it]. 'No, no.' I said, 'Oh no, this isn't for me.' I bought my little brother a pair of shoes, was about two dollars. When I got paid, I always bought him somethin' every week. I had to buy a ticket for Daddy and a ticket for me to Coastal City; that was three dollars each. So before we even left for home, that ten dollars was about gone. I thought, 'Nah, this not gonna work.' When I got to Coastal City, my uncle, who always had a new car, he gave us a ride home. Daddy said to pay him; that cost a dollar apiece. And I told Daddy, 'Daddy, I been gone for two long weeks and now I'm back home and I ain't got a dime.' And he got furious.

"So I went down the road there, to a little shop. Boys came along and we started buyin' sodas and stuff, you know how boys are. They had an illegal slot machine in there; the sheriff, he had those slot machines in all them little sto's [stores]. So I put my first nickel in and won the jackpot— 'bout thirty dollars in nickels. I kept playin' and in the end had about twenty dollars. When I came back home, I asked Daddy, 'Daddy, you think about some way for me to make more money?' And he said, 'No, I done spent that money. Had to buy groceries and such.' So I caught me a ride to [a nearby city] and I came back the next day and got dropped off in Conaty. Then I went to my brother's, BW's, in the Bluff. I stayed that night with him and got up on Monday and, on my way to Conaty, saw my Daddy headin' for the Bluff lookin' for me. Then I went to my sister's in Coastal City and stayed there. The next mornin' my sister said, 'Terrence, Papa out there.' I said, 'I don't want to talk to him.' But my sister said, 'Papa's an old man now. Workin' like that. Somethin' happen to him, nobody'll know.' They blew me up with sympathy and all that junk. So we caught the bus back to the camp. When we got there, it was rainin' but I went and ax'd the guy who owned the camp could we use the mule to go get some wood. He showed me where the wood was at and we loaded up the wagon and came back. Carried Daddy to a friend's house next door. He ax'd me could I cook so I put some food on and got it cookin' good and put it on the back of the fire. And when Daddy hit the back door, I hit the front door! Couldn't hack no more of that, man. I walked a long way on [Highway] 84 goin' to a club in the Negro section of Brookman. A Negro walkin' on that road in those years [the 1950s], man, you had yourself a problem, especially there. Every time I see a car comin' by I laid down in the ditch; then I'd walk some more. I got to Brookman and the club wasn't open so I waited there and a pulpwood truck came by and stopped. He brought me to Coastal City and there was a basketball game goin' on; we didn't have a gym at Alvin Johnson [the Negro high school in Colonial County]. Anyway, I got with them guys and caught the bus back home, just like them school kids. There was a man had a pulpwood operation near home and he gave me a job. By the time Daddy came home, I was makin' five times the money him and me was makin', period. I still lived at home and gave my parents some money but I was free."

BW, AC's oldest brother, has his own recollection of learning to work. "I didn't get a chance to go to school but once or twice a week. I was workin' in the fields for my grandpa, Mr. Weldon. When I was eight years old, I done got to rake boxes. See, a box on a tree. Chippin' the tree and the gum come down. When you rake boxes and chippin', that tar runs down. When that tar runs down, some of it misses the box and get on the ground. In them times, there'd be fires in the woods sometimes. So we'd have to rake it clean three to fo' feet 'round all them trees so the fire wouldn't run up the tree. See what I mean? That way that tree won't catch fire. Every tree what had a box had to do this. Had a big squad of people, thirty or fo'ty [forty] people, doin' this. I was seven or eight years old. I didn't get paid much; maybe twenty-five cents a day." I interrupted to ask, "Did you really get paid?" BW told me, "Not really. Daddy was the one gettin' paid."

Like his other brothers, BW also left home at a fairly early age. "I was 'round fifteen years old when I left. I left home 'cuz I wanted some money. I wanted to see why I was workin'. My Daddy took all my money; mighta give me two or three dolla's but that was it. One day a man came through

Yvonne and said 'We got a lot of pulpwood to cut in Homasville, y'all want to go?' I said, 'Yes,' and hopped right up on the van. We was livin' in a camp. Got paid in American money. Fellas from right here at home, they'd haul us up to Homasville. We wasn't nothin' but boys. They ax'd me did I want to go, so I went up there. We'd come home every other weekend, then we'd go back. Lived in a cabin one time, but most time we lived with a lady in a house, a bo'din' [boarding] house. We cut the trees right to the stumps and loaded 'em right then. I did pulpwood 'til I was 'round thirty-five or fo'ty [forty] years old. Pulpwooded everywhere. Had to be careful when you came through Ludowici 'cuz they hated black folk. Same way in Jesup, too."

For AC, timber cutting and processing was a fairly short-lived venture. Too much work, too little money. As he told me, "In '50 I quit pulpwoodin' and worked in Coastal City at a creosote plant where they dyed them poles, but I only worked there six months; I couldn't stand all that tar and I give it up. Then worked at a plant buildin' trailers. Then I went with the new steel mill. Eighty-five cents an hour; that was big money! Worked there 'til the plant quit. Didn't give us no option or nothin'. Three hundred head of us about the same way. We'd 'a mostly been fifty-two or fifty-three years old. They looked at all that money they'd 'a had to pay for retirement and they shut that plant down. We hired an attorney and filed a lawsuit but nothin' come out of it."[3]

The plant's closure occurred at about the same time that AC developed a physical disability. Neither slowed him down. Although Terrence and BW withdrew from working for wages, AC remained very active and has continued to work (by whatever name and whatever pace) to the present day. His "normal" day begins early in the morning, very early. The typical day finds him up before sunrise, making some biscuits, frying some meat, having a little coffee. Then, usually, he's off to go fishing for awhile before starting his other "jobs." The fishing is mostly recreational but it also helps to put food on the table—his, and others', for when he catches more than he can use he gives away the rest, often driving by people's houses and offering his extra catch for free.[4] And what people get simply depends on what's running—whiting one day, shrimp the next.

As a rule though, as AC tells me, he's out working for wages. "Most time I go and be out doin' somethin'. Don't axe a price. Most of 'em know me. Most time I can do it a third cheaper [than someone else]. Just ax' me what they owe me. Have a couple of fellas who help me most time. I usually have two or three jobs goin' all the time. When I get ready to fish, I go and forget about work. I can't run every day so I usually work three–four hours a day. Lot a' little jobs. Catch up with the little ones and then work on a big one."

AC agrees that much of this work is part of the informal economy. It is, strictly speaking, off the books—a cash-and-carry business or, occasionally, part of a bartering system (if someone has an item or service to be traded for). But AC's needs are quite simple, and it is almost always cash that he gets. He is worried about what he sees as the misfit between work available and workers to do it. As he told me one day, "Anybody got any little kinda' skill can make some money. We in great need of plumbers right now and electricians; I don't hardly do that. I got carpenter tools on my truck and I stick with that. Might take me a week or two weeks to get an electrician or plumber. Nobody else locally to do that work. All these young fellas here, if you learn to do something, you won't never starve. There's always a demand. But most of these young fellas don't want to learn nothin'; be with you two–three months and they quit. Can't do nothin' until you get back if you leave 'em on their own. I get so many calls; lots of 'em I turn down. But when I gets ready to go fishin', I go."

As I found in my time with AC, hiring him to do a job is akin to the frustration Peter Mayle recalled in hiring French workers to do jobs, some big, some small, on his house.[5] In all cases, Mayle stated, the rhythm to their work was dictated by them, not by Mayle; they came and went as they pleased. The same is true for AC. He works at his own pace. He is not the best person to hire if quick completion is required (unless a job is truly small). But if one's sense of time and priority are akin to his, with high tolerance for short and erratic work days, he does good work for fair prices.

Disability as Normative

There was one common refrain with every older man and most older women I spoke with: they had either worked until they were simply too old or tired to do so anymore or, more often, had become disabled.[6] For the women, the disability was usually related to some form of repetitive motion injury (e.g., from cleaning crabs day after day). For the men, the disability was more likely to be a respiratory or back injury; for AC, it was a lung problem from working in the steel mill. "I got put on disability when my lo'n [lung] collapsed. Put some kinda dipper in there. Doctor told me I couldn't hold a regular job no more." For BW, the problem was his back, hurt when he was working at the seafood processing plant. "I woiked [as pronounced] in seafood, with scallops. You could hear that truck comin', 'clop, clop, clop.' I'd go in there and water 'em down and kill 'em. Then that truck back up the vat where they gonna load 'em at. Come in a big trailer truck. Not boxed or nothin', just loose in the truck. And I'd wash 'em down with fresh water. After I kill 'em, they back the truck 'round the ramp. I pull the bodes [boards] out and get 'em out and put 'em on the belt. Then I'd wash out the truck. I wasn't in the plant. It was mostly women in there cleanin', and mostly men packin'.

"But eventually, I hurt my back and shoulders. When a truck start backin' up, I'd go get them bodes out where they cross the back. I'd put 'em flat there [pointing at an imaginary floor]. I got hurt that night when the truck wasn't 'bout half loaded. I'd got one bode out and laid it flat and I had to pull that other bode out; bode weigh 'bout 400 pounds. The truck done roll from me to you [about eight feet]. Brought that truck right down toward me and that bode went 'Boom! Boom!' when it crashed in. I had to jump under the truck. Worst part was I had to crawl out from theah. That man drivin' the truck just started to pull it away. I got workmen's comp, see. Befo' then, I went to one of them doctors to see what I could do for work. Said I could sit in an office. Then I tried to he'p'em packin' and stuff but I couldn't do much 'cuz I had to go to the doctor's two or three times a week and I had to go to therapy three times a week. Then they put me in a hospital. When I did that, they adjusted my neck and everything. I was in [for] a week, I think. They tol' me I could come if I want, to go ahead home. I went back and ax'd 'bout my job, 'bout light work, asked if they had anything fo' me to do; but they said 'nope.' And I been unemployed since then. I got disability."

The high incidence of disability seems understandable in light of the work that most people did. Timber cutting (in this case, pulpwooding) is one of the most dangerous occupations in America. Most of the work involves using saws, axes, equipment to haul and load or unload wood, and so on; and the wood itself is muscled around, which, even with the assistance of equipment, inevitably leaves one open to injury. For Terrence and AC, similar risk was encountered in the steel mill, another place of unusually high on-the-job injuries.

Factory Work

When AC first went to the steel mill, he was a happy man. The pay was the most money he had ever made and the benefits were comparatively good. He worked the night shift, from 4 P.M. to 12 A.M. At first he was a common laborer, as were nearly all the African Americans, but, in time, he set his sights on a better job. This, along with his willingness to challenge other prevailing workplace norms, led, inevitably, to problems.

I asked him what it must have been like, nearly forty years ago—in the 1960s, a time when whites and blacks simply did not work shoulder to shoulder in most southern factories. As AC told me, "It was dangerous. It was. The only thing we had to our advantage was a couple of fellas up in the cranes. Meantime, none of us could weld or nothin'. We couldn't be a fitter. All we could do was be a helper. We could clean the steel or clean up when they make a mess when they grind off, and get it ready to ship it off or pack. But all the better jobs were all white, all white. Then I put in for a weldin' job. They put it up on the bode [i.e., announced the opening on some type of bulletin board] and I signed up. They said, 'You can't pass no test.' And I said, 'Sign me up, anyhow. If anybody else can pass it, I can pass it.' I was workin' for a fella, lives right down the road here, John Colt; he's white. He used to ride me sometime [to work]. He told me, 'You can pass that test. When you over here sometime, come over and I'll show you.' And I told him, 'Okay, Mr. John.' And everytime I get a break, I'd go over and he'd show me. The other whites started not likin' him 'cuz he was helpin' me. But like I told you befo', in time everything was normal."

When I injected, "And you passed the test?" AC responded, "Yep, I passed. The man tried his best to dissuade me. After I passed that one, they give me another one. All the whites didn't have to pass but one, but I had to take two. I passed both of 'em. I was the first black qualified to weld. I paved the way for about ten more."

For AC and the other black men, the steel mill—as a newly "integrated" workplace—was much more than a place to work. It was a theater in which much larger societal dramas were continually played out. In the case of his becoming a welder, he challenged both prevailing norms and the authority structure that reinforced them; at the same time, he demonstrated a certain kind of "affirmative" action—that is, he let his actions affirm what he could do. Even though major social changes may be prompted by legal writs, or at least sanctioned by them, it is in these smaller, everyday ways that the true war for change is fought, in countless battles such as AC's challenge for a welding job.

As in all wars, those in power were not quick to yield any ground. Thus, AC had to take the test twice, much like having to pay a poll tax and pass an exam to vote. But he did it and succeeded, further reinforcing his sense of controlling his own destiny and of not being beaten down no matter how severe the odds. As he told me on other occasions, "Black people knew they had to be twice as good as white to succeed. Twice as good. But they bleed the same as me. Color's only skin deep. In the end, we're all the same."

Eating as Battleground

Working together in a newly integrated plant was only one of many ways the men had to learn to get along—and, in some ways, working would be the easiest, since it is so task-oriented. The more difficult and tense situations involved those small, everyday things normally taken for granted—such things as getting a drink of water, eating a meal, or going to the bathroom. Each, when it occurred in a new, racially integrated setting, provided opportunities to challenge and violate longstanding social practices. At the same time, the social forces inside the plant were not replicated exactly, outside, since there too change was going on—but at its own pace and playing out very differently in even neighboring locales.

I asked AC about what everyday life was like in the plant when black and white workers had separate facilities although sharing a workplace. He told me, "See, they had this little room on the back end separated from the cafeteria. The whites had a great big room, 'bout as long as this house [about fifty feet], probably two thousand square feet. We had a room with one little table. You had a pigeonhold [pigeonhole] where they handed your food through [a technique also found, before integration laws, in many southern restaurants, which would serve blacks only carry-out food, and only out of sight of white patrons, a practice AC and others vividly remembered as occurring in Conaty].

"The supervisor, the headman at the plant, he told us that everything was like that [uncertain due to the new emphasis on racial integration]. But the fellas didn't change it right then. Everybody knew it [the new legislation] was in effect, but some whites didn't want it, so what we did, the first thing, we'd go to the water fountain—they had a big old aluminum one, went from the flo' [floor] up, and we had a little old white [ceramic] one next to it with a little spigot thing sticking up. Me and two or three more, when we'd go to the fountain, we'd wash the steel dust off in the white one but we'd drink from the other one. And when we had our backs turned, two or three of the fellas would throw things at us.

"One of 'em, he almost hit me. Me and him used to ride together—called him Jack —over by Townsend. I looked up and saw him. And he came over and said, 'AC, I thought better of you than that. Me and you was friends and everything. You know you ain't supposed to do that.' And I told him, 'Jake, I'll drink from whatever one I want to drink from.' And he come over there and he done had a little hammer in his hand and he draw back, and I said, 'Jake, you ain't gonna lose nothin' but your swing 'cuz you gonna get my fist right back in your nose.' Two more fellas came up and we make a deal that when the cafe open up—now we used to bring our lunch, in those days—when the whistle blow, we'd run and be the first ones to get to the cafeteria, and we'd sit at the big center table.

"It was me, Charlie Sawyer, and Jimmy Jones. We decided. Charlie Sawyer operated a crane and Jimmy Jones worked by the ships in the yard. One day we started raisin' sane ["raising sand," meaning to stir things up] about it. Pretty good amount of blacks was there. We made our minds up to get this thing changed. Even if we can't get no one to go with us, we'll do it. So me, Charlie, and Jimmy got together, and whichever one of us got there first, we got the table in the middle of the building. Whites would come over and look and they'd go back in the shop and wouldn't eat. That happened for a week or so. Then the boss man who run the cafe, George, he told us that he wasn't makin' no money 'cuz the fellas quit buyin'. So we told him that they'd be back directly. After three or four weeks, people started easin' back into the cafeteria.

"Then we started doin' the bathrooms the same way. They'd catch us in there. And we said, 'Don't worry, they'll be back directly' [he laughs heartily at the memory of the white workers not wanting to use the bathrooms and the black workers anticipating that the whites will eventually give in].

When things started gettin' hot, the big man, the supervisor, he cut the water fountain down; he pulled down the little bathroom; and he pulled down the wall in the cafeteria. That kept us from having a riot or something. He talked to us and we told him we wasn't gonna back up."

I wondered if there were occasional fights, especially given the sanctity in which southern racial norms were held. As AC told me, "Well, one fella, white guy, they figured you was s'posed to back up and let 'em get their drink. One night he walked in front of this black fella called Smiley. And he shoved him out of the way and he swinged at him. And that black fella knocked him down. Everybody stopped him from doing anything else. And he didn't do that no mo'. Everyone just got in line. It took about fo' weeks, but that animosity didn't die down for two years or so.

"Sometimes they'd put nails in a bode and put it under your tires. And when you go to drive off you'd get a flat. They did that several times but they never caught no one doin' it. The security guard was white so never saw nothin'. He was with them. One time they had us park by the security office so nothin' would happen.

"After we got everything straight, they had me workin' cleanin' up the bathroom. A guy from Nehama, up that way [points and pauses for a moment] . . . we wouldn't have had so much trouble if it was mostly people from this area [near his home], but up there they was way mo' prejudiced. Those people by Waycross and Jesup and Nehama, they're real prejudice'. Them fellas, I'd been there since '63 and I knew everybody there. They knew I wouldn't back up from nothin'.

"These fellas was in the back stalls, and this one man was talking 'bout this 'nigger woman' he had workin' for him. He was talkin 'bout this 'nigger woman,' this 'nigger woman.' This one fella looked out and saw me and he just sat there [AC starts laughing at the memory], and I just started walkin' toward that stall. He saw me, and he just stood up. He didn't wipe himself or nothin' [more laughter]. He just pulled up his pants [more laughter]. I didn't smile or nothin'.

"I found out where he was workin' and I went over there. He jumped up and started apologizin'. I don't know what he thought I was gonna do. He said, 'AC, I'm sorry. I'd'a never said what I did. I respect you more than that.' And I told him, 'You know, practice make perfect. When you practice these things, that's why you do it. I don't want to hear it no mo'. If you want to talk, talk 'bout your color.' He was stunned. He thought sure I'd come out there to catch on to him. I was always kind of large anyhow and I didn't back up from nothin', no how. He'd had to whip me or I'd whip him, one of the two. But with the job at stake, I wasn't about to throw him down for nothin'. He started apologizin' again and that was the end of it."

Now, of course, it is much more common to see blacks and whites working together, but, as a huge amount of social science literature has shown, much of the workplace remains, despite such programs as affirmative action, segregated by both race and gender—blacks and women still the most likely to be in poorer-paying jobs, white men in better-paying ones. And yet, change has come. Even in a rural place like Colonial County, some jobs seem to have nearly as many blacks as whites. This is especially true at the new outlet mall, in the clothing and shoe stores. There, too, blacks and whites are found at similar entry-level jobs in the fast-food restaurants and convenience stores. The greatest racial mix of workers, at least in Colonial County, seems to be in the public sector. Walking through the courthouse, the town hall, the public schools, and so on, one perceives some sense of interracial job parity.

The impetus for this, according to local black folk, came primarily in the early 1970s—as a response to federal antidiscrimination laws becoming imperatives, but also, in a much more politically overt way, in response to the leadership of local black politicians. When Terrence, AC's youngest brother, was elected to the county board of supervisors, he essentially demanded that the county hire more minorities. This was a newer and more difficult case to make than with the county schools, which—in part from the legacy of dual systems—had always had a comparatively large number of minorities on the payroll. For Terrence, the final straw came with the opening of a new private facility, a bank. Terrence insisted that the bank hire a minority teller. When the bank argued that, being privately owned, it would hire whomever it wanted, Terrence threatened to lead a boycott, with local blacks depositing all their money out of the county. The bank then hired the person Terrence recommended (and who subsequently has gone on to her own political life in the county).

Without doubt, it is the youngest workers for whom interracial contact seems the most normal and natural. These are the ones who have always attended racially desegregated schools. By some estimates students spend upwards of fifteen thousand hours in school by the time they finish high school; it seems reasonable that this continual contact—plus possible interracial involvement in extracurricular activities and/or away from the school grounds—will foster a greater sense of ease in being with those of different races. This is at least somewhat akin to the sociological notion of the "equal contact" hypothesis that suggests, in effect, that the more time and the more equal the contacts people of different races have, the greater the likelihood of their getting along. This contact, in conjunction with the ruralness of Colonial County and the general foreknowledge people there often have of one another, enhances interracial acceptance (even if it is incomplete or flawed).

It is especially easy to see interracial contact and cooperation at virtually all retail stores (and even in restaurants, one of the most difficult places to desegregate). Whether at the outlet mall on the interstate, or at stores in Conaty or restaurants along the water, or in any of the area's public-sector buildings, today interracial work settings are commonplace. What was almost impossible to imagine for the older workers was a routine thing for younger ones. But even in rural Colonial County, as in more urban places, there was still a prevailing sense that, even in an era with comparatively less racial discrimination (especially for entry-level, service-sector jobs), one group especially had a tough row to hoe with a worrisome future—younger black males.

Young Black Males

Much like Mitchell Duneier in his book *Slim's Table,*[7] I spent my time almost exclusively with older people. (For Duneier, the point of contact was older black men in Chicago.) Also like him, I found some topics arose with little forethought or attention to how they advanced the particular research questions of central interest to me. The path was mostly serendipitous, not taken with intention, but trod nonetheless. Also like Duneier (and Elijah Anderson in his Philadelphia-based ethnography of an inner-city African American community),[8] I found that older black men were worried greatly about the future of younger black men.

As AC and I were talking one day, he told me how difficult it was to find help with some of his "little ole jobs." He lamented this, saying that if people would develop "any little ole skill," they would be employable. And indeed it is precisely the ability to harness such skills that gives his sons so much hope for their own business (a construction company) in Coastal City.

AC's sense of young people's lack of skills was coupled with a more general impression that too many young black males lacked a general sense of direction that would lead to a productive adult life. He was not sure exactly why this was so but, as he talked, the themes of family values and personal responsibility—the twin pillars of many conservative arguments about social programs—quickly arose. As at other times in our conversations, I recalled and reflected on some things Duneier had reported in his book about older black men and their views on everyday life and especially their sense of morality, knowing the difference between right and wrong.

For AC, too, such a distinction was clear, but like the men in Duneier's book he found it painful to think about how such clear choices and consequences were not apparent to young black men. AC was well aware of the high incarceration rate for young black males nationally. Regrettably, remote and rural Colonial County had its own problems, even if these did not seem so great as those in larger, urban areas.

"I wonda' . . . I'm a big churchgoer. Out of all the things happenin', I wonda' why we can't do nothin' with this generation. The Bible speak of the lost generation. Sometime I wonda'. It hurts me to wonda'. We talk about this in Sunday school in church sometimes. A person will see someone get his hand chopped off, like when blacks stole a hog or somethin' from whites . . . I knew that story and I think of drugs. They see what happen to the man ahead of him and he go stick his hand in the same place where they cut it off. Why put your hand in the same place?

"Only two things happen. Large man, not handlin' it, just puttin' out and receivin' the money; he gets by pretty good. But if you one of the horsemen carryin' it or usin' it, only two things happen: prison or death. Might have a hundred thousand dollars or even two to three thousand dollars, but as soon as the man get on 'em, then their money's gone and they're either dead or doin' time.

"They sell you that stuff even if you a stranger. Don't use no common sense or nothin'. If you go stop ova' in the Patch [the most notorious drug market in Colonial County], they'll be somebody up to your car door before you're even stopped good.

"Police have two or three roundups every year. They know everybody who sells drugs. They have to. They just turn their heads, or they get off when they go to court. But some do time. Got to be some big hade [head] in this thing. But when they bring a task force to clean it up, they take some guys but there's always little guys to replace them.[9] I could tell you all the spots where they hang out. Hot spot right down the road, but they don't come in' this area. Nobody mess with nothin' of mine." I interrupt to confirm that this is local people AC is telling me about, not people from Savannah or Charleston or some other urban area. He continues, "Sho'. The big ones start the little ones. Right behind the bank. I talk to their parents. Shoot, I have some of 'em in Sunday school. I fuss at 'em but they tell me they can't do nothin' with 'em.[10]

"We wasn't like that in my family. I'm not flexible. I mean what I say, what I stand behind. I stand by my decision. I'm not wishy-washy. My children tell me that they discuss things with their children. I tell 'em that's fine but when they in my house, they abide by my rules. And when they're in your house, then it's your rules."

AC's beliefs about this are similar to ones cited in other recent writings on the black community, but those cases concern the inner city, not a rural place like Yvonne. In his ethnography of young black men in Philadelphia, the sociologist Elijah Anderson comments, "The young men may have little desire to engage in the 'hard work' their elders performed, even if it were available and had long-term promise."[11] Or, as one of the characters in Mitchell Duneier's book says, "A man without things to do is not a man."[12] As another character laments, "The younger generations, if you make them lift fifty pounds, their backs hurt. We lifted hundreds of pounds and never thought nothing of it. It was like fun. And now if you tell kids to go get some groceries, they carry twenty-two pounds and they retired."[13] In this same conversation, "You always had a job. Sit around waiting on a check? Oh man," another man says, disgustedly. Duneier makes repeated reference to the disjuncture between the worldviews of older black men and of those much younger; ironically, these young men could easily be their sons (or perhaps grandsons). For the older men, personal responsibility is an integral part of life. They see themselves as living examples of following society's rules, of working hard and deriving a sense of pride from doing so. As Duneier says: "By living in accordance with principles such as pride, civility, sincerity, and discretion, these men confirm for themselves—rather than proving to others—that they possess some of the most important human virtues. Thus they make evident the extraordinary strength of their sense of self and their ease with their own selves."[14] Beyond this, though, they believe that "wastefulness, pretension, aggressiveness, uncommunicativeness, impatience, flashiness, laziness, disrespect for elders, and perhaps most important a lack of personal responsibility—all of [these] are taken by Slim and his sitting buddies to be features of a social disorganization that has ruined the ghettos of their youth. This pattern of values is 'unrespectable': It is beneath the level of moral worth that they associate with their own existence."[15] Again, these are urban men Duneier is talking about, not rural ones, yet how similar they seem to AC and many of the men with whom he is friends.

As AC told me, one day: "That group right down the road don't wanta be nothin'. What got a lot to do with it is the parents. They don't stop 'em. Children might do good but parents don't tell 'em. A lot of the parents see the money comin' in from this stuff [selling drugs]. No way they can't know. Got to know. Got to know what these children doin'. When I drive down the street, I see 'em. Not my children—I know what they doin'. Don't go to school neither. Parents must know."

For AC, everything comes down to personal responsibility: it should come from the family but should also be reinforced in the schools, in church, and everywhere in the local community. He often pines for the "old days" when norms were clearer, when the rod was seldom spared, to prevent spoiling the child. It was in this way that life's lessons were learned and not soon forgotten; this was the kind of learning experience to lessen the chances of erring in the future.

"Daddy used to say: 'If you don't look out fo' yourself, who is?' He'd say, 'When you got yo' hand in the lion's mouth, you don't snatch it out, you ease it out. And when you get it out, you can talk. But don't go snatchin' it out.' And them things stick with me. That's what you got to learn to deal with."

In time, nearly all of AC's children repeat this line and its lesson to me. "The hand in the lion's mouth" is a metaphor that says a lot about the need to be careful, to be thoughtful, to behave responsibly so as not to be put at risk. AC's son Samuel shares these views. He, too, feels that "something has been lost" with the current generation of young black males. He faults the schools, family values, and personal responsibility. As he tells me, when I ask him specifically about young black males:

"I think most of the young black guys will pretty much get by but their migration won't be to the military or jobs to take them out of Colonial County. Their migration will be to the jailhouse. And the school system isn't going to get better, it's going to get worse. We need to go back into our house and get control of it. That's why the military is good for these young blacks. They need to get an understanding, some discipline. They don't have it right now. Right now what they live is jail and once they come back, they're lost. You go to jail, . . . instead of your life improving, you've lost all likeness of yourself. You're a zombie. You're waiting around for your time to die and go to the grave. Most of these young guys coming out of school right now have a certificate; a piece of paper. They can't even pass a high school test. That's our future right there. You can consider this generation right now as not even being here."

Clorice, AC's first wife, had told me the same thing. As with nearly everything, Clorice offered a moral context for evaluating an issue and working toward its solution. A thoughtful, contemplative woman, she said she had begun a group to work with young black males: "There should be a man doing this . . . but they're not living up to that [moral] standard." So she too sees them at risk, and rather than let them be, she has decided to work on their behalf. She has done this in Colonial County by organizing a support group, a group that would have high ideals and would encourage lawful and moral behavior. She has tried to start a similar group in the neighboring county where she works, but was unable to, since the effort met little enthusiasm from her boss.

And Young Black Females?

Terrence predictably sees the failings of all young people as resting primarily with the schools. He sees an interrelatedness among the moral, social, and behaviorial problems of young black males and of the women they are most likely to marry, young black females. His analysis sounds strikingly like what a social scientist might suggest. For Terrence, things related to social structure dominate the explanatory landscape far more than do individual attributes. It is the schools that make children into delinquents or people with chronic difficulties.

As he, AC, and a friend are talking about this one day, Terrence's frustration is clear. It is palpable. His time in jail has merely reinforced his sense of how the power structure in America often works to the advantage of those already in power and to the detriment of those on the outside.

AC laments, "This group we got right here now, I don't know what we do with 'em. A third or more gettin' welfare could get along without it. A lot of 'em could get a job."

Terrence responds: "But AC, if these people on welfare get a job, where they gonna work, Burger King? If they get cut off welfare, the chirren got Medicaid, they got food stamps comin' in and a small insurance. You know good and well that their mamas got no high school education. To get a person off welfare, you got to have a job program or some kinda system to get 'em off. There's no way in the world that if I was on welfare I'm gonna get off for some four-dollar-and-eighty-five-cent job. My rent, take care of my kids, buy 'em clothes, take 'em to the doctor. There ain't no way!"

But AC doesn't yield: "You could have a job and still get help to take care of those children. There's never gonna be a place where they let people starvin' like that. There always be some kinda assistance. If you on welfare, I don't care who you is—once you in that rut, if you don't take some initiative, you go down that path and so do your children. I don't care who you is. What give people respect and a strong background and a strong family is when you gonna have to depend on yo'self. That's where you get it from. But as long as you stay on that welfare system, you ain't never gonna get off. Your children come along and they get the same thing. You have to take initiative to do somethin'. See, who's on welfare? The children come up, they all in that same system."

Terrence continues: "It's a governmental system. They've been taught by the system. The average person, a family of four, those people workin' in the office, the case workers and managers, . . . they make those little people makin' pennies look sick at the end of the month. They the ones makin' those seventy-to-eighty-thousand-dollar jobs. They's the ones benefittin' from welfare."

AC continues, almost as though he and Terrence are in different conversations, "So many people say they'll get off welfare if there's any way, but they got to have that initiative. You can find a way to get off; that ain't the problem. Some of my children been on welfare. But what they did? They either went back to school or learned a trade. My daughter doin' that right now over in Coastal City, learning to be a nurse."

Their friend chimes in: "That's right. You can't depend on others. You got to do for yourself."

AC gets in a final word, "Ain't nothin' guaranteed no mo'."

This conversation among the two brothers and their friend is a small window into a huge world. It illustrates well the disagreement even among older black males about how best to reform welfare and encourage work. And, importantly, it provides a kind of validation for much of what Duneier reports, since he, too, found this ambivalence among older black men about the role of the state in providing assistance for poor people. As Terrence sees it, the person who accepts welfare is merely recognizing that this is a more comprehensive form of income than is working for wages. But for AC and the brothers' friend, this is unacceptable, except purely as a temporary measure. AC's comment, "Ain't nothin' guaranteed no mo'," summarizes well the future that many welfare recipients face. It is a normative response to their life's situation. For them, the one certainty is uncertainty.

The Open-Air, Open-Space Drug Market

Driving around Colonial County at night is always disorienting for an outsider like me because it is so dark. There are no city lights reflecting in the sky, and few street lights to illuminate either the main or the secondary roads. Driving at night often gives the sense of heading into an inkpot, with light cast on things immediately present but on little else. Thus the simple task of driving requires a kind of faith for what lies down the road, a faith that there is something beyond the headlights.

Despite the general darkness in the county, there are some lights encountered—other cars, the occasional house or small community, and, most prominently, small "bonfires" (a local term for an outdoor fire of almost any size seen at night). In the black communities, bonfires are almost always accompanied by young black males. One might assume that on a winter's eve this is simply young men keeping warm while hanging out, but it is widely reported that a bonfire is akin to hanging out a business sign, as though saying in neon lights "Open." And the business is drugs. With the inky darkness and open spaces, it is easy to run for cover if the police drive by or try to raid them. To be sure, there is the occasional roundup of "drug dealers," but this inevitably catches the slow or most vulnerable—the low-level street dealers, not the "big money" behind them. I have discussed drugs in the county earlier, and shall say little more about them here, other than to reiterate: every black person I talked with, young or old, felt that the big money is white folk yet virtually every person caught and charged with distribution is young and black and male.

In a rural place like Colonial County, it is jarring to see "Say No to Drugs" signs—or my favorite, "No Drugs Aloed" (the spelling on the sign). It is clear, however, that, for at least some young black males, drugs are a way to make a buck. Like some of their "brothers" in inner cities, this work provides its own culture and support network. You may be an outlaw but you can hang out with others like yourself, and apparently, even in Colonial County, find some acceptance in the larger community by people who assume that your behavior is merely temporary and aberrant, not your true self. As AC tells me, "It's their parents. Them people know what's goin' on but don't do nothin' to stop it." As he says on several occasions when discussing young black males, "[They] may be a lost generation, like the Bible say. I don't know. I gots more hope for the next generation."

Here, miles from any urban place, in an area rural by any definition, with little population density or nightlife, young men sit on upturned logs or old ruined-looking kitchen chairs, selling drugs. My experience with this in Colonial County and my more general discussion with people about young black males remind me of Alex Kolkowitz's book, *There Are No Children Here*.[16] Although Kolkowitz did his work on one family's experience in a high-rise Chicago housing project, the title of the book conveys vividly the threat to children. I had a similar experience in Colonial County, wondering about the future of young black males. My best guess is that, generally, their futures are better than many of their urban counterparts', but are still too uncertain and too colored by the possible influence of drugs.[17]

These youths are not, of course, powerless drones in this drama. A term in vogue for several years in the social sciences is "agency," suggesting the ability to harness energy and do something. To be sure, young black males in Colonial County have the ability to influence—for good or not—their futures. But the harsh reality illuminated by their campfires is that, for many, life is lived somewhat on the edge, on a precipice with jail too often the social safety net.

Work—Past, Present, and Future

Colonial County's employment history reflects its rurality. Historically, much of the employment was in agriculture, especially timber and fishing (both harvesting and processing). More recently, the economy has
become far less agricultural, far more service-sector-driven. For about the
past fifty years, many residents work outside the county; for those working
in the county, the public sector accounts for nearly one in four workers. (Although the proportions may vary, the disproportionate influence of the public sector on employment is common to most rural counties.)

AC's lament (like those found in other ethnographies of older black men)
about the employment gap between his generation and the current one is
based largely on anecdotes and other impressions. Nothing is more common and widely known than an older generation bemoaning the state of a
younger one. But, in regard to the lack of jobs that pay a living wage or the
shortage of workers for some local jobs that might pay a living wage, there
is some truth to what AC and his companions say when they compare their
work lives to those of today's youth, essentially two generations younger.
This generation, in rural Colonial County and in most other rural counties,
has had far more educational opportunities and far fewer racial barriers—
but, at the same time, the economic landscape has undergone a revolution.
"Local" jobs may require comparatively little formal education (perhaps a
high school education) and pay comparatively poor wages; they may offer
dim future prospects, with little economic incentive. As is well known in the
research community, for example, wage curves for low-wage jobs are usually quite flat: where you start is not dramatically different from where you
finish. For example, a nonmanagement job at a place like McDonald's pays
(in adjusted dollars) little more after years of experience than did the
employee's entry job. Anthropologist Carol Stack and her colleagues describe this as "coming of age at minimum wage," something disproportionately applicable to minority and working-class children—the very children
most likely to attend Colonial County's public schools.

Thus the idea of "greater opportunities" may prove highly illusory for
many rural children. Absent living in a place where good jobs are available,
one is left with little option than to make do with local jobs (perhaps working more than one) or, as has been true since the advent of the industrial

revolution and its centralization in urban areas, to migrate out. But migration today is simply not the relatively attractive choice it once was. This is because, as sociologist William Julius Wilson has observed, the structural transformation of most inner-city economies has meant the massive out-migration of those industries that paid the best wages and best benefits, and offered the greatest likelihood of career advancement and all that comes with it—especially home ownership in increasingly better neighborhoods (whether in city or suburbs)—for workers who did not have college degrees but did have some education and, crucially, a strong desire to work.[18] The greatest casualties of this economic transformation have been inner-city residents, minorities in particular, who had a strong work ethic and desire to experience "the American dream." For such persons, whether present inner-city residents or rural folk who might otherwise have moved there, this desire has remained "American" and truly become a dream.

Recent U.S. Census data confirm (as though we need such confirmation) that black males die far sooner than members of any other race/gender group. Although AIDS is the largest killer of young black males, homicide is also far likelier for them. And the shocking statistics reported further document how great their risk is: With nearly one-half of young black males between fifteen and twenty-four caught up in the justice system in some way, their futures seem both grim and predetermined. Can one say this about any other group in U.S. society? Reading the Colonial County weekly paper provides a ready source of information on the outlook for local youth. The picture that emerges supports what many people have told me: young black males are the most likely to be arrested for selling drugs and to subsequently be sentenced. This tendency has become a perverse form of agriculture, with the community harvesting a crop on a regular basis, a crop headed for processing in the penal system.

In this sense, rural Colonial County is a microcosm of many poor rural counties and, sad to say, especially of poor rural minority counties. Lacking sufficient economic opportunities that pay a living wage, residents are disproportionately caught up in the legal system or in hustling to eke out an existence by combining whatever social welfare they can get with work in the informal, underground economy. This may include working at odd jobs for cash; bartering; and so on. What is very clear is that the younger generation, having grown up with fast food, is far less likely to—like their parents and, even more, their grandparents—grow and prepare their own food or (as AC did nearly every day) hunt and fish for their meals.

Even in rural Colonial County, much of the work that is and will be available is in the service sector. "Service" work has a long history of multiple meanings in the black community. It is most heavily laden with emotional baggage for older people. For them, being "in service" long preceded the arrival of the "service sector." The sector that older African Americans were most familiar with servicing was the homes of white folk. As the South became less rural, this work followed from the plantation's "big house" to the houses of the more affluent, both in older, expensive urban neighborhoods and in newer, suburban ones. There, "service work" meant quite literally being at the service of their white employers, or, as it was usually called, being a "maid." In Colonial County, every older African American with whom I spoke had direct experience of this, either having been "in service" themselves or having had family members who were; not surprisingly, it was women who disproportionately knew firsthand what this was like.

By contrast, being "in the service" (i.e., the military) was seen as a way out of the local economic structure. Especially with the all-volunteer force, beginning in the early 1970s, the military became an economic refuge for millions of African American men and women. Indeed, the military is the largest single employer of African Americans in the United States. About 30 percent of all U.S. Army enlisted personnel are black. The military is the one institution in which whites have by far the greatest exposure to blacks as equals, and the greatest likelihood of being supervised by them (in part because blacks even more disproportionately make a career out of the military, and thus are likelier to advance into senior ranks with supervisory responsibility).[19] This was the career path followed by three of AC's five children.

It is a certainty that subsequent generations of black children will have, collectively, an economic profile much different from their grandparents'. But how different it will be from their parents' remains to be seen. And nowhere is this harder to predict than in rural areas, places where economic opportunities have always been more truncated even if the regions offer far cheaper places to live.

Three

Strong Women

The black women of Colonial County have, like generations of black women before them, had to be strong. Every calamity that could befall someone was likelier to happen to them than to others: men running off (or running around even when living at home); having to work from a very early age, and having to work at whatever was available; bearing children at an early age; being a single parent for a disproportionate amount of one's life; greater probabilities of illness and of having to care for parents or other older relatives; providing shelter and care for "grands" (grandchildren).[1] In sum, there is little that came easy to black women in Colonial County, especially the women who are forty years of age and older. The younger women found themselves in new times, times made better by policies such as affirmative action and by new norms emerging even in southern rural counties, where some forms of employment, especially in the public sector, became more accessible.

The women I spoke with, at least most of them, did not benefit much from these programs, at least not until very recently. For them, much of life had been a struggle—whether schooling or finding work that paid a living wage or raising children or staying in a relationship with a man. None of these things was taken for granted. To the contrary, all were assumed to represent challenges. And yet all of the women I spoke with had immense hope, saw better tomorrows, complained little about today or the troubles their lives had seen.

I first became aware of the idea of "strong women" when speaking with two of AC's daughters, Alice and Grace. The concept was especially clear through their memories of their grandmothers but particularly of their mother, for whom they had immense respect. To them, she was in some ways a larger-than-life figure, someone who had to achieve over and over again to get what others might have with far less work. When Aretha Franklin says in her song "R-e-s-p-e-c-t," I am reminded exactly of how AC's children describe their mother. And it becomes clear when speaking with these children that her strength has found its way to them, as well.

Clorice

Clorice was AC's first wife. Their marriage lasted nearly twenty years but, as so many marriages do, it ended in divorce. Clorice is a very smart, very articulate woman in her early sixties. Although physically small, she is a force to be reckoned with. This becomes obvious when she interacts with her adult children; when she is instructing little children at church; or when she visits with an outside interviewer, like me. She is an imposing, impressive person. She speaks slowly, clearly, and with a sense of belief and importance in her own words.

"My father's side came from Carolina. My mother's side was from here. In this area, people did not leave—only the offspring, and, even then, many of them came back. I have one brother and two sisters. My oldest sister moved to New York for a job, and once she had children, my baby sister moved there to take care of them. My baby sister stayed in New York; she's a doctor now; she's been there a long time.

"Everybody in my family was taught the basics. We were taught to cut pulpwood, cut firewood, sew, embroider, crochet; there's almost nothing we couldn't do. Plant a garden—not cotton and stuff but corn, greens, and whatever. Things we could harvest.

"I was trained by my father to hunt. By the time we were twelve, we could go hunting. We could build houses, anything that came up. We were poor but we were not poor. My mother was educated. My father could have been superintendent; his ability was so strong. He didn't have much education but you couldn't tell. His English was clear; it wasn't 'flat' [meaning that he spoke correct English with little local idiom].

"When I was eight years old, within a block of here, I would get up every morning. I would spend the night next door at my grandmother's. I had to stay with her because she'd been ill. When I was twelve or thirteen, I had to get up every morning and slop the hogs, fix breakfast, grab my books, and go by my grandmother's, and catch the school bus. By the time I was fourteen, my daddy always cut wood; he would either pulpwood [work in the pulpwood industry] or log, cut crosscut ties. I'd load those ties and snake 'em out of the pond with the horse or the mule. I could snake out 120 ties in an afternoon. Then I'd go home and slop the hogs, eat dinner, study my lesson, and go to bed. All of us had to do those things, my brothers and sisters and me. There were only two boys, and the girls had to work just like them. We had to provide. We are where we are today because my mother taught us moral standards."[2]

Morality is an issue that arises often when speaking with Clorice. She sees herself as a highly moral person. She is someone who attends church regularly, and feels that others should as well. She has taught Sunday school and played the piano or organ at several churches for about as long as most people can remember. Beyond these things, she has a sense of herself as having always promoted values and morality with her children. This sense is folded, in ways conscious and not, into her everyday life (as I discuss later). Thus her everyday life is a blending of physical and spiritual strength. As I found in speaking with her children (and learned to a lesser degree from her), her strength was tested mightily when she and AC got divorced.

Until Death Do Us Part—Or until Divorced

One of the most intriguing aspects of life among black folk in Colonial County (as in virtually any place) is the relationship between men and women—in particular, their pre- and post-marital relationships. All of AC's brothers have been divorced; so have two of his daughters and one of his sons. Tellingly, though, nearly all of these divorced people had eventually married again and, once remarried, had stayed married. In this way, AC's family looks, statistically, like the larger rural African American population. There (according to the year 2000 U.S. census), about 85 percent of all married or divorced adults are still married and 15 percent are divorced or separated (figures comparable to those for Colonial County as a whole, white as well as black).

For the women in AC's family, divorce was discussed in two very different ways. It is easy to imagine these women presenting themselves as victims, and, indeed, this image comes through at times in their comments. But, more often, they present themselves as proactive, as the ones who initiated the divorce. At least for two of AC's daughters, Rhonda and Grace, having a man in one's life on an everyday basis is not necessary, maybe not even desirable. For them, part of the issue is an assertion of self. That is, they don't need a man to make them whole, even though having the additional income and person to share one's life with would, at times, be nice.

All of AC's children's feelings about and orientation to marriage have been shaped, in part, by their reactions to his divorce from Clorice. This affected the children and the sense of family among them all; their sense of themselves as a family, and their love and closeness, were severely disrupted and in need of either repair or acceptance of what seemed to be a new, less intimate and loving state. For all, the divorce was one more obstacle in life's path. And, importantly, much of what they say about this reflects their own willingness to step into the breach and not simply accept things as they are.

My curiosity about this matter was piqued one day when speaking with Grace. We had been talking about her parents' divorce when she paused and grew pensive. She feels that in Colonial County, it is normal for black men to have "fooled around" on their wives. She believes that all her uncles did this when they were married and that everyone knew about their actions.[3] Of course reports on such phenomena can be found in the academic literature, but there it is remote; here it was immediate and personal.

Grace said, "I always tell my son, 'Let one woman be enough for you.' Womanizing is just part of his culture. You may find some white men who mess around, but not at all like it is in the black community, and that upsets me. In the black community, it's acceptable. She is married and you're not! That's what they think. I'm not kidding. Like some black men will say, 'I'm not married but my wife is.'

"No matter what a man does and how much he runs around, if he gets wind that his wife is having any kind of affair, their relationship is over. He could have three or four kids outside of his marriage and that's supposed to be all right?

"This place is too small. What happens sometimes at school is that some kid will come up and say, 'Your daddy had a baby with my mama.' I would never be put into that position. Never. That's why I'm single today. I have no respect for men!" I interrupt to ask about her son, admitting that I'm surprised by how negative she seems. "I do all I can for my son's attitude toward women, to respect them. When he was dating this girl in high school, he was about seventeen. I called this girl's father and I told him, 'Don't take no stuff off my son. Give him the law. Give him the law.' And I told my son, 'Do not touch this man's girl.'

"A lot of black women, right here today, if they got sons, they think they can go out and do anything. But it's a different attitude if it's a daughter. I have the same attitude for my son as I do for my daughters."

Several weeks later, I asked Clorice how she felt about this, about black men in Colonial County. Given her own experience, having been born and raised there and spending nearly all of her adult life there, she would, I anticipated, tell me something similar to what Grace had. But she didn't, not entirely. Her strong Christian faith entered our conversation more than once, and it colored her sense of what had happened to her—and how she had urged her children to cope with it, to understand it. Equally, she had a sense of responsibility that transcended her own family. Black males, especially young ones, have been much in the news in recent years, often for the wrong reasons. This was not lost on Clorice, even in rural Colonial County, and entered our conversation.

Clorice started to tell me about her own attempt to organize a group for young black men. "There should be a man doing this. This is the time we need some moral standards. I have three men so far in my group in Colonial County. The young men need someone to look to as a role model, as a father, as a brother. We want the men as mentors, but we're not going to have that many from this area, because they're not living up to that standard. You can't have a mentor without some standards."

I told her that I had heard several black women be very critical of black men. I said that this critical stance seemed like what she was telling me, that she had to try to organize this group because no local man would do it. Clorice stiffened noticeably. That she was hearing this from a white man, an outsider, did not sit well.

"That's what they said? I don't see it that way. The only problem with most of our men is that they don't have this [she pauses for a moment]. . . . When I say 'mentor'—you've got to have a man who is faithful to his wife. Who keeps a good job. Who's a devout Christian. One who lives [for] the community. One who loves people. You don't have many of those. Most of our men don't spend enough time with their own families. Maybe I've been brought up different from most people to think that these men don't have the qualities that I'm looking for."

I told her that I had heard of an expression when a man is asked if he's married, that he may say "I'm not but my wife is," clearly implying both different sets of standards and cultural approval for running around. Clorice responded harshly, "I would consider those men trash. Most men would know that they are married and don't play around. We have a lot of good men, but their standards are not high enough for the boys that we want to reach." Then she paused again. It was like a scene from the movie *Waiting to Exhale*. A strong black woman not wanting to criticize black men but equivocating, knowing that the record locally was uneven and that, for many of the men, running around on their wives was not unusual. She continued in a very slow, measured way, "There are a few men around here who have these qualities [high moral standards], but not many."

Knowing Hard Times

It is clear that Clorice's picture of black men in Colonial County at present is set against a backdrop that is more personal, that involves her own divorce as well as the divorces of two of her daughters and the experiences of a third who never married. Remembering this personal odyssey and its consequences is painful but, at the same time, she was determined to deal with it and still affirm the value of her own life and her children's.

"There's things about this you would never understand because you're a male," she said, looking at the floor before slowly raising her head to look me squarely in the eye. "Are you a born-again Christian?" I was caught completely off-guard, but told her, "No, I'm not." She said, "I ask that because you have to really know the Lord to see the picture. You can see some of the picture without being a Christian but . . . and people can be Christian and not know it. You know that, don't you?" I give a noncommittal response, reminded that, while I may believe in God, I'm not a Christian.

Clorice continued, "When AC and I were divorced, children look for something. They had a beautiful picture of him and I tried to keep that alive. I taught them that if your father was crawling on his hands and knees like a snake, you must still respect him. I demanded that they respect their father. But you look for something. You know how children look for value in someone else? They kept looking and Grace, who was one of the most beautiful persons there was, doing church work and stuff, and she just turned, you know? And she said, 'I hate God! Mom and Daddy going to church all the time and now they're not together!'

"They were at that age," and she paused in a contemplative way, "like teenagers, that growing period. Something happened to those kids that I could never replace because I couldn't be their father. I tried but somewhere down the road they got lost. I tried and I still try today, but there's still something missing. Like they are searching for that father they once had.

"I had to change my whole way of living, because my life was for my children. I had to make them think I was happy when I wasn't. That same lady caught up in this [AC's new wife], I treat her just like I treat my own kids. She would call and say nasty things on the phone and all that kind of stuff. And the children would worry and I would say, 'Child, just look at your mother,' and I would be laughing. But I'd be hurting so bad inside that I didn't know what to do, until the Lord lifted me. I could see AC laying on somebody and it wouldn't even have curled my hair. Nothing. It was a blessing. I had to teach them love. I told my kids, 'If he's crawling in the gutter like a snake, he's still your father.' It goes right back to what I said before: it does not matter how someone treats you. What matters is how you treat them. And that's how we lived. We stayed in this place and prospered because, while many people had hate, we had love."

The strength of black women in Colonial County appears over and over in their narratives about their everyday lives.[4] For many—one would suspect, for most—life has often been very difficult. Almost no aspect of everyday life lacked severe obstacles. And yet, for them, this was normal, not unusual. What might paralyze some people was simply another card dealt by life—not always the card one might have wanted but part of one's hand nonetheless.

Dorthea, AC's nearly seventy-year-old former sister-in-law, told me one day about being a single mother (a state that all the women I met had been through). "I was in bad shape one time. It was so bad that I wondered where the next meal was comin' from. There was a place in the Bluff [the area where she lives] and the man who run the shop, a white man, saw my son one day outside his store. He asked him how we were doing? When he told him, the man said, 'I can't let you chirren starve. I know their daddy.' And he just filled up two boxes with groceries and said, 'You go home and feed them chirren. I can't see 'em starve.'[5]

"I seen hard times. I know how that feels. I know what it is. After those hard times, I said, 'I gotta learn to do for myself.' So I learned how to can— beans, peas, okra, tomatoes. I ain't canned in the last two years but I always got some okra. I put it in a jar with some salt and a little water. I can always buy some cans of tomatoes and mix 'em with that okra to make a soup."

As Dorthea tells me, her behavior and strength of character is directly attributable to her mother. "My mama died when I was fourteen. She was a person say at night, 'Let's sit down and talk. I'm not gonna be with y'all always, so you're gonna have to do for yourself.' She tell us what you'll have to do. 'Don't let nobody run over you; learn to do for yourself.' So I learn to cook. I had to take it in here [pointing at her head]. She died fifty-five years ago. If I hadn't taken in what she tellin' me, I'd a-been a bum in the world. So I thank God for what she did."

Amazing Grace and Others

The idea of personal responsibility and standing on one's own two feet arose again and again. No matter with whom I spoke—man or woman, young or old—AC's family had an incredible strength of character and a determination to not be beaten down by the obstacles in one's path.[6]

Grace told me about her sister, Alice, who had retired recently after twenty years in the military and moved back to Colonial County with her husband and children. Life had not been easy for Alice. "I'll tell you how strong she is. When Alice went to Germany that first time, [as a young solider], she had a baby and a six- or seven-year-old. Didn't know anybody. Didn't have a husband. Had to live on the economy. She had a bicycle and she took her kids to the babysitter, one on the handlebars. She and James weren't married yet. She was on the waiting list for the benefits on base like housing and whatnot. Now, let me tell you, friend, that's a strong girl!"

But Grace also told me about herself—a proud black woman who knew what it was like to rely almost solely on herself. Although she had loving family members close at home, she almost always chose pride, independence, and obstinacy over reaching out for help. Being around Grace for any length of time makes clear that her beliefs are strongly imparted to her children. I learned this when we spent a long evening together.

Grace's house sits back a short way from Route 17. It is a quarter mile or so to her father's home in one direction, to her mother's in the other. Her sister Rhonda also lives less than a mile away. The house is a place that had special meaning for Grace. "I remember being a little girl and walking by and it looked so big and white from a distance. The man who owned this house died. It's about forty years old" (about Grace's age). Now the little girl has grown up and owns the "big" house she remembers so fondly.

The house is actually quite modest, perhaps fourteen hundred square feet. It is still white but could definitely use a coat of paint. Like much else in Yvonne, it looks a little tired. Grace is aware of this, and tells me, "I got to get my father to do some things here." The yard is mostly dirt, including the path from the road. Directly next to the house sits a pile of old furniture and junk, covered by what looks like yards of old carpet. Indeed, when Grace's income rose sufficiently, she essentially replaced her old furniture and carpeting—but the old sits outside as a reminder of days not long past. Too, it is a reminder of her admonition to me, at her sister's house one day, when she asked what I really knew about "poor people" and then told me that what things look like from outside are not always what they look like on the inside.

The interior of the house is very tidy and well kept. Grace and I sat in the living room, which contained a comfortable couch and chairs as well as a large television. For hours, we were mostly by ourselves, but her children dropped in occasionally and sometimes joined us in conversation.

Grace had her first child immediately after graduating from high school. She wasn't married, and for awhile she joined her older sister, Alice, living in another part of the state. But when Alice joined the military, Grace returned home and started working at whatever jobs were available.

"I worked at the shoe factory in Conaty and then I started cookin' in the islands. . . . Me and my sister, Rhonda, could do any kind of party. She and I supervised the food preparation at the Radisson. We had a big job one time and got people off the streets and out of the woods! We worked some long hours—I'm talkin from three one mornin' to one the next. One night we did over nine hundred steak dinners in one spot, three different rooms of people [she laughs, remembering this occasion]. We worked at Shuckers; it was a restaurant on the island, run by some people from Atlanta. Rhonda used to work there. They wanted me to manage one shift, and I told them that I needed to bring my sister back. We did that till we got tired of workin' and I decided there's got to be a better way."

The "islands," where many of the black people in Colonial County work, are forty-five minutes to an hour's drive away. There is one road to them. When it is foggy or stormy, the driving, as on many roads in the Lowcountry, gets treacherous. The roads will have water on top, and even on a clear night, it is often inky black where the main road (U.S. 17) runs like a path through a forest. There are no streetlights outside towns, and houses and other possibly lighted buildings are few and far between.

Grace, like her brothers and sisters, reached a point in life where, as she told me, she was determined to find "a better way." This way was to go back to school and find a career that would be more rewarding, financially and otherwise, than continuing to cook. In the end, she decided that, if she was going to be on her feet much of the day, it would be as a nurse—an occupation where the pay and benefits would be worth the physically tiring work. But like much else in her life, this was not easy.

"I went to school when I was in my thirties. See, what happened was that I was gettin' up at four in the mornin' and my children were raisin' themselves. I took a nursing assistants class. I came out of there in six months with a one-hundred accumulated average. I got out of there on a Thursday and started college on the following Monday. I went two years and got an associate's degree; passed my state boards; and became an R.N.

"When I started clinical, I had to be at the hospital at six forty-five in the morning. I had to be there earlier before the inspector come. I would walk down to the corner and catch a ride with people goin' to work. Or if I could connect with someone, I would ask them to pick me up here. Lots of times, I rode with a girlfriend of mine, a white girl. . . . One girl came from Fort [pronounced, as by many Lowcountry black people, Fote] Stewart and when she found out where I lived on 17, she said I could ride with her.

"When I got off at nights, at ten, I'd be standin' out in front of the hospital tryin' to get a ride home. My brother said, 'You should quit and take care of those kids.' I told him, 'If I have to wait that long, I need not go. I'm gonna go to school if I have to sleep in that old broken-down yellow car [still parked in the yard] with my kids.'

"I had this nursing assistant's certificate under my belt, so I tried working during my last year of school. One of my girlfriends had an old car she sold to me for five hundred dollars, so I used my loan money from school for that and drove the car to work on the islands and then I'd study when I got home. I would work all night and go to school during the day and then come home. I could maintain my grades that way.

"My time was so difficult that the newspaper did a story on me and what I had done. About how I caught rides and what I did to finish school. That was [the summer she graduated]."

I told Grace that I was getting "this incredible sense of people doing whatever they have to do to exist. And I'm not so sure that it's any different in inner cities, despite what much of the public [and especially whites] may think. Here, in Colonial County, though, people just seem to work very hard, like all these women who still work on the islands or more locally in seafood processing plants."

Grace responded, "All these years, all these years—and they still go! My daddy's sister raised her kids workin' at the crab factory. When my aunt stopped workin' at the crab factory, she was makin' $350 to $400 cuttin' crabs! Can you imagine?!? That's a lot of crabs to clean, let me tell you!

"Back then you didn't have to have transportation because [the employers would] send a little bus around to pick up people who worked. I had friends who got a twelfth-grade education and they never went anyplace else but that factory [processing seafood] and they're still workin' there. I'd never do that or be a maid in a motel. I don't know why but I would never do that."

I told Grace that other women had told me that working in seafood or "being in service" (as a maid either in a hotel or in someone's home) were the only two jobs available to most black women. She reiterated, "I would never do that."

But just because she wouldn't do it didn't mean that thousands of black women had not, or that they would not, continue to work in service or processing seafood. Although the demand for domestic work may have declined sharply in some places, in a rural area like Colonial County, especially with relatively easy access to "the islands" (with the kinds of houses and hotels there), the demand for domestic workers is relatively constant; and as one generation quits, another takes its place.[7] Indeed, virtually all Grace's older women relatives, including her stepmother, had worked at one of these jobs. Her oldest living relative, her Aunt Flo, had told me about doing this. Flo is in her mid-eighties. Illness has slowed her down considerably and she spends most of her day lying in a recliner fixed up like a bed. She is lightskinned and has wispy straight hair. Her eyes are sharp and her hearing is good. With her sock-covered feet sticking out from under a crocheted blanket, she talked with me in her family room.

"I did factory work around here, in the shrimp factory. And before I married I used to have little jobs—washing, ironing, cooking. I did some of everything you could do. I worked at a seafood factory down here [up the road about three miles from her house]. Used to walk there each morning and back at night. I worked everywhere. I worked until 1989 [when she was in her seventies], Christmas week, until they shut down. That was in Coastal City. I worked there thirty-six years. When I first started workin' there, they had a bus. But they took the bus off and you had to get your own way. Some of us who drive took turns. I worked on the line and did all different things— french toast, oysters. I was workin' as a packer.

"At first you got two cents a box for packing shrimp. Could make two to three dollars a day. Then you got forty cents an hour, in 1967, I think. Then when you got a dollar an hour, that was some money [she laughs hard]. At forty cents an hour, it wasn't by the piece no more. At a dollar an hour, those mens got mad 'cuz they said we got a dollar an hour and they got a dollar.

"Over to the islands, where I worked before Coastal City, that was hard. Those ladies got used to it. You sometimes had to wait all day [for the seafood to come in]. Over time, you got so much an hour, but with SeaPak on the islands, you had to drive over there and it was like you were workin' for nothin'. It was better workin' in Coastal City. You had good benefits, medicine, and all like that."

Patrice, AC's second wife, also remembers those days. She and AC have been together over twenty-five years. Patrice is not a native of Colonial

County but her migration was short, from the next county over. Like Flo, she too worked until quite recently—until, in fact, she could not work anymore. "I peeled and headed shrimp. Process, cook, pack it. All work with my hands. Used to ride the bus but when they quit that, I'd drive a week and someone else would, another week. Used to send a school bus to Liberty County. It wasn't no pile of money but you had to make a livin'." Like Flo, she had also worked in service: "I cooked for white folks."

Again, all the older women had done this—worked in service and seafood, the two jobs most readily available to women. Dorthea, AC's former sister-in-law, had first worked in service in Miami, where she moved to live near her older sister (with whom, eventually, she lost all contact; the sister just disappeared). But then Dorthea, when she was still a young girl (about eighteen), returned to Colonial County and "went to work in service for a couple of years but it didn't pay nothin'. Then I met a cousin of mine and she said 'Watcha doin? Why don't you come to work in the crab factory? You can make twenty-five dollars in three hours.' There was other jobs, like the shoe factory, but I didn't want to work there. I worked in a local place for eighteen years, off an on. It didn't used to pay much but the price of crabs went up and up. I got paid by the pound. I worked until I averaged fifty dollars a day, from seven to two-thirty. That was in the seventies. After I get a speed, I had schoolchirren to buy for. I wanted to make $185 a week to take home. So I'd work hard the first four days of the week to get that amount. And then, on the fifth day, I made $54.74—the govamint take the fifty and leave me four! [she laughs heartily]"

But she is much more pensive when I ask about women still working in the plants, especially on the islands and in Coastal City. "All the colored women who workin' go to Coastal City." She looks around, visualizing her neighbors, and says, "There's Lidia, Sarah, Sheila and Mary, Liana, Alma down the road. They go to Coastal City every morning. The mens, too, go to Coastal City." The big difference today is that it is primarily only the older women, and those few younger ones who cannot find anything else, who still work in the seafood plants. As Dorthea also tells me, "You have to buy your own gas. Long way to drive. Take about an hour. Don't pay no money. They only want to give you about five dollars an hour. . . . But you have to leave Colonial County to find work."

Their Mothers' Daughters

Grace was practically legendary in her family for being a hard worker. Some might say she was virtually consumed by work. Her daughter, Sheila ("not," Grace later tells me, "one of those fashionable ethnic names"), characterized her mother as a "workaholic." For Grace, working hard is important not only for economic reasons but also for expression on a deeper level of who she is—and for sending her children the message they could do this.

"I 'double up,' like on Sundays. Last Sunday I worked at my regular job, at Gateway, where I do drugs and mental health. Then I did my other job [caring for a homebound child] until seven in the evening. Then, instead of coming home, I'll go to my aunt's in Coastal City and take a nap. Get up; take a shower; and go back to Gateway. I'm gonna tell ya, one year I worked so much . . . I worked at the hospital in intensive care. I refuse to be a floor nurse or a nurse taking care of someone any can take care of. My home patients, I take care of the critical patients, I want them on ventilators. I need the challenge. Like I tell my sister and them: 'To me, I don't want to be a housekeeper or stay home and raise children. What I want to do is here— if I can work sixteen hours a day, that's what I like to do. That's who I am.'"

But Grace also tells me she feels trapped in Yvonne. Even with the love of her family, she feels constrained, fears she can never become fully what she otherwise might. She worries that she might repeat a mistake her mother made.

"Like my mom. She was so naive before she left [and lived in New York for two years], and her eyes were wide open when she got back. I was seventeen when she went up there. Rhonda was with my dad for a little bit then. I got out of high school when I was sixteen. My mom got married to a man up there but they got divorced and then she came back here.

"I remember when I was sixteen or seventeen years old, when my oldest son was born. My son's father came here and wanted me to leave to go back with him so we could get married. My mom never liked him and she told me 'no.' And I had been raised so that whatever my mom said, that was it. I never thought about goin' against her wish. That's how we were. To this day I regret that. And shortly after that I decided that any decision I make is gonna be mine. I might regret it anyway but it'll be my decision."

Grace and I also spoke about the issue of assuming control—over ourselves and others—so that if there is blame to be placed, there is no question on whom it will go. Her father had told me about this side of Grace. He thought that she would never hang onto any man because "She has to wear the pants in the family. Ain't no man gonna put up with that."

As she told me, her desire to control goes beyond any man in her life. "I'm a control freak with my children. They don't have any privacy. I don't believe in privacy. I don't believe you should have a diary that I can't read. I don't believe that you should have anything to hide from me. My daughter had a couple of diaries that Alice brought to her. My daughter wanted to go to her friend's house and she was begging me to go and I didn't like the friend's mother that much. I was hesitant to let her go and I told her, 'But I don't want you walkin' the streets again.' When those little girls walk the streets at night like that [really just a local form of hanging out], I call 'em 'little hookers'—to me, that's what they look like. Then, here on my bed is her diary saying that she's goin' to Conaty to walk the streets. When I saw that, I didn't let her go. And she burned her diary, never kept another one since. I told her, 'I don't care if your diary is locked, I'm gonna do anything I have to save you from the world and from yourself. I'm gonna know what's goin' on in your mind; I'm gonna know where you are and what you're doin' at all times.' Now they're used to that. They try to pull quickies, but they know I'll find out."

I wondered about Grace's grandchild; I'd seen the child and one other infant in the house while I was there. Always, the children were being looked after by their nieces or nephews or, in this case, their aunts or father.

Grace told me, "That's my son's child. My daughters know they aren't having no babies, not as long as they're under my roof. I told them, 'You can either not get pregnant, or get pregnant and have an abortion. What's your option gonna be? I cannot tell you when to have sex and I can't tell you when not to. You're gonna do what you want to. But you can always tell me what you're thinkin' about and I'll make sure you're taken care of. It's all about bein' responsible. You can go with birth control on your own, but, first thing, if you don't use a condom, what you're telling me is that your life is not worth a screw. Under no circumstances are we having any children in this house as long as you're in my house.' So, Sheila's almost eighteen and Sandra is sixteen and they know I mean that.

"My son will be twenty-one in August. He took this quarter off from school; he's a junior in college. His baby was born in January [two months prior to my visit], and he wants to bond with his baby. His girlfriend is going back to school next quarter, over in Coastal City. They're getting married in August. I can say he made me proud, because you know the reputation black men have for walkin' out and leavin' their children. He didn't do that. He came home and said, 'Ma, I've got some bad news for you. Cynthia's pregnant.' I was so hurt. I was so upset. I talked to him and to her. Her mother never told her anything about getting pregnant. I was so hurt, you know? But then after the realization came that I had a grandchild coming, I had to change my feelings."

I interrupt to ask if her son has custody some of the time. "Where's the mom?" Grace points at the room next to us, and I hit myself in the head: "Geez, she just walked in, right?" And we both start laughing, since it was hard to tell who the mother was, given that Grace's daughters, nieces (two of whom were visiting at the same time), and the mothers were all nearly the same age.[8] Grace continued, "Even if the mom wasn't here, the baby would be. That was my biggest fear. Usually, when your son has a child and he's not married, you lose touch with the maternal grandparents. I told Cynthia, I don't care what happens to them, they can get married or not, but this is my grandchild and it's gonna be part of my life.

"It's gonna be hard for them, working and going to school. My greatest wish for my children, what they can do for me, I want to see my grandchildren with two parents—a mother and a father."

As her father had told me one time, not only had Grace had a smaller family (three children) than he (five children), and not only was her family drastically smaller than the one he was born into (thirteen children), but now, in turn, Grace wanted her children to have even smaller families.

Grace tells me, "I told my children" [and she turns to her daughter], 'How many grandchildren do I want?' Sheila responds, 'Three.' Grace continues, 'And if somebody has more than one, what does that mean for the others?' Sheila, as if their conversation had been rehearsed for my benefit, answers, 'They can't have any.'" We all laugh hard at this little family drama.

Welfare Queens?

When we talked about welfare locally, and how tempting it might be for some young people, especially single mothers, Grace quickly tried to dispel the notion that the number of persons on welfare was high. She saw this as mostly an image blown out of proportion by, in part, the media, especially television, which she felt went out of its way to show black people in poverty, on news stories.[9] "So who are the poor in Colonial County, and what about welfare?" I asked her one day. "It's mostly the younger people," she said (something also stated by her daughter and Janice and her friends, when I was visiting with them). "You will find a large percentage of single mothers in this county buyin' their homes, even if it's a house trailer, and they will have a car and they're not on welfare. That's what a lot of men here say. Even where the husbands have forgot they had children. These are a hard-working bunch of women.[10]

"Now there's a certain group of women who are not goin' to do anything. There's a certain group of women [she says this disdainfully] think that their goal in life is to get a husband or a boyfriend. But that's a minority. It's like, in America it's only a minority of young doin' drugs but if you listen to the media you'd think every black young man in America was doin' drugs. But it's not, it's only a minority.

"Blacks in America are the fastest growing economic group, but that's not what you hear. I've got single friends who make forty, fifty thousand dollars a year in Colonial County. People wouldn't believe it but it's true. It's not a huge number but they are there. Hard-working women.

"Let me tell you, when I went to school, for the first year, we got food stamps, nothin' else. We weren't no welfare queens. A girl I was goin' to school with had the restaurant up the street [in Yvonne] and I'd work for them as a cook. I would give my mom forty dollars to buy groceries for my children for two weeks, and whatever she bought, we ate—beans, okra, peas. I had no car. School was thirty miles away. But I did it.

"My sister works two jobs; neither one is top-paying. But she works at the college during the day and Walmart at night. Before I went to college, I left the house at four-thirty in the morning and my children raised themselves. I worked out on the islands until five in the evening, then I went to the Quality Inn and worked till closing. When I left home my children were in bed, and when I came home they were in bed. They knew that they could only visit my mom's or my sister's. No one else was allowed in the house. And I've got fine children that went to school, obeyed the laws, don't get in trouble.

"But then you hear on television that it's single parents that are causin' the problems. That makes me mad, 'cuz it's not single parents that cause the problems. It's ignorance! All the single mothers I know, nine times out of ten, the children had to raise themselves because the parents got divorced."

For Grace, there is the potential of a self-fulfilling prophecy in much of the common, taken-for-granted, media-created sense of what life results from single parenthood, especially for young black women. But her own sense of these women is that they are strong, hard-working, determined to do the best that they can. Her sister, Rhonda, shares much of Grace's belief. She, too, is single. But, unlike Grace, Rhonda has never been married. She has lived with men but never married one. Like Grace, Rhonda has three children, with one grandchild—born to her oldest daughter, who is in college and single.

Many scholars have addressed directly the strength of the black family and its ability to adapt continually to changing circumstances, whether in slavery or in post-slavery years. Historically, the prevailing image was of people moving away in search of better jobs or, more recently, having to adjust to life in some inner city with its decaying industrial base and loss of jobs that pay a living wage.[11] But usually these scholars provide empirical data analyses far removed from people's everyday lives. It is only in discussing their lives with them, directly, in the places where these lives are lived, that the people's strength comes through. There, they seem less like victims of an unkind welfare state or institutional discrimination (or any one of a half dozen other possible "explanations" for their "plight,"—all of which would have some merit when applied to their lives). Indeed, the women I spoke with seemed far less like victims and far more like heroines.[12]

As Rhonda told me one day, talking about women in her family, "We refuse to give in. We fight to the last." At this she laughed. "I was thirteen when my daddy left. I remember that. It was really a blow. It really affected me. That's why I had children early, because I felt the love wasn't there. He left me way out there. I stopped seeing him for awhile. It made me stronger. It made me depend not on this man but on myself.

"I watched my mother fix whatever had to be fixed. She didn't have a man to do it. And I did everything my mom did. A lot of people tell me that

I'm just like my mom in a lot of ways. But I'm not as creative as her. She's a little fanatic. Well, not a fanatic but she's always doing [here she speaks very rapidly] busybody, busybody, busybody! I believe in keeping it going. I can't keep a boyfriend because, if a man is here, he has a certain thing he has to do [to this she gives great emphasis—and then pauses before continuing] or he has to go. And that's just the way it is.

"I've never been married and, the way it looks [she starts laughing hard], I never will be [she keeps laughing hard]. My sister tells me, 'You gonna run 'em away, you gonna run 'em away!'" Indeed, the man she had been living with for some time, the man her father told me she was going to marry in the summer, had moved out the day before I stopped by.

But this man was in his early forties. I had met him previously and thought he seemed a nice guy. But he didn't measure up for Rhonda, in part because he was not religious enough (for she has a strong moral streak, found especially in her mother but also in her father and oldest sister).

Discussing her youth and her age when her children were born ("I was sixteen with my first child, eighteen with my second, and twenty or twenty-one with the last one"), we started talking about her recollection of how prevalent it was for young women to have children as single parents. It was not unusual. Thus Rhonda, one of these young women, simply made her way as best she could, with some regrets but determined to carry on.

"They [her children's fathers] were young and I don't really put the blame on them. I was young, too. I didn't really know how to choose a man. A lot of the things you're taught now we didn't know then. My children's father? If I had to do it today, he would never have been their father. I tell my children that, today; I apologize to them; I didn't really give them a father. But, you know, all things happen for a reason, so I accept it and keep moving. My oldest children's father never participated in their lives. My baby's father does come and do for her. He's a lot better. He tries to be a part of her life. He's still not the father that he could be." But, sooner than lament this, Rhonda goes forward, and nothing has been more gratifying and fulfilling than attending college.

Like Grace, Rhonda has found college far more than a simple classroom learning experience. Instead, it has been a realization of self; a celebration of self; an opportunity to explore herself in ways she had never imagined.

"We used to take life one way and reality another. We got off somewhere. We missed the boat. Our parents tried hard, but we weren't taught life, you know? We just took it for granted. When I got older, I realized it. When I went to school, I really realized it. I used to think that college was some kind of great big disease and, if you go, you'll get this thing." We both laugh hard. But when I started going, I was like 'Man, this is great!' You know? 'Man, you know the things you learn!' We both laugh again.

So, working two jobs, facing a forty-five-minute drive morning and night, attending college, having little time to herself, Rhonda has discovered not only what she can do for now but also what she can look forward to doing as she accomplishes her intermediate goals. And this ability, this newfound sense of self-worth, has underscored her sense of herself in dealing with others.

"I know that I can do anything I want to do. I like nice things. What I want tomorrow is nicer than what I have today. But, if I don't get it, I'm not going to lose sleep over it. I have to be happy. I go to work everyday and I have to deal with these bosses that can't stand me because I'm a very strong black woman." She pauses and then continues, saying very deliberately, "[be-cause] I'm not just a woman, but I'm a black woman. My boss cannot stand me because I do not sit under him and act like 'Sir, what can I do for you?'" She assumes a very meek posture, telling me this, to dramatize it. "That's how I feel."

I wonder aloud, "So he wants you to act like he thinks a black woman should be?"

"Right," Rhonda says, "and I can't do that. I can be who I am. I can't be who he wants me to be and he can't accept that. But that's okay. He's just a man like my daddy is; he puts his pants on one leg at a time just like him. I go to work and I'm happy and get my check. If I was so worried about him, I would've left that job a long time ago."

The Weaker Sex?

The time I spent with women was some of my most enjoyable time in Colonial County. It was akin to being allowed into the inner sanctum for some secret organization. I was made privy to people's lives as they saw them, not as reflected in demographic tables or other analyses in which they were depersonalized and their spirits killed. Here, they were experienced face-to-face—strongly spiritual and full of a kind of self-determination that would astound many social scientists, never mind flabbergasting many politicians who wish to blame or ignore them.

Such meeting is instructive about the fundamental relationship of individuals to the society in which they are born and raised. It has led some theorists to postulate that our selves are formed in a lookingglass, becoming what others wanted us to be. For the black women of Colonial County whom I spoke with—admittedly, in only one family—wringing one's hands and seeking self-pity has not been high on the list of things to do. Instead, it is survival and thriving as people of worth that has been important. And they have done this in a place that, to some, might seem most unfavorable, a place where many difficulties—some of the subjects' own making—were encountered. It is a place that has given birth to a certain frontier-like spirit. It is a place in which these women have not just sought respect but have earned it.

An eloquent independence is found in the words and deeds of these women. They did not merely tolerate the eras in which they were raised, and the associated opportunities; rather, they embraced them. As greater economic opportunities presented themselves, and as gender roles changed, the women acted to take advantage of these new chances. They did as much as they could to take control of their lives, almost always in the context of considerable family support. Since gender is an important part of people's lives, it may be empowering or debilitating—that depends. Clearly, for these women gender was a life force, not a death knell. It was a fusion of race and gender that empowered them, emboldened them, embraced them in their search for self and realization of family—that made them strong women.

This fact was captured beautifully when Grace told me how difficult things had been for her mother and the children after Clorice and AC got divorced. Despite the divorce, life had to go on, painful as it was. Money, always in short supply, had become even scarcer, but for Clorice this was merely one more mountain to climb and conquer (of course similar mountains have been faced by millions of women, who are almost always hurt most financially in a divorce).

As Grace told me, "If it wasn't for my mom, I don't know what we would have done. We would go to bed and it would be like little elves had come to the house. We'd get up and there'd be two new dresses there, one for me and one for Rhonda. My mom had stayed up all night making those dresses for us to wear to school."

It is easy to imagine Clorice doing this. She is a whirlwind of activity on the most normal of days. Tireless in her determination to succeed at whatever she is doing, she fits her daughter's characterization of her as an "elf." Clorice, the diminutive woman, is a tower of strength, one strong woman in a family of them.

Four

What Did You Learn in School Today?

Homilies such as "the children are our future" seem both self-evident (since, absent the children, society will not replenish itself) and ringing with important implications for what the future may hold. Schools, long envisioned in America as the levelers of social distinctions of all kinds, and as the places where "created equal" is supposed to have a chance of being realized, have, of course, been a battleground over these very issues. Nothing has been more divisive and politically potent than legal squabbles over desegregating the public schools, and this has been as true in rural places as in urban ones, although it is assuredly the urban places that have received the most attention. The great debate over integration has faded considerably, as the urban public essentially resegregated itself through housing choices. Whites continued to migrate into the suburbs, leaving behind increasingly minority-dominated urban school systems. But in rural counties, which typically have one unified school system for a whole county, such choices were not possible.

In Colonial County, the schools are organized at the county level; there are no independent school districts within the county. Until the late 1960s, there were two separate school systems—one black, one white—but that changed in the late 1960s when the Supreme Court modified its 1954 *Brown v. Board of Education* ruling and mandated that school desegregation was to occur "with all deliberate speed." It was then that one of the greatest so-cial experiments undertaken in American society was begun.

True, there were no control and experimental groups with random as-signment of individuals, but it was an experiment nonetheless. It was tam-pering with a social system in place since the birth of public education in America, especially in the South with its history of de jure segregation. "Ne-gro" and white public school systems were not only normative, they were legally mandated, and all southern states kept records on students and schools organized around this distinction. Stories abound about the radical differences between the white and black schools, with the white ones al-ways receiving the best physical facilities, equipment, books, curricula, and teacher training. Black schools lived a hand-me-down existence, receiving the old equipment and books trickling down from the white schools.

It was widely assumed in social science as well as in legal circles that creating greater equity in these areas would help to improve educational outcomes. In part, this was assumed because there was a jarring contrast between relatively more affluent white schools (and their relatively more affluent student bodies) and the comparatively poor black schools (and their comparatively poor student bodies). The white-black contrast was not only in the schools and in who attended them, but in the unequal outcomes from the experience, with black students and schools having lower test scores, higher dropout rates, and fewer graduates going on to college, with subse-quently poorer occupational and income attainment. But in the mid–1960s, little was known about exactly how unequal these things were and to what degree schooling mechanisms, versus familial and community factors, were responsible. To help unravel this mystery, sociologist James Coleman un-dertook the most comprehensive assessment of schooling, and indeed the largest social research project on any topic, ever done in American society; it came to have the most serious outcomes. So closely linked was Coleman to the study that it was usually called the "Coleman report."[1]

The study's aim was to determine to what degree aspects of the school-ing process (including physical facilities) affected educational outcomes. Us-ing sophisticated social science research techniques in study design, data collection, and analysis, Coleman and his colleagues concluded several things that confirmed and contradicted prevailing wisdom. The two most crucial follow. First, contradicting what many believed, physical facilities had little relationship to schooling outcomes; whether in old schools or new, using up-to-date textbooks or not, kids did about the same on achievement tests. Second, confirming what many believed, the more affluent the families from which schoolchildren came, the better the children did in all aspects of their schooling and in adult outcomes. And, importantly, there was a "school effect" for poorer children who benefited from attending school with the comparatively more affluent children.

This latter finding was to have a revolutionary impact on public education in America. Once the magnitude of the relationship between family background and educational outcomes was more precisely defined, the most expedient path for creating not only "equal opportunity" but also more equal outcomes was at hand—through schools in which classrooms were desegregated to mix the comparatively affluent white children with the comparatively poor black ones. Both the hope and hypothesis was this: the poor children would have their scores go up and the more affluent children would see their scores affected little, if at all. It was also hoped that white parents would understand that desegregation was the law of the land and that good faith by all would, in a myriad of ways, benefit all.

This was the hope, but not the reality. The reality was that white parents feared the outcomes of school desegregation. Although perhaps glad that black children would receive improved schooling, many white parents were not anxious to see this occur at their own children's expense. It was widely assumed that for those at the bottom to benefit so much, those at the top would have to suffer; disproportionate attention given to the least prepared would, of necessity, take time away from the more advanced ones.

Coleman's findings that smart kids do well almost in spite of school notwithstanding, white parents pulled their children from the public schools in massive numbers. This was usually done in one of two ways. First, many southern white parents quickly established a system of private schools. Often done in conjunction with their churches and called "Christian academies," these schools were later referred to by social scientists as "segregation academies."[2] Almost no southern county with a sizable black population was without these alternative schools, and only the poorest white children continued to attend the local public schools.[3] A second response of white parents to school desegregation was to move away; to get out of their present school district into a nearby but not yet racially desegregated

one. This decision was often reflective of two forces: (1) school desegregation itself, and (2) "forced bussing" to transport children from their neighborhood schools to achieve racial balance in all of the schools. Thus, white
parents often saw their children transported away from the neighborhood
schools (a benefit of where people chose to live) to attend comparatively
poorer schools in considerably poorer neighborhoods (the very places that
almost no parents would have chosen as their residence, and from which
many white families had moved a generation or two earlier). Once again,
James Coleman was the main voice among social scientists to address this
issue. Coleman analyzed data in the mid–1970s and concluded that school
districts where desegregation had occurred were experiencing massive
"white flight."[4] He worried openly in his writings and in his "expert witness"
testimony that many urban school districts with forced bussing were on the
road to becoming racially resegregated, and that this process was inevitable
and had speeded up as whites found they could simply relocate to other
public schools in districts nearby. Although Coleman was nearly run out of
many academic circles (especially sociology) because of these statements,
his predictions were proven largely correct. Thus the person many thought
of as the father of bussing (the court-ordered "remedy" to achieve racial
balance, accompanied by the hope for better schooling) was to become its
gravedigger.

What Coleman worried about in terms of racial resegregation was con-
fined primarily to large urban school districts, and not just in the South. Indeed, the school districts in such nonsouthern places as Boston, Detroit,
and Los Angeles had fierce fights at all levels of the school desegregation
process (from public hearings in school board meetings to courtrooms to
protests at neighborhood schools receiving newly imported, and mostly
inner-city, black children).

What few gave much thought to was that, in the South in particular, many
children in the late 1960s attended rural schools and, for these children,
riding busses was a way of life. Thus when school desegregation occurred,
there were few instances of white children being bussed to formerly black
schools; instead many of the comparatively older and worse-off black schools
were simply closed, with their students bussed to the formerly all-white
schools. Teaching staffs were Cuisinarted in a blend that had little thought
other than to integrate the teachers along with the children. A simple axiom

involved was "teaching is teaching," no matter where or with whom. The fallacy of this was soon apparent, since black children were as unfamiliar to white teachers in the classrooms as were the teachers to the children; and the same was true for black teachers and white students. And, of course, equally odd were the children to one another, as well as to administrators of a different race. Parallel universes had collided, and from the collision new universes were born.

Some Things Gained, Some Things Lost

When confronted with the mandate to desegregate the local schools, the (then) all white school board in Colonial County began to implement a plan. This involved closing some older "Negro" schools; Alvin Johnson (the high school named after a legendary black educator in Colonial County, and in which the principal was also legendary) was closed and its students merged into Colonial County High School. This, at least according to the local newspaper and comments from people recalling the era, occurred with little difficulty from local residents. The only protest of any size came from the Ku Klux Klan, which staged a rally in downtown Conaty. The Klan and its supporters were outnumbered by a counterprotest of local black people—still recalled by many older black people, over twenty-five years later, as the largest protest in Colonial County.

In the fall of 1970, black and white children in Colonial County began to attend school together for the first time. The great hope for many proponents of school desegregation was that the children would be able to lead the way toward a brighter, more hopeful, racially integrated, more equal society. In a remarkably naive approach to social life, black and white children were simply thrown together, with virtually no preparation by the adults to assist them with their new circumstances. This led some scholars to describe the newly desegregated surroundings as "segregated students in desegregated classrooms." In other words, the familiarity of the old (old friends and social norms) was not neatly nor easily replaced simply because the students found themselves in new circumstances. Instead, the children quickly (and in retrospect, understandably) clung to what was familiar. But in time this changed.

Almost anyone observing these older desegregated schools today is struck by the ease of conversation and interaction among many white and black children. To be sure, there may be some worries about continuing racial animosities or about the fact that some children's friendships rarely cross racial lines, but millions of children attend integrated schools every day and there are few racial hostilities. Thus, to some degree, this one hope for school desegregation has been achieved.

It was assumed by nearly everyone, including black parents and educators, that the black children would be the principal beneficiaries of the newly desegregated schools. They would have access to better everything, especially facilities, equipment, and textbooks. But, I found in Colonial County, people's views of what happened when the schools desegregated initially, and of what has happened in the nearly thirty years since, are at times highly negative—and these are not the views of hardcore white supremacists but of local black folk, many of whom were in the schools when they desegregated.

Although social scientists, some politicians, and others who wanted to see the schools racially desegregated had laudable reasons for their beliefs, few gave any thought to what would be lost in the process—to what sociologists call "unintended consequences." It is fair to say that the backers of integration were blinded by their vision of a better society and saw school desegregation as a key way to achieve this. Indeed, who could not be moved by Martin Luther King Jr's. 1963 speech looking toward a day when people "would be judged not by the color of their skin but the content of their character" and when "little black and white children can join hand in hand"? This is precisely the kind of imagery that came to mind for school desegregation's advocates. For many of these people, school desegregation was seen in a one-sided way: Black people would benefit; they would benefit by attending school with the relatively more affluent white children. The hope of "better everything" included assumptions about the normative structures in place in the formerly all-white schools. It was assumed that these schools' educational expectations would be higher and that the maxim that "all boats rise on a rising tide" would apply for all of the children, especially the black ones. What few gave any thought to was that the schools black children had attended having been poorer in some ways did not necessarily mean that those schools were poorer in all ways.

Indeed, silly as it sounds now (but a tough argument to make thirty years ago, or even to voice at that time), the comparatively poor black schools had one thing going for them that could never be bettered in the formerly white schools: no matter how poor they were, they were still theirs with a strong sense of community pride and ownership! This is the one thing that no one (least of all, the social scientists) seemed to recognize. Yet this sentiment is heard often when talking to black people in Colonial County—heard from everyone from students to parents to teachers and administrators.

"Where There Is No Vision, the People Perish"

The issue of local control arose one day when AC and I were talking. Like many white social scientists, I assumed (wished) that integration would have had almost uniformly positive results. Also like most white social scientists (or many members of the general public for that matter), I see this from a "white" point of view and, when I think about it at all, compartmentalize it, thinking of integration and schools, integration and work, integration and housing, and so on. But, for black people, such things—housing, schools, jobs, church, etc.—aren't neatly categorized. Instead, they blend together in the wholeness to people's lives (as is true for anyone, but here race is an important part of the taken-for-granted context). This was reflected while conversing with AC about the role of religion in people's everyday lives; suddenly, unexpectedly, the conversation took a turn toward integration:

"Now Janice [his granddaughter, whom he helped raise], she'd get her lesson and I made her work hard. If she came to me with '90' on her card, I thought she could get '100.' But she was the exception. A lot of the kids in the crowd didn't get their lessons. Just gettin' by, they satisfied. You'd be surprised."

I was, because I hadn't thought of linking integration with negative effects on everyday life for black people in this historically black place. For AC, it was clear that one side effect to school desegregation was that to be lazy and not do their work became much easier for many black children. AC's hypothesis (although he, like most people, would never call it that) was that with school desegregation came a new set of norms that the black children quickly figured out. These new norms tolerated their doing worse in school and finding that, in time, as with all things made normative, they would also be acceptable at home—at least, in many of their homes.

As AC went on, "Before integration, everybody had good sense. Had to work twice as hard as a white kid to get it. Had that embedded in 'em. Since integration, don't care if they do or not. The family or someone, white or black, think you supposed to get things for free. Parents go there and buy 'em a car to drive to school; but no one bought me a cycle. I bought one myself and learned to appreciate it. But they buy 'em a car and stay in the street. Two-thirds of 'em stay there. They sayin' 'I don't want my children to come up the way I did.' But they killin' their children, messin' 'em up. Sacrifice was good for me and it should be good for my children."

One day, AC's oldest daughter, Alice, and I sat in her living room, sipping ice tea, and talking in general about her life in Colonial County. Alice is someone who lived nearly all her adult life away from the area, having gone into the military as a very young woman. But there was never any doubt about where she would return once she retired (after twenty years); this is her home. She feels a responsibility to her own children to make all local things as good as possible, and this includes especially the schools, which she believes are in real trouble.

Alice is the family's only child to have always attended racially segregated schools. It was the year after she graduated that the local schools "integrated." Her recollection of this is vivid, as is her sense of the situation today in the schools. Her knowledge is not second hand; she works there as a volunteer.

"When they first integrated, there were people pulling their kids outta' school. When they went over to A.J. [Alvin Johnson, the black high school], a black kid couldn't look at a white. We were living in the same county all our life but they [white people, including school authorities] thought if a black child did something, kids would call home and say this one did something to me. It was so bad that they got them a private school 'cuz they didn't want 'em in with the blacks. That was in '69 or '70. They go to work together every day; they can't work separately. But now, it's still segregated! Believe it or not. Most of the whites ride on one bus; most of the blacks on another. When the kids are together in one group, you have mostly white or mostly black. There's no togetherness. What we used to do—like I told my son [a graduating senior]—is pull together. Like, did you see the girls who ran for homecoming queen last time? I think they were all black except one. Well, if you have only two candidates on the white side and fifty on the black side, who's gonna win? They [black kids] started pullin' together and doing things. And that way some of their candidates can win."

As we talk, Grace stops by. As soon as she realizes what we are talking about, she enters the conversation. Grace's is the harshest assessment I hear during my early days in the county. But it is an assessment that sticks with me and influences much of the information I seek in the weeks ahead. Grace was in the first cohort of children to attend the desegregated high school— the place where one would assume that desegregating social processes would be most difficult, given the well-established friendships and norms that children would have established by then. Indeed, this turns out to be the case, but the heart of the matter seems far beyond that.

"When the schools were integrated, it made things worse. Worse. People hate it when I say that, but it's true. You never heard black children curse, and we heard white children tell their parents where to get off. We had no children like that. We weren't allowed to wear shorts in our classrooms at A.J. For awhile, you couldn't wear pants 'cuz Mrs. Cooper didn't allow that. There was a pride about you—about the way you dressed and behaved. There were always a few, like those whole families who are caught up in drugs now. You had trouble with them even then. But some do-gooder white person came in, looked around, and saw that in the black community you got your butt paddled when you misbehaved. They said 'These [black] people are abusing their children.' My mom and dad striked my butt. My dad wasn't much of a butt spanker but my mom got it by the root! My mom left many a welt on my legs with a switch, but I've never felt abused. It's because of my mom that I knew I had a punishment coming. It kept me in check. When my friends were gonna do somethin', I might think about it, but I knew I had to answer to my mom. What's happened now is the check has been taken 'way; the check has been removed. It don't matter if it's true or not, if your children say something about you when they're at school. You've got a social worker in your house. You've got this to deal with along with everything else. There's been a downside to integration. There's been a downside."[5] Alice interrupts, saying, "You didn't know you weren't together until someone told you that you had to be. You didn't notice the separation. You were living and working together all the time, and all of a sudden you don't want your child to go to school with this one 'cuz of race."

Grace, who is now sitting on the edge of her seat, clearly anxious to continue talking, starts again: "We are a different culture. What works with the
white culture doesn't work with the black culture. We didn't come here on
our own, we were slaves. We got whipped as slaves, but it was alright then;
we knew what was expected of us. This is like evolution. We grew up with
an iron hand; I'm not talkin' about breakin' their arms or legs or bruisin'
'em up. But we had an iron hand; we kept 'em in line. All my mom had to
do was look across the room and it checked me. But once we got with the
white kids, it wasn't like that. You had white kids smokin' in school; you
had a tree out there on the school grounds where they did it. In the black
community, if you had smokin', it was sneakin' over in the Patch, or those
Monroe boys or somethin' like that. It was just a very few. But the whites
always smoked. The kids chewed tobacco. We had no exposure to this type
of stuff."

Grace's sense about having "a social worker in your house" reminded
me of Duneier's similar account. As one of the men in his Chicago study
stated, "This little social worker had a grandmother in front of the judge,
who was black. And she said, 'She beat him unmercifully.' She wanted the
court to take the kid from the grandmother. 'What did the child do?' the
judge said to the grandmother. Grandmama said, 'I came out from the bathroom and I caught him with his hand in my purse.' 'Say what?' said the judge.
'Case dismissed.'[6] The little social worker was enraged: 'This is brutality.'
Judge said, 'You do not understand the black experience. You do not steal
from your grandmother. That is the one looking after you. And he steals
from his grandmother? I ought to put him in jail. Case dismissed."

As someone who wrote a doctoral dissertation on school desegregation,
and who has followed the subject, if somewhat loosely, ever since (i.e., for
thirty years), I was not surprised to hear these remarks. When I worked at
an all-black, inner-city school in Dallas, at about the same time that the
schools were being desegregated in Colonial County, the white professional
staff had a sense of bringing enlightenment (as we saw it) to the hard-
pressed, disadvantaged black staff and students. When one black teacher
provided corporal punishment to her students, we cringed. We thought we
knew better what would benefit the local children. As noted above, the assumption was "better in all ways." Clearly, this view was at odds with what
Alice and Grace were telling me. When I asked them about standards to-

day, and how the situation compares to the early 1970s, their general sense of problems continues.

Grace tells me: "They're not getting the education they used to get before integration. At all-black schools, those people cared. You didn't have to worry about drugs or behavior. All that teacher had to do was talk to your mother. Or they could look at you and say, 'I know your mother, you behave and do your work or I'll call your house.' A few years ago, my cousin had a child who acted up so bad in school. A sub [substitute teacher] came in one day, who was related to him, and said 'You actin' like that, I don't believe it. I'm gonna call your daddy.' And that checked him; no problems from that day forward."

Alice chimes in, "That's the same thing with my kids when they went to A.J. One of my classmates was the principal. If one of my kids did something wrong or anything, I knew about it. I had no problem out there. They knew that, whatever they did, someone would call and tell me. And I would check him. But you don't have that now." The rural sociologist William Freudenberg refers to this quality of small-town life as "watchfulness," one more casualty of rapid social change.[7]

Grace says, "I believe things were better when they were equal but separate, even when we got the leftover books. We got the old books from the white schools. Even with that, we got a better education. I know, 'cuz I went to both. I was in the ninth grade when integration came down. Alice was in the last class at A.J. It was totally different. Those black teachers cared whether you learned or didn't learn. Now they just go through the motions; they got to pass enough to make their quotas so their contract won't be challenged. If you got the whole class failin', someone will wonder about your teachin' ability and you'll lose your contract."

Alice has been working on this with the local schools. She believes that the teachers are, in fact, scared of losing their jobs. "The likeable ones, they're gone. The others are scared of losing their jobs. I'm serious. I'm working with 'em. I can't believe it."

This, it turns out, is the tip of the proverbial iceberg. When I return to Colonial County nearly one year later, the teachers' situation is a front-page story in the local paper. Some of the teachers (who are not unionized or represented in any very organized way) have appealed to the state board of education for an investigation of their treatment by local school administrators.

Are the Schools Really Worse?

All of AC's children feel that the local schools have suffered since integration, although not all blame integration itself equally for the problems. But the net effect is the same: the schools are worse. This is like a mantra with nearly every black person to whom I speak for the first time, especially the older people, and it is not unreasonable that the same sentiment would have been expressed by the region's older white people; indeed, it is not unlikely that I would have heard such a lament from older people everywhere in the United States, when discussing the local schools, for this is one canard that just never seems to go away. But negativity about the schools is tempered some for Rhonda and Samuel, AC's youngest children— the ones who were in the desegregated schools the longest.

Samuel is the only one who spent most of his schooling in desegregated schools. He says: "I was in the sixth grade when they integrated the schools and I just had to accept it. I went straight to C.C.A. [Colonial County Academy, the county's largest public school complex, containing both middle and high schools]. They had a private school that got cranked up then. During the first year everybody was looking at each other but kept their distance. The next year, though, when the kids who couldn't afford to go to the private school came back into the public schools, I had what you could say is the best year out of the history of C.C.A. The class of '76 is still a tight class. We have a reunion in June. Black and white both come. We had one prom. The guy at the filling station in Yvonne is Mark; he used to pick me up by the side of the road and give me a ride to school [a distance of about twelve miles]. Our class stuck with it. We didn't have as many problems within the class, with sports programs and everything else. It made a big difference. I never felt threatened or nothing. Growing up here and watching things around me, I never had any problems."

And apparently, that is true. Samuel's characterization of both his class at school and his relationship to it are supported by his sisters. AC is always quick to brag about Samuel, about his ability to get along with everyone; Samuel is a kind of junior version of AC, a case of the expression "The apple doesn't fall far from the tree." Janice has visited him at the military base and come away with a sense of him as a very tough person. As Janice told me, one time, "Those soldiers stood at attention when they spoke with him. And he made them go and redo something. Whew, I wouldn't want to work for him!"

Even though Samuel is very positive about his own experience in newly desegregated schools (and feels that this better prepared him for his career in the military, where whites and blacks have to work and live together) (and perhaps it is relevant that Samuel has a white wife), he is—like his family—very negative about the Colonial County schools today. "There are kids in school today who never graduate. It looks bad. It's something the school owes kids but they don't get it anymore because the 'old school' is gone. In the old school, the teachers, most of whom lived nearby, would stop by the house and say, 'Look here, that boy of yours has totally disrupted my class. He's a real problem.' But now nobody does that except maybe by telephone. I hate those little meetings at school. I don't believe in that. They should be able to tell us about these problems because they see us where we live, because they live with us.

"I'm not going to send Alan [his son] to the Colonial County school system. That's why I'm over here [in the next county] right now. I went to two graduations before I came home [from the military]. I went there checking the teachers out. They were so substandard—no motivation, no positive attitude. They marched like there was no cohesion, nothing you'd want to be a part of. And I went there twice. And then Alice tells me what's going on [about the problems she's seen] and I said, 'I could tell you that just from watching the graduation.' But she's working hard in the schools of Colonial County trying to get the board of education to do something. You just can't get the families to come out. Today we've lost the black families and kids."

His Aunt Althea, who is in her late sixties, agrees. When I ask her about the schools (through which she has put eleven children), she is more sanguine: "I hear 'em complaining about the schools. Got white teachers favor certain children, give 'em good grades, don't get some good grades. I always tol' mine, 'Study ha'd [hard] and do the best you can. If they don't give you credit for it, you'll still know it.' I know I hear my grands [grandchildren] say that some kids ax' [ask] to go to the bathroom and don't get to go and then others ax' and they get to go. Sometimes black teachers might favor white children, or white teachers might favor blacks. It's mixed;

it's not because of race. Some of my kids love the white teachers. You neva' know. It could be the kids just don't want to get along." I interrupt to ask Althea if she thinks maybe the problem rests with the adults, with the parents, since this is something I have heard others say. "When the kids get along with the colored children, then their mamas and the parents don't want 'em to be bothered with 'em. I know that my kids had two or three white kids as their fra'nds [friends], but some of 'em don't like it. This works both ways. If the white got colored fra'nds or the colored got white fra'nds, some don't like it. If some of those children are prejudic', their parents taught 'em to be like that. I see that. If the parents stay out of it, then the kids don't be havin' all that prejudice against one another."

Her former sister-in-law, Dorthea, speaks to this same point, one day when she and I are sitting in her kitchen talking. "The [white] parents didn't want the chirren to go to school together but they get along good. If the adults don't get along, the chirren do."

So for Dorthea, who is now about seventy years old, the relationships in school (especially those concerning race) reflect directly the attitudes of the parents. Her own range of experience, living in Colonial County since a time when the races were kept apart through legal means—for instance, blacks got food from a local restaurant out of a small window at the back: they couldn't go in to eat even though they could work in the kitchen— shows how varied one person's experience can be. In general, over time slowly emerged a kind of grudging acceptance of the new norms and much of the social change that came with them. Yet, even though everyone I spoke with seemed to feel that, in general, race relations are better now than before, problems with schools continue.

Rhonda, like Samuel someone who attended desegregated schools for several years, also recalls the role that parents played in making things more difficult. Like Samuel's, her experience was more good than bad, even with some early difficulties.

"When I was a child, we had a lot of problems going to school when they desegregated. We graduated from elementary school and went straight to high school. It was a job. [She says this with real resignation in her voice.] It was a time. Whew, it was a time! Because everybody had to feel each other out. We could have done good if it wasn't for the parents. We had a lot of petty fights, arguments, you know.

"In the segregated schools, if your teacher told your parents something that you did, you got your butt whipped once you got home—and that was after the teacher whipped you at school. You had more respect for those black teachers, because you had to go to church with them and they see your parents and it's like, 'You either behave in this class or I'm going to talk to your parents.' When we desegregated, we had white teachers and you didn't have to behave like you had. We had more freedom to be loose. We get out of our parents' eyesight, you know, we gonna act up anyway. You had a lot more freedom and you tried to imitate the white kids, do whatever they did—wear those little short things, what do you call them, 'hot pants.' White girls kiss their boyfriends in the hall. Wow! That was something for us because we weren't allowed to do that kind of thing. Kiss a man in school? You kiddin'? [She laughs.] You'd get your mouth washed out with bleach and. . . . Yeah, when we desegregated, we focused more on other things and not on school. We had to do our schoolwork, we didn't have a choice. Then when we desegregated, we could blame . . . you know, we could say, 'Well, they can do it. Why can't we?' We had someone else to put the blame on."

No one was more critical of the local schools—before, during, and after desegregation—than Clorice, AC's first wife. She sees herself as representing a black elite in the county. Her parents were very bright, her mother being "educated" (unusual for black folk of that age group) and her father, although lacking much formal education, being remembered by all (especially Clorice) as very smart.

Clorice feels strongly, passionately, about the local schools. Nothing, she feels, is more disgraceful than what has happened there, in part as a result of desegregation. "I can say truthfully that the only good thing to come out of desegregation is that we no longer got all the raggedy books. Before, what we got was no backs [on the books], nothing. All the new books went to C.C.A. [Colonial County Academy, as the high school is now called]. But, despite it all, we made it.

"Teachers have lost their personality. Like I'm a nobody, like I'm just here. We lost that care we had for each other. I guess, too, that prayer out of the schools changed things a lot. We know there's a God. The child can be in the classroom and, if it's not my friend's child, it's someone else's child, but this child today gets no consideration. I mean, we would never put our kids in a detention center. To us, that's lowering our moral standards. A black child's mind is destroyed sitting in that detention center. Now you might say, 'Where you coming from? Darkness is nothing. You get nothing out of darkness so why put me there where I can't get nothing?' So the child thinks, 'I'm just going to be no good anyway so I'm in here.' So what's happened to that child? You've taken something away from him. There's not a bad child in that school. There's kids that need to be worked on . . . if you are a good teacher; like I said before, teaching is not teaching if you cannot make a child learn. Learning is the important thing. What we lost with that desegregation deal is the children's learning abilities. No one learns anything now. Only those few who want to do something with their lives."

I told Clorice that I had heard from many people, including her children, that to the black children the teachers were just like parents. As she told me, "They were mama and daddy away from home. There used to be respect. Respect mattered. But not now. It's horrible now."

Trade Schools Long Forgotten

One day I was visiting with Terrence, AC's youngest brother. He had only been out of prison a short time (in what virtually everyone in the black community felt had been an entrapment case to imprison the county's most publicly irritating, politically active black man). We talked about a wide range of things, and moved from inside the house to the driveway. I had gone out there with him, thinking I would go on down the road to see AC, when AC pulled up. Soon after he arrived, another old friend, Daryl, drove up. So now we had Terrence's old Plymouth Voyager, AC's pick-up with its highly used look, including a toolbox that fit across the bed right behind the cab, and Daryl's sporty-looking truck with special wheels and fancy dual exhaust, looking like anything but a work truck. As we stood there, Terrence shifted into a gear of holding court—a position he was used to, the center of attention. But more than anything, it was three old friends (two of them brothers) and me as the outsider. It was much like watching a play.

AC was talking about his strong belief in the need to learn "any little ol' skill." "These young guys, you can't tell 'em nothin'. They gonna be really messed up. Everything goin' to computers and they gonna be messed up. They cain't do nothin'."

Terrence responded, "The thing that bothers me the most is certification and qualification. That's what people will start lookin' for. The whites movin' in, they gonna look for someone that's certified . . . qualified. If you don't have those two things, they won't touch you. Now AC, he's been doin' it long enough that he's qualified, even if he isn't certified. But now if I get out there and try to do the same thing he's doin', I don't have the certification or the qualification. Eventually you're gonna have to have a license to get recognized for your job. We gotta get some kids in school who can get qualified for these jobs like electrician and plumber."

I wondered if the schools, though, were training kids any longer to do these kinds of things. Was there sufficient interest? AC quickly responded: "They gotta have their own interest. You can't depend on someone else for that. You want to do something for 'em but. . . . " Terrence interrupts, speaking in a frustrated voice: "You can only build interest with the smarter children." I ask if it now seems everyone must go to college, or at least think that they are supposed to go or else are a failure, so there's no longer as much interest in learning a trade. Daryl chimes in: "Oh yeah, I can give you an example. I had two kids graduate from C.C.A. My son, he went to Tennessee State but he only stayed for a year; he couldn't cut it, so he went into the military. My daughter, now, she went to Columbia University and got two degrees. But we had to pay for her tuition and get her a tutor; these local schools didn't prepare her for college. She didn't have it. Those schools now are worse than when she went."

Terrence, always pensive-looking, responds: "Now when I went to high school, we had things like F.F.A., Future Farmers of America, raisin' hogs, chickens, plantin' trees, layin' blocks and bricks, all them type things. With integration, all that ended. F.F.A. wasn't nothin'. Maybe see a little sign by the side of the road but you didn't find the boys out there laying bricks or fattenin' chickens. That all went down the drain."

AC turns his attention back to the schools themselves: "See, the white, it's not gonna benefit them whether you get anything or not. All they want is for you to go through the system. See, if you go through that whole system and don't take no initiative to get something out of it, you gonna be lost in the soup. You might find two or three teachers who will make you learn somethin', but if you won't take the initiative, you' lost. Now black people, they got to push. Janice [the very bright, very motivated grandchild he helped to raise] wouldn't a-got what she got out of it if we hadn't pushed.

You gonna have to do somethin' yo'self. You can't depend on other people. You gonna be in the soup. That's happenin' to black people all over the states, not just in Colonial County. You see a lot of these children, all they wanna do is fool around. They could be a lot smarter but all they wanna do is pass, make a 'pass.' Just get by. If they can get by without workin', that's all they want. A lot of smart kids come out of Colonial County, they could've taken the initiative and made somethin' of themselves but they don't do it. All they wanna do is pass. It's that way everywhere. They think somebody gonna give 'em somethin'. They don't wanna work for it." AC looks down and says quietly, "All these young children think somebody gonna give 'em somethin'."

Daryl quickly agrees. "A lot of that comes from the parents. These kids today don't respect their parents. I graduated from high school. The kids now, throw some modern math in front of them, they don't know nothin'. It's like Greek to them. In [their state], 46 percent of the teachers flunked a test. If the teacher can't pass, how can they teach anythin'? How you gonna teach my kids somethin'?"

In the midst of this exchange, AC states his belief (which I've heard before) that the hope lies with the youngest kids. "These children now, even the youngest ones, they'll figure it out. All those computers and everything on TV, but I'd never get it 'cuz I'm so slow. But these young kids can get it. They in the system. But you can't hardly learn them old people [meaning his generation] anything."

Terrence joins in: "When I went to prison, there were computers and certain math you had to learn. I'd never seen it before but . . . in prison you could put your mind to it, and it was simple. When I first came home, my daughter came over and I told her that any problem you had, sit down and study it; let your mind wander and go with it and you can figure it out. And that's what I do with 'em. If I didn't learn this in prison, I'd be lost. There's so many people around her, that why they're havin' problems; they don't have it. A lot of people don't realize that tax assessor's office is math; the calculations of what they's assessing your property by and for, [and if you don't realize that, then] you' in trouble. That tax assessor is rippin' them off."

AC says, "I've had some of these young guys want to work with me and they don't even know fractions [something he had learned at night from one of his children's teachers]. Fractions used to be taught in Head Start. They take an apple in so many parts. They taught that in Head Start. There's no excuse. A lot of times, these children leave that and do what they wanna do; they don't pay no attention." And, returning to a theme I've heard him speak of before, AC concludes, "When you get through this generation right here, you get the next group, everything gonna be better. The whole system is gonna improve, 'cuz the youngest children seem mo' smarter, mo' brighter, and they wanna do somethin.' But this group we got right here now, I don't know what we do with them."

It was clear to me that, for these men, the schools are part of the larger fabric holding the community together. As they discuss these things, they also express—albeit not in sociological terms—what happens when the norms change, and not always for the better. The issue of the current lack of trade school programs worries them because having a trade is an area from which they (especially Daryl and AC) have benefited and yet there seems almost no emphasis on it anymore. And Terrence's comments about the lack of an F.F.A. is a much larger comment on the change in his lifetime from near-self-sufficiency—from growing up with hogs and cattle and chickens roaming around, as AC would say, "back in them woods." But those days are over.

Teachers Old and New

I spent several hours one day with a man who is the most widely recognized black politician in the county. He had served on the Conaty City Council as well as on the county board of supervisors. He, along with Terrence, was very active in promoting opening up the electoral process in Colonial County and electing more blacks to office. He is a thin man, medium height, with a kind of quasi-Afro—hair much longer than is found on younger black men, but similar to what is seen, locally on many older black men, including AC and his brothers and their friends. Besides working on the City Council, this man teaches elementary school in another county and serves as a pastor for a local church. Everyone calls him "Reverend Jacobs."

During our day together, he asks me if I've spoken with Mr. Warren, the former principal of Alvin Johnson and the most senior black politician in the county? When I tell him no, he calls and asks if we can come for a visit. It is only a short drive. Mr. Warren lives in a large brick ranch house; it looks like millions of other middle-class houses built during the 1960s. We enter the house through a carport and, after introductions, we all sit in a large, nicely furnished family room. Mr. Warren and Reverend Jacobs reconstruct for me what life was like when the schools desegregated; this description also provides a basis for commenting on the schools today. Both men express openly and frequently their worries about what did happen and what has continued to plague the local schools. Once again, much of what they say comes as a shock, but not entirely.

Reverend Jacobs was very deferential to Mr. Warren and let him begin our conversation: "There were good and bad things to come of integration. It meant different things to whites and blacks. For blacks, it meant being able to sit by whites in a restaurant, attend schools with them, and so on. For whites, however—they resented it. For them it meant one thing: a loss of power. The most worrisome thing for them was economics; that was the important thing. Whites controlled the local economy, and they couldn't stand the idea that that wouldn't continue as it always had.

"Once integration started, each group adopted the worst of the other. I'm sorry to say it but it's true. Each group stereotyped the other. A story black people used to tell about what whites believed was 'The only time a black tells the truth is when he says: "Boss, I ain't no good!"'

"Each group felt that the other was untrustworthy and manipulative; to some degree, that's true right up to the present time—each feeling like the other might get something that they don't really have coming to them. In fact, right now I've been dealing with the City Council and its mayor. There had been a motion over a year ago to name a street after me but the mayor didn't want to do it, supposedly because it would mean changing the name of an existing street. Anyway, after a year of argument, they finally approved doing it, just the other night.

"You see, whites had always been in control in Colonial County. They didn't want to share their power. The sheriff controlled who got what kinds of jobs, and a lot of local black people liked him; or if they didn't like him, they at least knew where they stood with him. But once we got integration, that too changed, because the rules for everything became confused.

"What white parents really resented when the schools integrated was that black teachers could discipline their children. Before integration, black teachers had full control in and out of the school. They were just like the child's parents. And when it came to disciplining them, they treated them like their own children. I believe that 'Unless you know the culture, you can't understand the child.' In that sense, integration was to the detriment of the child, because black children knew the teachers meant business. With all due respect, nobody knows what it's like to be black unless you're black.

"After integration, they didn't allow all of one race to be in any class. They were seeking 'balance.' I had a case where a new, white, young teacher came to our school. A white lady came in one day and told me that she wanted her daughter assigned to the woman's class. She thought that woman would be best for her. The child was already in a class with a black teacher who had considerable experience. So I told the woman I thought that was best and would have to say 'no' to her request to move her daughter. So the woman went to see the superintendent, who was white. The superintendent then called me up and said, 'For peace' sake, let's do it. Let's move her.' It was like I got shot through the heart. I cried when she did that. I really did. I said, 'What about for peace' sake with me?'

"The next day the husband came in with his wife, and met with me and the superintendent. The husband said to me, 'Stand your ground and put her back. I didn't know my wife was such a racist.' She just didn't want her daughter taught by a black person. So I put the girl back and she stayed there the rest of the year.

"It's funny, though, what you remember about those times. [He turns to Reverend Jacobs.] Have I ever told you the 'Yes ma'am; no ma'am story?'" Reverend Jacobs says, "No." So we get to hear it.

"A woman called one day and my daughter, who was a student at the time, answered the phone. This was after we integrated. The woman said, 'Is Mr. Warren there?' And my daughter said, 'No, he's not.' She then asked, 'Do you know when he will return?' And she said, 'No, I don't, but I will be glad to take a message.' Then the woman asked to speak to Mary Lou, my secretary. And she said, 'Mary Lou, was that a student who answered the phone?' And Mary Lou said, 'Yes, ma'am, it was.' The lady said, 'Was it Mr. Warren's daughter?' Mary Lou said, 'Yes, ma'am, it was.' 'I knew it,' she said. 'Do you know that she never even said "ma'am" to me?!?' 'No, ma'am, I didn't,' said Mary Lou. When I returned, Mary Lou told me what had happened. I knew the lady would call the superintendent so I went to see her. I told her what had happened, and she asked me if I thought it was expecting too much of my daughter to say 'Yes, ma'am; no, ma'am.' I said, 'I'll be damned if my daughter is going to say 'ma'am' to her when her daughter says to me in the store, 'Hi, Charlie!'"

Reverend Jacobs and I both laughed at this story, as did Mr. Warren. But clearly his recollections of the early days of school desegregation have a painful side to them. And the central issues—(1) control (with black teachers and a white power structure), and (2) prevailing norms that were not to be violated *and* were a reminder of local race relations—were crucial. Indeed, it turns out that this former issue, control, remains crucial today.

Reverend Jacobs taught in the local schools when they were desegregated. As he told me, "Prior to integration, the teachers controlled problems in the classroom. Their authority was unquestioned. Sometimes you'd have a parent upset and they'd talk with you, but you almost always knew these people, and they didn't undercut your authority. You could encourage the potential in a child. Now, when you tell a child to do something, he will say, 'I'm not gonna do that. You can't make me. My mama will have your job.' That never occurred before.

"Now, little kids get sent home. Integration took discipline out of the schools because white parents didn't want black teachers to strike their white children. There's so much concern about child abuse now that you can't touch them. You're afraid to, really."

I wondered if this simply reflected some larger change in society—for example, our sensitivity to children and our not wanting to see them beaten or abused, especially not by people in positions of public trust and authority.

Reverend Jacobs felt strongly and sadly that, although this was true to some degree, deferring too much to the children and their parents was most worrisome for blacks and as a result had made him wonder about the whole educational system. "I hate to say it but separate [white and black] education might be better. Honestly, it's worse for black kids. Very rarely do young white children sass you or misbehave in class. But, black children, that's another story! They learn at home and from watching television. All they have to do is call 9–1–1 and you could be charged with child abuse. I hate it. I really do. It's made me want to get out of teaching."

But It's Not All Bad

One Saturday morning, Rhonda and I sat in her trailer, having coffee and visiting. She lives about one hundred yards off of the road, at the end of a dirt lane. Her trailer looks a little tired, sagging some, the kind of thing that AC could repair as one of his "little ol' jobs." Rhonda and I talked at length, but on this Saturday we talked especially about the role the teachers played in the local schools. I told her that I had heard repeatedly, from former and present black teachers among others, about the loss of control in the classroom. As we spoke, it became clear that, although Rhonda sees such problems, she also sees benefits that can only accrue from white and black kids being in school together.

"I've taught my kids to respect those teachers, doesn't matter who they are. I tell 'em, 'You come home; let me handle the teachers. Don't go there cursing them out. I don't care who they are or what color they are.' They got into a lot of trouble with teachers who were prejudic'. I said, 'Let me handle that.' I don't sit and discuss it with them; I go and talk to the teachers. I think it's made my kids a better person because they have to deal with it and keep their mouths shut. The kids got along with the whites fine. They still do. Even now they bring white friends home all the time. We have no problem with the kids. It's the older people in the school we have problems with. They don't know how to talk to the kids."

I asked Rhonda, "And you think that's because of race, or age?" Without hesitation, Rhonda says, "Race, definitely. There are some people who are real strong about what should and shouldn't be: 'Whites shouldn't be with blacks and blacks shouldn't be with whites.' And that's true on both sides, whites and blacks. But then you've got these people who say 'To each his own.' People are starting to adjust more and it's not so—Oh! [she clutches her heart and sharply draws in her breath for dramatic effect]—shocking, anymore. Now it's like 'Oh, yeah.' You make a comment like 'Why would that black man be with that white woman?' Or vice-versa. Now people just go about their business. That person, if it makes him happy, so be it. If it makes her happy, so be it. My generation, in our class reunion, we've had classmates bring in their white wives and nobody paid any attention to it.

"Our class, the class of '75, was the first one where we had the proms together. We talked about it at the reunion. I didn't graduate with my class [having dropped out to have her first child], but that was my class and it always will be. I spent all of my school years with them, my whole life. So they're still my classmates. We were the first ones to become black and white then, and we are the first to have a class reunion with white and black together, and we felt good about it. I videotaped it. We had a good time and we're going to get back together in the year 2000."

Rhonda's feelings about this were echoed by her brother, Samuel, and her sister, Grace. Samuel continued to have white friends from the local community, even though he had been gone for much of the past twenty years, serving in the military. Grace is the better marker of the radical change from old to new, since she was in the first class to graduate from the newly integrated school. Clearly, for them accepting the new was difficult. I asked Grace one time about her senior prom: was it integrated? "No, no. We had the prom but the only ones who went were the blacks. The whites had their own, away from the school. The same thing was true for class reunions." "Still?" I asked. Grace said, "It still goes on. When blacks get together to have their class reunion, we always notify the whites to participate or whatever, but they don't. But my children, now, they have mixed proms. So, I'll tell you, I think it has gotten better. For the young people, yes. I think for the older people, though, it's still more of the same."

So, on a happier note, the sociological notion of the "equal contact hypothesis" (that people perceive one another more equally, the more equal are their contacts) has some support from the integration experience in Colonial County. The schools are, in fact, somewhat of a leveler. To be sure, the advantages that local whites, especially the more affluent ones, have are not dropped off when they walk through the school doors. But, that said, black kids become aware of their power by virtue of their numbers (as is clear in Alice's descriptions), and desegregation also puts the black and white kids into regular contact in and out of the classroom. This contact becomes normal; it is not unusual. So even if all of the kids don't become best friends, nonetheless interacting every school day makes them all more aware of, and savvy about, the multiracial world around them.

Janice, admittedly a somewhat exceptional case, is a good example of this. She had good white friends in school and, as the kids got older, they continued to hang out together. When Janice comes home from college, she sees one of these young women. One of the people most influential on Janice is her Uncle Samuel, who is married to a white woman.

The Schools Today: A Postscript

It was clear that many I spoke with in Colonial County felt the schools today were in trouble. Some of the problems stemmed, people thought, from the early days of school desegregation and the resultant erosion of black authority. But much of the problem stemmed, they felt, from a more historical and seemingly intractable issue—the white power structure. Further, there was a sense that some local black "leaders" elected to office were "acting white." In other words, once elected, even the black officials quickly learned the normative (viz., white) way of doing things, so the race of the participants in the process did not matter much. This was a frequent lament of Terrence, talking about times either old or new.

The present unhappiness over the schools flows from several causes. The superintendent is relatively new, having come from outside the county. Although in some places this might be seen as an asset, in Colonial County it might be seen as a liability. As the superintendent of a small school district (with 1,500 students) that is rural and historically black, the superintendent has something in common with all former superintendents of the Colonial County schools—she's white. Even though this does not mean that she cannot be an effective administrator, it does give her one more obstacle to overcome with many black parents. A not totally surprising corollary is her salary, eighty thousand dollars. This is over three times the median income in 1990 for the county, and seven times the per capita income for black residents.[8]

Colonial County's schools had among the poorest test scores in the state. There is the seeming contradiction, according to Mr. Warren, of "high grades in the elementary schools, but no achievement in high school. Why not? It wasn't like this when the schools were segregated. Then, even though the schools were physically poorer, the teachers and the administrators pushed the children to succeed. You didn't have children being sent home from school except in rare cases. I think that's disrespectful of the child; it sends the message that you've given up on him. We just didn't do that."[9] Terrence told me the same thing. He thought it was disgraceful that the schools routinely expel children. As he told me, "And then they go do what? They see that they aren't valued in the school so they're on the street. When they get on the street, the only things they can learn are drugs and getting in trouble and the only people they can hang out with are going to teach them about these things. So, see, we've kind of created a system than ensures their failure. It makes me mad, really mad."

The teachers that Alice and Clorice had mentioned who were losing their jobs did not lose them, after all. A grievance was filed with the state school board and an inquiry was begun. As happens with many grievances, after awhile it became difficult for either side to sustain the energy necessary to continue the process. In the end, peace was restored. Whether or not the attempted dismissals were other than political depends on where you stood on the issue.

What Did You Learn in School Today?

The schools, like all of society's institutions, are not immune to larger social and historical forces. School desegregation was and is, of course, only one of these; any analytic assessment of problems in the schools would identify many potential culprits. During the time that AC's children were in the public schools, the schools were also experiencing other revolutions, such as the increasing importance of standardized testing, increasing class sizes, changing gender roles and expectations, and no doubt a myriad of new pedagogical practices (which seem always in flux). At the same time, in economic periods good or bad, rural schools always struggle; they must always make do with less, even as the expectations being set for them by outside groups are increased.[10]

But the political and interpersonal ramifications to school desegregation were of paramount significance for all of AC's children. Their experiences with the local schools demonstrate the kinds of challenges that the schools present, especially in rural school districts where there is usually limited "school choice." Instead, the students must make do with what is presented to them. This brings to mind the folk song "What Did You Learn in School Today?"[11] with its memorable lines like "I learned that Washington never told a lie, I learned that soldiers seldom die," "I learned our government must be strong, it's always right and never wrong." As this song makes clear, there is a mythology to much that we are told and subsequently accept as true. The schools are major purveyors of these tales, most often wanting to share knowledge widely assumed to be true even if (as in the song) much of it is folklore or myth or would be hard-pressed to withstand careful scrutiny and rigorous assessment. The one certainty is that in Colonial County, the schools have never been particularly good—and, for African Americans, the days prior to school desegregation may have provided better schooling than the ones since.

As everyone I spoke with confirmed, even if not in the most statistical, analytical way, all social arrangements have costs and benefits; in the case of the schools, the old norms were displaced by desegregation, equal opportunity programs of all kinds, and evolving gender roles and relations among other social forces. But, in the end, how much do we know about the new norms? My sense is: not much, and this would apply equally to virtually all southern rural school districts that did and still do have large black populations. Those were the places where segregation academies (by whatever name) were most likely to arise on the heels of federal court orders to desegregate. Many of those schools failed, but many did not and are still in business; they are a reminder of a form of de facto segregation that still exists, paralleling much of the social life not only in rural counties but in highly segregated urban places as well.

Five

In the Lord's House

If we had a continuum for racial segregation within American institutions, schools would be at one end, as the most racially desegregated; churches would be at the other end, as the most racially segregated. No affirmative action program affects churches as it might school or work or the right to buy a house without suffering racial discrimination. There is no legislated "equal opportunity" imperative when it comes to church attendance. If any place reflects "freedom of choice"—albeit buttressed by residential patterns—it is the church. And no matter when you look at who is there (that is, whenever church meetings are held), one thing will be paramount: racially, the people will all (or nearly all) look alike. This is true regardless of whether the church is in the city, the suburbs, or a small town.

In rural communities, religion in general and local churches in particular take on greater significance than in most urban and suburban areas. In rural areas, religion is often easily infused into everyday life and, because the local population is less heterogeneous than in urban areas, relatively greater proportions of local people have the same religious beliefs and church affiliation. Too, the church almost always refers to a local place; it is far less likely to be thought of in some larger denominational way. As with nearly all things rural, there is a sense of ownership profound and intense; it is "ours" (the local population's), with the pride of ownership and degree of caring this brings. Then, there is a sense of community around the church in part because a church serves as a multipurpose place for sacred and secular functions. Further, in rural areas the church is more likely to be accompanied by a "born-again" fervor. Such religiosity is especially true in the rural South. Sociologist John Shelton Reed, citing Flannery O'Connor, notes that the South is "Christ-haunted" and that, to understand the region, one must understand the role that religion plays in southern life.[1]

Scholars have long noted the importance of the church for African Americans and African American communities. Sociologist Andrew Billingsley has stated, "Fully 70 percent of black adults belong to just one [organization], namely the black church."[2] In their book on the black church in America, C. Eric Lincoln and Lawrence H. Mamiya note, "Historically, black churches have been the most important and dominant institutional phenomenon in African American communities."[3]

The church, then, is a place of social organization around which much community activity occurs. In the process, it reinforces norms of all types, not only religious ones. "It was," Lincoln and Mamiya say of the black church, "lyceum and gymnasium as well as sanctum sanctorum. [African Americans'] religion was the peculiar sustaining force that gave them the strength to endure when endurance gave no promise, and the courage to be creative in the face of their own dehumanization."[4] Historically the church helped to make manageable the inherent tension between African- and European-based belief systems.

In Colonial County, as in the rest of the Lowcountry, a novel aspect of the region is a sense of local history in which there is a real contrast between African- and European-based belief systems. Current attempts to preserve African American history in the Lowcountry often focus on items of religious significance. This is true of St. Helena Island, South Carolina, of Sapelo Island, Georgia, or of St. John's Island between the two. Not only have physical artifacts been retained, but attempts have been made to retain certain forms of worship, especially in the barrier islands, where it was comparatively easier to sustain belief systems and forms of worship unique to western Africa (place of origin of most slaves).

The historian William McFeely tells movingly about the retention of beliefs on Sapelo Island. He makes reference both to important historical African American figures and to contemporary practices.[5] Sapelo Island is a very small barrier island off the Georgia coast, and still has about seventy residents who are direct descendants of slaves who lived on the island. The county in which the island is located is home to a group called the "Sea Island Singers" well-known both nationally and internationally for its "chants" (as a musical form) and for preserving and using indigenous language (specifically, Gullah-Geechee). McFeely's story is mirrored in some ways by the conclusions of Jacqueline Jones-Jackson, who spent time living on St. John's Island and came to know well the local people and their cultural practices.[6] And in the much earlier book *Drums and Shadows*, written by the Georgia Writers Project, a W.P.A. project during the Great Depression, the sole intent was to document the use of African-derived practices in religious services.[7] So there is good reason to believe that, for African Americans in the Lowcountry (as well as elsewhere in the South), having their own churches and worship services was not only a way to value and preserve cultural practices but a way of retaining something over which local whites had little influence or control.

In Colonial County (with a population in 2000 of a little over ten thousand), there are over forty houses of worship. None are Jewish or Islamic; all are Christian, with Baptist churches accounting for fully one-half. Several churches are Methodist, and there is one fairly large Presbyterian church. It is easy to identify some of the "black" churches, not only by location but also because only they carry the identifier "A.M.E." (African Methodist Episcopal). Also, they are without exception the most rundown-looking from outside, usually surrounded by that cheapest of all parking lots, dirt. Driving past any of Colonial County's churches on a Sunday morning reinforces the sense of racial separation that exists. The one exception is the Jehovah's Witness Hall, which does seem to attract a noticeably interracial crowd.

Religion and Everyday Life

Religion is, to some degree, a prism through which life is experienced, internalized, and interpreted. Although thousands of ministers have no doubt delivered sermons in which they urge their congregations to be "godly" on other days as well as Sunday,[8] it is on Sunday that the church (writ large and small) is most on people's minds. The day is special in a variety of ways, especially in rural communities, where certain traditions—such as going to church and having a family meal—are more likely to continue. Sunday is a day of being religious (as a kind of ontological and existential statement about one's existence).

In rural areas, the rural South especially, religion is also likely to have a greater carryover effect in everyday life. This is in part due to the greater probability of evangelical, fundamental beliefs there. The specific form of these beliefs varies considerably across the South, with cultural practices in the almost entirely white upland South being different than those elsewhere in the South; nevertheless, the South, wherever one is, has a near monopoly on famous and infamous preachers (Billy Graham, Jerry Falwell, Pat Robertson, and Jimmy Swaggart, to name a few). Their attempts to institutionalize and socialize others into their beliefs have occurred through tent revivals, auditorium revivals, and not only television programs but entire channels owned and operated by their Christian "ministries." As further evidence of these preachers' influence, consider the prominence of such fundamentalist Christian colleges as Oral Roberts, Bob Jones University, and Liberty University; and one can hardly visit a rural southern county and not find a precursor to these—a "Christian" academy of some kind, often affiliated with the largest, always white churches.

It is difficult, if not impossible, to find something comparable to this outside the South. And in the South, almost no matter where one lands, strongly held fundamentalist beliefs are more likely to prevail—not just among whites but among blacks. This is well documented in the scholarly literature and easily determined in casual conversations. It is underscored throughout this region, where, in local restaurants, individuals or families may be seen praying before meals; where—the U.S. Constitution be damned—prayers may be offered before, during, and after school and school-related events; where city halls, judge's chambers, and other public places may exhibit religious symbols: where, in short the separation between church and state may be a constitutional ideal but is one often and sometimes overtly violated in many areas, rural ones in particular.

In rural communities, white or black, no special mention need be made of religion, but it crops up in everyday conversations and situations. "God" is thanked formally at meal times and acknowledged at others in a variety of ways. Indeed, the concept of God as a force in people's everyday lives seems easier to grasp and somehow more believable in rural than in urban or suburban areas.[9] The relative calm and beauty of rural areas offers the sort of scenic backdrop in which a term like "God's majesty" appears more fitting, especially if compared to the aesthetic quality of most urban areas, whether expensive high-rise apartment buildings or urban ghettoes. This distinction is especially true for African Americans, as noted by sociologists Larry L. Hunt and Matthew O. Hunt, who state that "the black church was the central institution in African American communities in the rural South . . . and has become a less dominant institution in the urban North."[10] This is, I believe, relatively easy to understand. In urban areas, family and community bonds—and the religious beliefs that in many instances buttress them—have been more weakened and the population is more mobile. In rural areas, with comparatively less mobile people, hence comparatively more stable family and community bonds, the individual (and the individual's family and community), nature, and God seem to merge, creating their own synthesis. As geographer David Hummons says: "American agrarianism . . . does not simply avert the superiority of rural over urban life but involves a system of beliefs and claims: that rural life is closer to nature, fosters greater interdependence, supports democratic citizenship, and nourishes moral and religious life."[11]

Religion is, at heart, important because it distinguishes some things from others. It accords comparatively great importance to ideas and beliefs that involve a willingness to suspend an emphasis on "this world" and project oneself into an "other" world, a world essentially "beyond" this one. In this way, religion—of whatever kind—may involve a kind of transcendence in which one believes in the supremacy of a "place" quite distinct from mundane, everyday life. At the same time, a very sharp distinction is drawn between "sacred" and "secular" realms; indeed, the most damning comment that can be made (by Christian fundamentalists) about much contemporary social thought and practice is that it is based on "secular humanism," in contrast to Christian (sacred) beliefs, thought by those who practice them to be more rooted in morality.

Without respect to any one religion, the sociologist Peter Berger has written very poetically about its larger and, perhaps, largest premise:

> It is well at this point to recall the definition of religion used a little earlier—the establishment, through human activity, of a sacred cosmos that will be capable of maintaining itself in the ever-present face of chaos.

Every human society, however legitimated, must maintain its solidarity in the face of chaos. Religiously legitimated solidarity brings this fundamental sociological fact into sharper focus. The world of sacred order, by virtue of being an ongoing human production, is ongoingly confronted with the disordering forces of human existence in time. The precariousness of every such world is revealed each time they dream reality-denying dreams of 'madness,' and most importantly, each time they consciously encounter death. Every human society is, in the last resort, men banded together in the face of death. The power of religion depends, in the last resort, upon the credibility of the banners it puts in the hands of men as they stand before death, or more accurately, as they walk, inevitably, toward it.[12]

Sociologically speaking, then, religion is a way of bringing order to the world. It posits a belief system that helps to create social order and stability. It is, for Berger, a "sacred cosmos," a world built, to some degree, upon religious belief. It posits an "ultimate" world that can only be experienced by fervently held beliefs, beliefs that may assuage one's fears about the chaos of everyday life and, ultimately, death. The strength of one's belief and one's need to sustain it is captured well by the concept of the "Protestant ethic," unique in Western thought—and, for the sociologist Max Weber, something merged in Western experience with the rise of capitalism, as he writes in his famous book, *The Protestant Ethic and the Spirit of Capitalism*.[13] In the ethic's grand synthesis, salvation came through one's own hard work.

Small Books, Big Thoughts

During my stay in Colonial County, I became very aware of this synthesis and the importance of religion in everyday life, at least as it played out in one small community and in one of that county's churches. In part, I became aware of it because AC was a pillar of the local church—for years he had served as its superintendent of Sunday school. But, beyond that, the church had been crucially important in his life in some fundamental ways, not only as a place in its own right but as a prism, a lens, through which the world was interpreted (much as noted in some of the quotes above).

More than once, I entered AC's house to find him reading from a very small book, no bigger than two or three postage stamps wide or high. It was a tiny Bible. AC read very slowly, but inevitably he would comment on the passages at hand, drawing lessons from them and, in effect, saying that much that was important about life could be drawn from this small book. For AC, the Bible was more than just a compilation of stories and weighty moral principles; indeed, it was a window to the world. Actually, it was not just *a* window but *the* window, for the Bible had been the one book with which AC had developed familiarity early in life. AC's schooling had stopped at age ten, at a time when he could neither read nor write. He had left school to work with his father. Where did he learn to read?

"I learned how to read from the Bible."

I asked, in a dimwitted way, "In school?" as though that would be the logical place to learn to read. AC said, "No, suh. I didn't learn how to read in school. I learned how to read, sho' 'nuf, in Sunday school. I always liked to go to church. My habit was to be right there in the front and they'd call on me to do certain things or say certain things. I learned by memorizin', 'cuz I couldn't read. When I'd git up there, I prayed and asked God to help me to learn how to read. I worked on learnin'. I picked up the Bible or a book. The more I read, the more understandin' come to me. I used to spell every word befo' it come to me, but later on I got to where I could spell the first letter or two and the rest of the word would come to me. I could pronounce the word and keep on goin'. It wasn't that hard for me. When I go to bed at night, I read an hour or two, readin' the Bible. That's mostly what I read now. When I do that, it just picks me up. These children go to school now, finish the tenth or eleventh grade. I give 'em somethin' to read and they'll be stumblin' over that. Some of 'em tell me that they don't learn how to read in school no mo'. I say 'What?' Seem like that's the most impotant thing you can learn in school. If you want to be frustrated, be some-place where you can't read nothin' and everybody around you can. You're scared somebody is gonna call on you. I was thirty years old when I learned to read."

One of AC's daughters had told me this story, but its poignancy was en-hanced considerably in hearing it from him. As AC told me, I could see how important it had been for him when—as a thirty-year-old man—he had ac-tually learned to read. Hearing this was akin to hearing Helen Keller's story about the first time a deaf child learns to sign; as Keller reputedly said, "It made the hair on the back of my neck stand on end." AC's wistful way of telling me about learning to read, and of his years of worrying as he sat in the front of the church "scared somebody is gonna call on you," was one of the most moving experiences in all of my time with him.[14]

Buildings—Large and Small

The church AC learned to read in is located an easy walk from his home. Like nearly everything else in Yvonne, it is built along the highway, set back a hundred feet or so. And like much else in Yvonne, it looks a little tired. A sign in front conveys the church's name, Shiloh Baptist Church; sometimes biblical sayings or announcements about meetings or future sermons appear below. Most often, though, the sign conveys the church's name and nothing else.

The church looks like most churches. It is a one-story structure, with a good-sized sanctuary with front doors facing the highway. Abutted to one side of the sanctuary is another large building, containing Sunday school classrooms, a kitchen, and a large meeting hall (where church suppers are held). The building is made of red brick, wood painted white, and gray cinder blocks. Like all else in Yvonne, it sits on a perfectly flat piece of land; the parking area is unpaved and a few live oaks stand between the church and neighboring residential houses.

AC's relationship to his church is unusually personal—he built it. "All of it, like the wiring and everything?" I asked. AC said, "Aaron did that. I did everything else. I laid every block, thirty-five hundred of 'em! I tried to get my sons to learn but they didn't like that part of the job. I had to lay every block. In that church down there, there's thirty-five hundred blocks and about four thousand bricks. I did it all, includin' puttin' tile on the flo'."

I asked, "Where did the money come from?" AC said, "Well, we'd raise a little money here and there. I didn't get nothin' for my work. Everything I did was free. We'd go to [a nearby city] if we'd get a good deal. If I bought a couple hundred dollars worth of stuff, man in [a nearby city] would give me a hundred fifty of other stuff."

I asked, rather incredulously, "But it's a big church, none of the other people in the church helped?" AC said, "Well, I had two fellas for helpers, but they only helped when I was there. William did the wirin' and plumbin'. Robert would mix the mud for me most times when he was home. But most times I'd be workin' in the mornin' with no one but me and I'd have to mix the mud myself and tote and lay the blocks."

I asked, "What about the kitchen?" (in which I had eaten, that Saturday). AC said, "Yep, all of it. Him [Robert] and I put up twelve-foot-long sheetrock in that kitchen." I wondered, "Did that sheetrock come from the truck that tipped over, the one reported in Melissa Greene's book?"[15] AC said, "Yep, that's where it came from. A boy had it who used to work on 95 [the interstate]; he got a bunch of it. He had it at his house. He told me he'd give us that twelve-foot sheetrock. They had all kind on there [on the truck that tipped over]—four by eight, four by ten. He gave us twenty sheets that was all 'treated'; it was blue. I put that up in the bathroom."

No one would describe the church as an architectural thing of beauty, but it is functionally designed and well used. AC, ever the pragmatist, had even found a steeple from a church that had been rebuilt in a neighboring town. However, much to his frustration and dismay, "[I] couldn't ever get nobody to help me load it up and bring it over here," so the church was finished as it now stands.

Being Laid to Rest

Building this church was not the only religious construction work that AC had done. In fact, he had built or helped to build five churches, locally. Beyond that, he had built an even more personal related item—caskets. Actually, we got into a conversation about this in a roundabout way. I wondered about what happened to local black people when they died? That is, who served as an undertaker? I wondered about this because (1) I had not seen a funeral home in any of the black neighborhoods, and (2) I was familiar with the kind of itinerant undertakers found throughout small, historically black, rural communities in the South.

AC told me, "We didn't have no undertaker 'til Mr. Cooper came down. Mr. Cooper's been here since the 1950s. Mr. Cooper's a black man; he's real fair, real fair. Been here since the early fifties. Before he was here, Colonial County used Sidney Jones from Savannah." I asked AC, "And you say he was real fair?" AC responded, "Mr. Cooper's real fair; he's almost fairer than you. He's a little redder." I laughed and said, "Oh, you mean he's lighter skinned than me." AC laughed back and said, "Yes, suh. He's real fair."

Our discussion of dying in Yvonne and Colonial County soon led me to ask AC about the caskets he had built. One of his children had mentioned this once, saying that AC had built a casket for a nephew. AC told me, "Well, I made a casket for my sister's little boy. This was back there in the sixties. The most recent one I built was for a lady in the Bluff. I built one for her son. That was in the early seventies. I just looked at him [to gauge his size] and made it and lined it. They didn't have no vaults in those days."

I wondered how the costs of a burial were covered. Some people have burial insurance but, I knew, in many rural black communities this was not true. I had been told that, aside from building some caskets (five, as it turned out), AC had also been responsible for fundraising to pay for burials. "I tried to help out, gittin' around some of that expense. You'd be surprised, when people die here, since Mr. Cooper was here, we'd take up enough money to bury people. We'd go around house to house to take up a collection."

Whether building churches or caskets, or collecting money for burials— the activities related to these things reinforce and strengthen the sense of community. Most of us have never built a casket or could imagine doing so. Nor have we gone around and collected money to help cover the costs of a funeral, just "to help out." It is precisely such things that reminded me over and over how far we were from the view that many Americans have of a black underclass, often stereotyped as helpless and hopeless. This story served as one more reminder that AC and his family, much like the characters in Duneier's *Slim's Table*, embodied personal responsibility on a regular basis. Their lives were organized around "helping out," not "a handout."

This of course, is hardly unique to historically black counties. All rural places and their residents are known for reluctance to accept government assistance except as a last resort. It is especially in rural areas that the ethos of rugged individualism is heavily valued and publicly touted. Indeed, rare is the politician who campaigns in a rural area who doesn't make reference to the hardworking local population. For black families, in particular, especially in rural areas, there is a prevailing sense of resiliency, of refusing to be beaten down regardless of life's circumstances. Sociologist Michael Thornton makes reference to this when he comments that "self-sufficiency is often thrust upon black families . . . and the lack of financial resources has meant that they must rely upon themselves."[16] Or, as McCubbin et al. note, "The support systems for African American families have been characterized as deeply rooted in the church and other healing forces in the community."[17] In a similar vein, Harriet Piper McAdoo states that "the patterns of resiliency have continued to provide protective cover for entire families and communities."[18]

Buildings Out There and In Here

Much of religion—and its integration into daily life—is an internal thing. It is the basis for much moral reasoning, our internal conversation on occasion when debating right and wrong. Some people refer to it as a "moral compass," or as helping to "keep us on the straight and narrow." In the process, though, there is a sense of religion as strengthening our character—not only as providing a moral certitude but as providing a framework within which we learn to behave honorably. As stated earlier, there is a pragmatic quality to religion in everyday, taken-for-granted, ways.

One night, Clorice and I were talking about Grace. Grace had had some difficult times as a teenager and as a young adult. As discussed earlier, she had worked as a cook, and had eventually decided to go to nursing school but that wasn't easy. Clorice told me about one particular incident involving her and Grace, and the way religion was integral to it.

"I told her that you might think I'm silly, but, I said to her: 'If you don't have any food to put on the table, you wash those kids' hands and put them to the table and say your prayers and thank God for what you have and God will make it work.[19] He is the way.' Grace was over there crying one day; she never told me. Sometimes I threw out so much food; nobody but me [living in her house at that time]. She never said a word because I could have gotten something. I made a big pot of stew and I said, 'I'm going to surprise them and take them something to eat.' And her children had folded their hands and were sitting at the table and I walked in with the food. Grace sat down and started crying. She said, 'Mama, you told me.' And I said, 'Whatchou talking about?' And I saw the kids at the table, and they did not have anything to eat. But she lived by what I said. And God sent the food. Then I started checking [on them].

"She's a private person; she didn't want anyone to know what was going on in her life. She closes herself away from everyone. She will not let you in. Never, you couldn't get in. Got to be something drastic. She keeps you out. So I started going by. She had a hard time. She'd be out there late at night trying to catch a ride [home from school, about thirty miles]. And sometimes it didn't matter what time it was, I'd get up out of my bed and go pick her up. Sometime after she finished, she said to me, 'Mama, if it hadn't been for you, I wouldn't have made it.' But I was glad. Sometimes I didn't have gas money myself and I'd think 'How am I going to go to Coastal City and back and go back the next day?' [she laughs a little, remembering Grace's struggle to achieve and her own role in it]. But like I told her, I had to look to Him, too. I said, 'Am I my neighbor's keeper?' And I answered, 'Yes.' I needed to get her home so I found a way."

Although Grace's remembrance of this story is slightly different than her mother's, religion is a part of her life, too. But in a way different from her mother's and father's. One evening, we got into a discussion about this:

"My youngest daughter goes to Shiloh [the church AC built, and where his former wife is the assistant superintendent of the Sunday school and a pianist regularly accompanying the choir]. My oldest daughter is a Jehovah's Witness. My son goes where he feels like it. And I don't! If my mom and them aren't there when the church doors open, they think the world is going to end. To me, I'm radical. I think a lot of problems black people have as a whole are due to religion. When people think everything is pray, pray, pray, I think you have to get out there and go do something for yourself. Get off your buns. God gettin' tired of you beggin' and askin' for things you can go get for yourself. I'm just radical. You talk to all of us, maybe my brother is a little radical like I am, but I'm radical in a lot of ways. When we were children and my parents was teachin' us things, the rest of them would take it to heart. I started out with what I wanted and didn't want. There's a whole lot of things [ideas] in the pot to choose from, and I would decide I needed that and I didn't need that. I go to church two or three times a year now. I go to church missionary society 'cuz my mom always wants me to be a missionary. I go to a couple of those meetings just to pacify her."

I interrupt to ask: "Is that a women's group?"

Grace says, "Yeah. I try to make sure I'm working otherwise! [we both laugh]. I love working Sundays. My mom is the only one who can nag me into going to church."

I told Grace that I wondered about her family's going to church because I knew how important it was as a regular part of her parents' lives. "I tell my dad all the time, 'My church is in my heart.' I have conversations with God, usually in my car. There's where I feel closest. I have this reoccurring dream when I can feel the Holy Spirit all through my body and I'm callin' out to pray. I have this two or three times a month."

I commented that there seemed to be lots of good psychiatric stuff in the dream. Grace quickly responded: "My birth started with that. You know my mom lost the baby before me; the baby before me died. Doctor said for her not to have any more children. My pregnancy was so hard on her and difficult, and there was this little white lady who ran the flower shop; she was gonna take care of my mom everyday. Miss Rosa was her name. She told my mom, 'If this baby is born and lives we will name her Grace—'cuz it has taken faith and the grace of God to pray us through this.'[20] When I was a small kid, this lady, my godmom, gave me my first Bible, and she was always very religious teaching me about the Bible. But I'm the free-spirited one, in the end. I don't fall for anything. And I don't go where the wind blows. I have a path of my own. I do things my own way."

This, of course, illustrates well the distinction between individual spirituality and the church as a societal institution. Even in the most fundamentalist religion, individual practitioners may have their own idiosyncratic beliefs and interpretations. Phrased differently, even where dogma is the rule of the day, not everyone may believe with equal fervor any given religion's most central tenets. For evangelicals, all of whom have "the Spirit," it seems reasonable to posit that they do not all experience that spirit in exactly the same way or interpret it identically. This will be even more true for more liberal religions or those less fundamentalist in orientation. For Grace, who admits to having religious sentiments even though she does not attend church regularly, this point may be stated as "My church is in my heart."

Grace's youngest sister, Rhonda, however, both attends church more often and seems more like her parents in religious demeanor. She is a believer in the power of religion in everyday life, and she sees in it a powerful venue for forgiveness. She lights up when she talks about it.

When her parents were getting divorced, and later when her uncle's criminal trial was under way, she told me that her father's faith never wavered. He still believed in the importance of the church, and it was very much part of his life (any moral questions linked to his divorce notwithstanding). As Rhonda told me, "He was always active in the church. Always, always. He was superintendent of the Sunday school. He didn't stop going during those years. But just because you keep going to church don't make you live the life. You can go to church all your life and still go to hell. It's not being in the building, it's the building being in here [pointing at her heart]."

How better to state the power that religion can have? Sociologist Peter Berger's notion of "sacred canopies"[21] comes to mind as a more intellectualized, sociological way of putting it, but "buildings . . . in here" seems truly well stated. And for sociologists attracted to the concept of "structure," the "building in here" is a normative frame of reference —one fusing intellectual and emotional elements, evoking respect and reverence.

Even when her parents had divorced and the children did not take kindly to AC's new wife, religion (and the church) became a mediating influence. But for Rhonda this occurred in a way that was unexpected. She told me, one time, that her stepmother had "rooted" her father. "Rooted?" I wondered. "You know, kind of voodoo-like. Some people would look at you like, 'Rooted? Are you crazy?' But my Bible tell me that stuff exists, that it's real. If you believe it, it can be a part of your life. A lot of people might not believe it but, for me, if that Bible say it, I'll eat it, sleep it, drink it. It's real. Oh yeah."[22] Since being "rooted" was not an expression I was familiar with, I wondered if others, locally, would know it? Would it be part of what Berger calls a "common stock of knowledge" (in other words, things widely known across a population)? Rhonda assured me that she would not have to explain "rooted" to local people as she did to me. For them, it was more or less a colloquial expression, suggesting the ability of one person to spiritually influence another (usually for one's own purposes).

A Whole Freedom

The church is of special significance for many southerners, and for none more than African Americans. The preaching and hymns, both before and after the Civil War, often have addressed (even if cryptically) the issue of freedom. "Free at last" was not uttered only upon one's death. In the 1960s, as the civil rights movement became more prominent, the church (not only in the South, but nationally) became the most visible institution fomenting major civil disobedience and social change. It is difficult today for many to remember what it was like then, especially in the late 1960s and early 1970s after school desegregation was federally mandated and the

South felt disproportionately its impact. Not only school desegregation was then going on; at the same time, voting rights issues were still being debated and the larger civil rights movement remained very much alive. And the church played a major role in all of this, whether one of the churches focusing on the bombing in Montgomery or Ebeneezer Baptist Church in Atlanta, or any one of hundreds of other black churches throughout the South; (for that matter, churches—white and black—nationally got involved in the civil rights movement). Churches, as such, provided legitimacy as a societal institution and could therefore challenge prevailing practices in ways no other societal institution could. But, laudable aims aside, there may have been an unintended consequence to these attempts to create a more equal society. What AC told me about this with regard to local people was a surprise but sociologically understandable.

"I think, seem like black people was better off livin' off fear than what we call 'whole freedom.' People had more respect for one another. I don't know if they was afraid to do what they do now, or what. As long as you had something to pray for or need something, you'd pray. That's how I was raised up. A long time ago, black people went to church. Mornin' church full; evenin' church full. But no more.[23] But white people, now they's churches full mornin' and night.[24] Before integration start, church full mornin' and night 'cuz old people used to say they was praying for our freedom. Like the story say, white and black boys and girls play together and go to church together, hand in hand. [Note: Here AC is citing Martin Luther King's call, in his 1963 speech, for true equality between the races.] The old people [are] what brought about the change [integration], I guess by doing all that readin' the Bible and all that. So in a sense it good, and in a sense it bad. But when black people figure they got it made, they quit goin'."

Hearing AC talk about gaining "whole freedom" was a vivid reminder of how recently he had experienced a sense of freedom denied—not some vague philosophical notion like "equality" but a more basic thing, *freedom*. He had left school at age ten, been married and become a father at age eighteen, lived in a mostly all-black world until working at a steel mill and, once there, for years been denied promotions purely on the basis of race. So when he speaks of seeking "whole freedom," he is speaking of something that had been personally relevant. But his comments about it reflect an interesting aspect of sociology: social change brings normative change. And whereas things may have been done one way heretofore, this changes when new norms come into play. AC's account suggests that there were pluses and minuses to this result. For, when church brought people together regularly, this was a way of maintaining a sense of community; further, given the nature of the challenges that confronted people (i.e., the pursuit of freedom), consistent togetherness was also a way of maintaining a sense of moral imperative. Once this imperative is removed, what is there to replace it? Clearly, for African Americans, the gains from the civil rights movement have not been sufficient to create equality with whites, but where are the moral imperatives to substitute for the search for "whole freedom"?

Let God's Light Shine

Given AC's regular church attendance, and the role religion plays in his everyday life, it is not surprising that religion would also find its way into his subconscious and appear in dreams. Like Berger's "canopy," religion is a kind of cloak that can be thrown over us. When Christian ministers say "Let the Lord's light shine upon and protect you," it is this cloak-like quality they mean. Religion is part of the social matrix within which our lives make sense. It helps to provide order and, for some, is the most meaningful source of inspiration and guidance.

When AC had worked for nearly twenty-nine years at the steel mill in Coastal City, his lung got infected and he had to quit work. AC is a very proud man. He had always stood on his own two feet, and had insisted on the same qualities in others. He had no patience for slackers or layabouts. So, when he got sick, it was a difficult time. He was not doing something he had always done, and he had no desire to simply hang around the house or to go down to Jack's (a local gathering spot, named for its owner) and hang out with the other men who regularly gathered there.

When he applied for disability income, he had to fill out many forms and be examined by a physician. When the first physician denied his request for disability, he got a second opinion, this time favorable. However, the state sided with the first physician and AC had to go to court for the matter to be decided. He had, by that time, "a pump put in my lung to draw out the fluid";[25] this meant that he tired more quickly and hence working was more difficult.

Shortly before he went to court, he had a dream in which he saw a long street and two lights on, one dim and one bright. He decided he would go to the farther light, the brighter one. And when he got there, there was one of his doctors in the disability case.

When his case went to court, both doctors he had seen testified, one for, one against. It was the one he had dreamed about under the light who testified for him. The judge heard the doctors and AC, and read through the case file. He said that he was ruling in AC's favor; that he did not see how AC had even managed to come in for the hearing, given the damage his lung had sustained. When I asked AC how he interpreted the dream in light of this, he said, "This was God intervening and pointing him in the right direction." May His light shine upon you. Indeed.

Religion as the Opiate of the Masses

For sociologists, who are trained to be skeptical of nearly everything, religion has always been problematic, even though accorded considerable importance by sociology's founders, especially Marx, Weber, and Durkheim—the latter two of whom wrote entire books about it. Nor does religion get considerable emphasis in most contemporary accounts of black life, whether in the inner city[26] or rural areas.[27] Billingsley, however, who titles his book *Climbing Jacob's Ladder*, recognizes the importance of religion for African Americans and deals effectively with it.[28] My experience in Yvonne, and in Colonial County more generally, was that the church still has a powerful influence on many local people, especially older ones. In this, I echo some of what Billingsley finds.

The rural church is a peculiarly powerful institution, in part, of course, because it has fewer institutional competitors than are found in larger, more densely settled urban areas. Too—cable television notwithstanding—rural areas still are more traditional, and hold to certain values with less disruption, than urban areas. As Christopher Ellison puts it, "family members who pray together may not only stay together, but they may also find their relationships highly satisfying."[29] More specifically, Lincoln and Mamiya say that "[Black] families contributed the building blocks for black churches and the children, through their preaching and teaching, symbols, belief system, morality, and rituals provided a unity—a glue that united families and the community to each other."[30]

For AC and his family, religion has been a shared frame of reference, with its importance not questioned by any family member. Even Grace, the most skeptical and "radical" of the children, admits to finding some comfort in her sense of God, and all her children maintain some contact with the church. As Berger and Luckmann say about all institutions, they are there before us and they will be there after us.[31] John Shelton Reed has noted that the family and the church are more powerful in the South than elsewhere.[32] "The South," as writer John Egerton says, "remains the most preaching, believing, testifying, proselytizing, evangelizing region of the country when people are looking back for the sense of roots, connection, and history."[33] Family and church blend together for families like AC's. The lines of fusion are so subtle that no one needs to comment on them. Religion, as belief and practice, is fundamental to creating, maintaining, and perpetuating a sense of community. And so it is for AC and his family. The "Lord's House" becomes a mutable, mobile thing. As AC's daughter says, "You can go to church all your life and still go to hell. It's not being in the building, it's the building being in here [in your heart]."

Six

Race and Everyday Life

In writing about either southern or urban places, it is impossible to ignore race. Race is there, like it or not. And in the South, it is almost always there in the starkest possible terms—black and white. African Americans and whites account for about 95 percent of the population in the South. To be sure, the South has had large increases in recent decades of Hispanics and Asian Americans, and so is more diverse than it once was. But the Hispanic and Asian immigrants have settled mostly in large urban places, leaving the rural South to look, demographically, pretty much as it always has.[1]

For the past one hundred years, the South, the rural South especially, has become decreasingly black, increasingly white. This shift was fueled primarily by the huge outmigration of rural blacks, not only to the cities but also to outside the region. Blacks from the Delta moved in massive numbers to Chicago, and also west, stopping perhaps in a place like Dallas but often continuing on across the country to Los Angeles and/or the West Coast; blacks from the central South moved to places like Atlanta but also northward to Detroit and Pittsburgh; and blacks from the easternmost parts of the South moved especially to Washington, Baltimore, Wilmington, Philadelphia, New York, and Boston. Nearly every city of any size on the East Coast now has a large (in some cases majority) black population. Indeed, Washington, D.C., was known for years by many African Americans as

"Chocolate City" because of its large black population; in the ensuing years, it has developed the largest African American middle class in the country, including the first majority black suburban county (Prince George's County, Maryland).

Having lived my entire adult life in the South, and having spent much of that time writing about life in the region, I was more aware than some outsiders might have been about the historical presence of majority black places there. In this case, these places weren't byproducts of immigration or urban ghettoes. These were the birthplaces, the roots, and the historical homes of most African Americans, including millions who eventually moved to urban areas. For whom else could it reasonably be said that their culture in America was grounded almost entirely in one region (the South)?

In the South, as nowhere else for blacks in the United States, blacks were not a novelty but rather were, in some ways, the very definition of the place. That is, one could only understand the place in light of their presence. No blacks, no slavery. No blacks, no cotton industry. No blacks, no Civil War. No blacks, no Reconstruction. No blacks, no *Plessy v. Ferguson*. No blacks, no "race as the most vexing question of the twentieth century." No blacks, no civil rights revolution, no school desegregation, no integration of all public facilities, no affirmative action. In short, no blacks, no continual reminder to *all of America* about how far is the reach to "e pluribus unum." As Langston Hughes says in a famous poem, "I too am America."[2]

It is probably not an overstatement to say that African Americans have been the measuring stick for the United States's progress on virtually all aspects of civil rights and the ideal of achieving an integrated society—the mythical ideal of the "melting pot" or, as it is sometimes called more recently, the "color-blind society." But, in general, the South, whether rural or urban, is a place where racial segregation is more common than not. In this, it is much like the rest of the country.[3]

For many white adult Americans, the very word "race" suggests problems. It is more than a demographic qualifier or personal attribute. It is a millstone around Americans' necks and, at the same time, an attribute socially constructed and to which has been given considerable emphasis.[4] Hardly a day goes by when something newsworthy does not happen that has a racial aspect.

In my time in Colonial County, I was interested in hearing what African

Americans had to say about race. It was not something we usually discussed; it only arose, as a rule, when I prompted such discussion, or in conjunction with something else (e.g., race in the workplace or race and politics). Only on a rare occasion would anyone ascribe to race a quality that suggested having been a victim (though surely this is a common way many white people think about being of a dark race, as a form of handicap). Instead, most of the people I spent time with didn't think about race much, at least not when I was around; to be sure, they were African Americans, but for them this was mostly a trait taken for granted; they did not have to contemplate its meaning. But, as we shall see, race did arise, and often in ways that said a lot about how race was and is historically situated and, like all else social, mutable, changing over time.

Race in Yvonne

One thing was always clear in AC's family: for his children, race was not a pressing matter. The children were well aware of it but it never deterred them; as with many families, the children's socialization experience did not lead to a "one size fits all." There was considerable variance among the children on how they dealt with race in their personal lives, but in general they adopted both Clorice's and AC's view, to keep their eyes on larger prizes than short-term worries about race.

As Clorice told me: "In this community, there was not white and black taught. We were taught by that Bible [pointing at one in the room]. It said that everybody was created equal. We lived where it said 'Colored' and stuff on signs, and we would come home crying. And you know what my mother would say? 'Dry your eye, child. God is love. You don't have to pay for how they treat you but you will have to pay for how you treat them. Take that person out of your house!' That's how we grew up and that's what I taught my children."

But, having said these things, Clorice is also quite open about admitting that not everyone believes as she does nor does everyone act in ways consistent with her beliefs. As she said, "The only trouble you might have would be in a public place. You have a few dirty people, black and white. But it wasn't something that happened everyday. I think you have more of that now than you did then. This county has gotten to be like a 'white supremacy';

the whole thing is nasty. It's just changed so much. Whites have more political power now than ever.

"The people who moved in, white and black, did so because it was peaceful. A lot of people came back home because it was better here than where they were. What I like about living here is that if a person hates you—black or white—you know it. If you were in another city, the black or white mean person would be coachwhipped, strike without warning. But in this town, you have the rattlesnake type person. You'd never be struck without knowing it. So living with that person is easy. But rarely would you have a case like that."

AC agrees. On numerous occasions he tells me about having lived all his life around whites, working with them, and also for them in some of his "little ol' jobs." As he does with nearly everything, AC is quick to put race into a historical perspective, seeing how this has changed in many ways, improved in some, and deteriorated in others. But with his usual optimism, he sees things as getting better in the long run.

"What we did when we was younger happened, and we learned to live with that. I guess you learn at Sunday school, you can't make it in [to heaven] by holdin' things against your sister and brother. I don't care what color you is. See, what happened yesterday [when segregation was the rule], you can't live with that same thing today. A lot of people want to think about what white people did to black people years ago, but I don't think you can do that. Yesterday was yesterday and today is today. Whether it was wrong yesterday, I won't say. The things you can change, change, and the things you can't, let God handle it. You can't affo'd no time to hate people 'cuz you might die tonight or tomorrow."

As much as I admired AC's eternal optimism and pragmatism, I wondered about what some of his relatives and other local black folk had told me: whites and blacks spent little time together, other than at work. Did this bother him?

"You gonna have some of 'em . . . like a lot my age, the average white, when they want somethin, you see 'em. But with me and my status (as an older, well-known local person), I get along with all of 'em. Like, if I see one, it's just like another black. I don't expect nothin' out of 'em. See, some people think you s'posed to give 'em somethin'. I don't expect nothin' out of 'em.

So when they see me, it's 'Hi, AC. How you doin'?' But a lot of people expect somethin' and they don't wanna give it themselves. I always learn that, if you want respect, you have to give respect. Just like anything else, it's a two-way street. You take younger blacks, a lot of 'em can't accept that."

I wondered, though, if maybe their experience, especially in school but also through popular media, made them more sensitive to the historical hardships that blacks had suffered. AC wasn't buying that. "You can't live in the past. If you do that, there's always gonna be resentshun [resentment]. You say two or three words and your thoughts start flashin' back. People you resent may have nuttin' [nothing] to do with you." "So," I interrupted, "you might resent them for what they represent [i.e., being white, hence by implication having treated blacks unfairly], not for what they did to you?" AC responded, "Yeah. Some of the younger ones in school got these attitudes from their parents, and they think a lot of the teachers discriminate against 'em. I tell 'em, 'If you' a teacher and you have thu'ty [thirty] head of children, you ain't got no time to give any of 'em special treatment. It's up to the individual if he want to learn it. That's not the teacher's job. They got their education; they gittin' paid. You wanna git you education so you can git paid.' I ain't find no white people I couldn't git what I want. I don't care how many of 'em there is or how mean they is, I can go to 'em and git what I want.

"Some people might still want you to go to the back [of the bus or restaurant, e.g.], but they ain't gonna confront you with that. Like we s'posed to have some people 'round here in the Klan, but that don't make no difference if they in that organization. So long as they treat me fair, that's all that matters. If he want to be in that Klan, that's his decision. I git along with people, I don't care who it is. I ain't got nothin' to do with what they do behind my back."

As AC and I continued our conversation about race (the only time we focused specifically on that topic), I prodded him to say more about whites and blacks together. How could he be so accepting, knowing that at times people might dislike him or resent him purely because he was black?

"You will find some people in both races will look for any little excuse to start somethin'—black and white. The main issue is to keep your cool and give everybody the respect they should have and you won't have no trouble. Whites call me to do some work all the time." And here AC paused, as though he was tired of talking about race yet also recognized its ongoing aspect in his everyday life: "A lot of people just don't know how to act. They think if you're bein' nice to 'em that you're bein' fresh [at this, we both have a good laugh]. Really, a lot of 'em just don't know how to act. You can't be nice to some people. All you have to do is respect people and treat 'em like you want them to treat you. Everything else will fall into place. A lot of people call me 'crazy' 'cuz I say what I want to say and I don't hold any animosity."

It is important to remember that AC's optimistic and pragmatic outlook has been forged over a sixty-six-year period, all lived in the same place. He has seen people come and go, norms evolve and change, situations get better and worse at the same time. Perhaps most striking of all the changes he has seen is that blacks and whites, even if not embracing one another with wild enthusiasm, get along better than not.

He told me one day about when he was a younger man and some black workers were effectively in a peonage system. This, of course, was similar to the stituation of all sharecroppers and tenants. They would be terribly indebted to the landowner and, since the owner controlled the books recording both crops grown and items bought at the company (or plantation) store, it was nearly impossible for them to escape from debt; hence they were living in a form of peonage. AC's recounting of this took on a very personal note: "One man, what he did was sell his nephew off to a farmer and went and got money on him. You ain't never earning it off. It was in the early fifties when that happened. We had to go steal him back by night. We took a chance. Those people would hang you up good. Only time I know of like that and . . . you wouldn't go back nohow. They wouldn't even allow you to go to town in '49 or the early fifties. Took the governor, in the end, to make those people mo' acceptin' of blacks. He had to come down personally and make them do it, but that wasn't till the sixties." With a story like that part of one's experience, how could things not look better?

But my own sense of how whites and blacks relate in Colonial County is that—like those of whites and blacks in the rest of America—their relationships are mostly at arm's length, maybe cordial but rarely involving much knowledge of each other. This sense was well captured one day when I was talking with AC's sister, Althea. Barely younger than AC, she too has lived her entire life in Yvonne. She remembered when "colored people" owned stores in Yvonne and never went to Coastal City (which was and still is majority-white). Whites were a group with whom Althea had virtually no contact.

"Terrence and AC, now, they know a lot of whites. But if I see a white person, if I see 'em again, I don't know who it is. I know 'em when I work around 'em every day. Probably a lot of white people around heah know me and I don't even know who they is. I really don't know."

AC's former sister-in-law, Dorthea, a nearly seventy-year-old woman, sees race problems as anchored primarily in the older adults, not in the children. And she believes in accepting people pretty much as she finds them; in this, she voices an opinion commonly heard, and akin to some of AC's remarks and general stance toward life, of acceptance, as he might put it, "without animosity."

As Dorthea noted one day, "They [whites] didn't want the chirren to go to school together, but they get along real good. If the adults don't get along, the chirren do. I'll tell you the truth, now I got a girl raised up here with me, she's white. Her family used to live behind the church. They's white but they's like a family to me. They always come by and them two people love me and I love them. When they come by, they say, 'Dorthea, I ain't leavin' 'til you give me a hug.' I don't care where I see them at, we have a hug. If they see my daughter, they always ax' after me." This, as it turns out, reflects well the kind of bimodal response people often give about race: hot and cold, sometimes both at once. It is a sort of realpolitik about race in the county and, in a larger way, race in the entire country.

Terrence, AC's brother and the youngest member of the family, is also the most overtly political. He was, for awhile, the county's most high-profile and charismatic black politician. Talking with him is like sitting around a university coffee shop listening in on the latest intellectual machinations about how the world works (as seen from the ivory tower—but, in Terrence's case, as seen from his burned-out shell of a house at ground level). He has a very political-economy view of the world.

As he tells me, "As long as I'm makin' money offa you, and my family's makin' their livin' offa you, and my friends makin' their livin' offa you, I'm gonna treat you with respect"— he pauses dramatically before continuing— "as long as I'm talkin' to your face. That's the part that whites in Colonial County plays. Reachin' out for a piece of land, a swamp or an ol' car. Somethin' they want. Not all of 'em now, not all of 'em. We have some people here fo' years. They'll be prejudic' to a certain extent, but they will do you a favor without asking for a favor or getting anything from you. That's what Colonial County consists of right now. 'Cuz all of your businesses in Colonial County is owned by whites. Who got all the money invested in those sto's [stores]? Who gonna git the proceeds from 'em? They're not gonna hire you. Because they don't want to pay the insurance on you. They're smart in your face but you go in certain areas at night and you'll see they got them big ol' fires goin', discussin' their situation.[5] That don't bother me none. It worries me, though, because I believe in callin' a spade a spade. Then you know how to deal with that individual. But when someone's a spade and he wants you to think he's a heart, that's the problem. That's what we got in Colonial County right now. Everybody says we get along good. Sure! You pay your taxes and insurances. All these white guys and women come into your house. They treat you good, sure—'cuz you makin' 'em money! And I told 'em, 'Don't come by my house, for nothin'. Period. If I owe some insurance, I'll mail it.' They're not gonna let you in their house to collect no insurance. If a black man got to collect insurance from a white man, you know where he gonna get it at? On the porch. On the porch."

Race and Politics

Race seems to have always been a part of politics in Colonial County. Beginning in the early 1950s, an older black man was essentially "given" a spot on the county council by the other council members, all of whom were white. This gave the appearance of black representation in what was, at that time, a majority black place. After awhile, having one older black man on the council became normative and, when the first one left, another took his place. But this changed dramatically in the early 1970s. At that point, a small group of younger black men (mostly in their thirties and early forties) decided that it was time for more proportional representation. To do this, they obtained the help of the state legal services office and filed suit in federal court. They lost initially, but in the end they won.

I spoke at length with the person most widely regarded as having led their fight, Terrence. I wondered especially how someone like him, a high-school dropout working in a steel mill at night, had decided to get involved in politics, to aggressively become a politician.

"It was when a white cop shot a black man, that's where it all started from. See, I was working at [the steel mill] and, when I came through Conaty on my way home, I see a lot of cars parked there. By the time I got to the house, a lot of people came over to tell me what happened: That a white cop had shot . . . [a black man] in the mouth. So I'd just got home from work, sweatin' and all, and I said, 'Well, I'll tell you what we'll do. Call some people you can trust, and we'll go into Conaty tomorrow monin' and we'll talk to the city council and find out what happened.' People called me back at about seven o'clock and said we may not have but a hundred . . . , but sho' 'nuff, there was about a thousand theah!" He laughs heartily at the memory. "We had the streets all blocked. So the mayor, who worked at the Ford place, he didn't want to act then 'cuz the city council wasn't in session, but we took over city hall and started makin' our demands. The sheriff sent a deputy down there to tell us to go on home. And we'd got word that he'd called all the merchants and told 'em, 'Don't sell no damn niggers any ammunition!' So I gave the word, 'Tell [the sheriff], You don't go to war and buy ammunition. You bring ammunition witcha [with you] when you come to war!' After that, I was on his bad side from then on. They had that man in jail with a bullet in his mouth. Thank God, the bullet had lodged in his jaw. Musta been a bad bullet or somethin'. After that, they tried to prosecute him. The po-lice went on private property—said there was a disturbance call but theah wasn't. The problem was that the white po-liceman was datin' the same girl as him. And when he went theah, that was where the disturbance came from. After that, the national NAACP got involved, and I was the president of the Colonial County Civic Association, that was right before the NAACP came into Colonial County. After all that, we eventually got reappo'tionment.

"It's funny, you know, Reverend Jacobs was tellin' me the other day that there is a group now in Colonial County filin' suit for reappo'tionment. We did the same thing. We couldn't get a black elected at large. Once upon a time, that was what we did—paper ballots, at-large vote. But you'd find boxes of ballots in the river. They were always transported [from the voting places] by the sheriff's department—now that was when the sheriff was still in control. We found out that the federal government had fo' [four] voting machines, and we started to buy them and that stopped the voting problem.

"We told the federal government how we would split it up equally. We only gave ourselves assurance of two black commissioners. And the judge was very pleased and the county did not challenge us with it. Still pretty much two black and three white. But we left ourselves open that if we got a good black candidate, the people—white and black—would support the person and we could wind up with three black. So far it works, and it can work. Just like you can get a black sheriff elected [the current sheriff is black], you can also get a black commissioner elected at large. Now though, they want to say that from the census you need reappo'tionment. That what's John Saunders [a prominent white commissioner] and them tryin' to do right now."

Of course, as Terrence noted, there was a great irony to this. Only twenty years earlier blacks had filed suit for reapportionment, wanting to expand their representation. They had been underrepresented historically and sought to right this wrong. Now, twenty years later, whites (always in control of all important matters in the county, especially economic ones) were filing suit to effectively expand their own base of power. History repeating itself.

Race and Land

When Terrence mentioned John Saunders's name, it made me wonder about something else that has historically been a bone of contention between whites and blacks in the Lowcountry: land ownership. Nearly all the barrier islands along the South Carolina and Georgia coast were, at one time, inhabited primarily by blacks. Indeed, most had nearly all-black populations. This is true for nearly every major barrier island, which, in the past twenty to thirty years, have become identified with second homes and island "resort" living. Most notable would be such places as Hilton Head and St. Simons Island.

That blacks were the majority population in these places did not stop white developers from coming in and buying up vacant land. Although, on the one hand, there may have been nothing technically illegal about this, on the other hand, the land acquisition was often done in sheriff's tax sales— where it was not always easy to prove what taxes had been paid or even who owned the land. It was this latter issue that proved especially difficult since, as families died out or moved away, title to their land was vested in the heirs. But if the heirs did not live there and were not in touch with local people (many of whom, of course, could not read and so would not have necessarily known what was going on, in any case), there was no way for these heirs to know they were at risk of losing their land—often for the sake of a pittance in back taxes.

The first large-scale effort to slow this process was begun on St. Helena Island, off the South Carolina coast. It is an historically black place, located across the St. John's River from Beaufort (pronounced Bew-fort), a beautiful, quaint coastal town—in fact, the place where such films as *The Big Chill* and *Prince of Tides* had scenery shot. Antebellum homes, live oaks draped with Spanish moss, and a truly "southern" way of life abound. But crossing the river (as, metaphorically, in Pat Conroy's autobiographical account, *The Water Is Wide*[6]) is a trip far greater than the span of the bridge. It is to step into another era, captured wonderfully at the Penn Center, a place established to preserve "Negro" culture, complete with basket weaving, Gullah language and customs, and general barrier island life, for African Americans. In recent years, this preservation has included organizing to challenge land grabs by white developers at tax sales, with organizers arguing that all reasonable efforts must be made to contact the legal heirs to give them the opportunity to retain their family land.

I wondered about how this activity had occurred in Colonial County, since I knew that whites had bought up virtually all the waterfront property. As Dorthea had told me one time, "Friend, white people will kill to live by the water." And, among blacks, it is widely assumed that white population growth in the county will continue as long as land along the water can be bought and developed. Indeed, AC, in one of our first meetings, had commented on this, noting that "Blacks didn't think the land was worth much. Didn't mean that much to me when I was a young man. I, myself, had a chance to buy land at ten dollars an acre. But we already had a lot of land, so we didn't need it. In those days, they'd swap you an acre of land for a hog, cow, goat, chicken, anything. Blacks owned the waterfront from Colonial County all the way up the coast. Most now own it is white. Most blacks don't like to live on the river. Maybe one or two, but not most. They built their houses way back on a hill. Never near the river even though they owned the land. They's the ones sold out, mostly. Too late now, 'cuz it's mostly gone."

There was little history of sharecropping in the county; blacks had, in fact, owned land ever since Reconstruction. In the Lowcountry, most sharecropping was played out long ago, and it was never as prevalent there as a bit farther inland, where larger, more easily tilled and planted acreage was available. Thus, in a place like Colonial County, the more dominant form of land ownership and usage was as a residence with, perhaps, some land used for a garden, with the produce primarily intended for consumption, not sale. Above all else, owning the land was, as AC saw it, a way of keeping the family together. But he well recognized the difficulty of doing this. He told me one time about how he came to own the land where his own house sat.

"This piece, right here, is an acre. I got it from my aunt right here [pointing next door]. Before I moved up here [from down the road a short distance], my grandfather's uncle owned it. Then my grandfather's uncle died and my grandfather got it. Twenty-seven acres in Yvonne. Then, when my grandfather died, my father got it. Then, when I got big enough, he showed me everything and he had me take it over. He figured I wouldn't get rid of it. Had the sense to hang on to it. He knew I wouldn't sell it or nothin'. He put it in my hands to have it. I still own it.

"My mother died the other day [actually, a year earlier], and she and her sister had seventeen acres. They messed me up [by willing pieces of it rather than the entire amount]. As long as we all split up, everybody will start sellin'. If you keep it together, you all right. But if you start splittin' it up. . . . Now my Daddy gave the first five children an acre each. When my brother died, his wife sold his acre. Sell it piece at a time. This crew now, they want money. The young crew won't have no land around here. They sell it all off. Just like the blacks along the water. People borrowed money on land but won't pay it back. They run off. Some got land for an old car, or borrowed two–three hundred dollars but they won't come back to pay it.

"Black people just don't understand the value of land. Somebody put it up for sale at a sheriff's sale. Some of them older white people—take a lot of them right now don't let a week pass and they goin' through them books [to find buyable land]. See who don't pay their taxes, and they buy it up. That's what happen on a lot of land. Still happen, a lot of places."[7]

So, for AC, the loss of black-owned land is something that has occurred for years and has shown no signs of slowing. Indeed, black people seemed to him their own enemies in this, essentially defaulting the land to others in a position to buy it, and most often those others turned out to be whites.

AC sounds much like Dorthea when he tells me about whites wanting to live near the water. "Average white folk likes the island, for some reason.

They likes the water. If there's water, they flock to it. Get off the waterfront, don't see themselves makin' much money on it. Ain't no one goin' to put a two-hundred-thousand-dollar house out here in these woods." He laughs at the very idea."We gots to be a long ways from there."

In telling me this, AC sounds at times like longtime residents on barrier islands and coastal lands, more generally. Without degrees in geology, they understood a simple principle—the water comes in, the water goes out. On the seaward side of an island or on the coast itself, the land erodes regularly. On the backside, it is more likely to build up. There is a kind of "Lord giveth, Lord taketh away" rhythm to this. The same is true for other coastal properties characterized by what AC calls "hills"—those areas where the land rises above sea level. The land accumulates inland from the coast, whereas the coast itself, usually slowly, but sometimes helped by storms, wears away. So, for longtime residents the issue of "Who would want to live by the water?" is not a silly question but one with a history. Their time to live in the area is not a few years, in a home built for retirement or as a second home; rather, they live with a much different sense of permanency and, for that matter, a much different sense of place.

It is axiomatic that the closer one lives to the coast or on the water, the greater the probability of experiencing flooding. Hurricanes or tropical storms often bring tidal surges or, minimally, unusually high tides that bring water into the marshy lowland closest to the coast. Also, because this same area is at, or sometimes barely above or below, sea level, any heavy rainfall is slow to subside. It is no exaggeration that, when driving on the main roads after such rain, some of the side roads look like ribbons winding their way through huge lakes, and this is true even a short way inland, where the land has yet to rise much above sea level. Occasional flooding, it may be noted, has only marginal effects on the area's land-based agriculture, since it occurs only in the most western part of Colonial County (about thirty miles inland from the coast). In general, houses along the water do not flood often, in part because both the older homes and the newer developments have been built along rivers and creeks that are tidal, thus making their high-water marks known on a daily basis.

Clearly, for whites, living by the water is desirable, and they will pay whatever it takes to accomplish this. But even in Colonial County, there is some intra-racial unhappiness about this—that is, among whites. Few local whites can afford to buy houses near the water, anymore; it is simply too expensive. Instead, as one person tells me, "Developers from Atlanta are the ones who buy it up." Thus, there is a sense that new growth is largely fueled by outside money and outside interests.

This is most clearly the case at the pricey "plantations," a name often tagged on to upscale developments catering almost entirely to white buyers, sending a subliminal message that the good old days have not completely gone away; indeed, Hilton Head Island is one big series of "plantations," as though the name is a synonym for development or neighborhood. In Colonial County, the newest, priciest "plantation" development is found at the southern end, along the river, with another large waterfront development along the county's southeastern side.

I asked Terrence one day about his sense of black land ownership in Colonial County, specifically about what role tax sales had played and to what degree he felt that local black people had essentially had their land stolen. I say "stolen" here because this is a term often used by local black folk in the Lowcountry when they talk about white developers coming in. They believe that the developers stole the land from the original owners and that there is no sense of right and wrong (in a Biblical way) about how this was done. For white developers, a land transfer is a simple business transaction: elementary capitalism with profits to be maximized. For local black folk, it is anything but this: it is taking something from families whose roots in America are found there, usually back to the Reconstruction era. For them, the issue is not dollars and cents but rather a cultural identity tied to the land.

More than any other local person with whom I spent time in Colonial County, Terrence understood this. He, too, saw what was happening as far more than an economic situation. He saw it as persons' rightful heritage being taken from them—or, alternatively, being sold away (even by the person involved) without thought as to what this loss might mean in the long run.

As he told me, "A lot of the people who migrated to New Yawk, they lost their property or they sold their parents' property. If they got ready to migrate back, they got nothin' to migrate to. When I was commissioner, anytime I'd see a piece of property for sale, I'd make them write—I wouldn't care how many times. And no land was sold from the tax assessor during that time, and that's the whole sixteen years I was commissioner.

"I saw that it didn't happen. As of right now, they got a tax amnesty. That's double taxes but a lot of people sittin' here today don't realize that. If you don't pay your taxes this year, they are doubled. A lot of guys don't know how tax amnesty works. They aren't forgiving you with amnesty; it's a way of creatin' more money. We got old people on fixed incomes and people who own land away from here but they don't get any relief. I tried to get tax equalization, for people on the riverfront to pay more taxes. I felt like people inland should get some relief but people here in Yvonne were paying more than the ones on the river.

"For awhile we had tax equalization, but I went to prison . . . and now it's all gone. Two or three blacks want to live on the river but most folks, their property is gone. Before I got indicted, I had a crowd of lawyers from North Carolina who were land specialists. And a whole lot of white people thought they were going to lose their land 'cuz we were going to look at the legalities of how that land had become theirs. Our people were ignorant about this, a long time ago. They'd put up their land on property bonds and the sheriff didn't tell them that they had to pay taxes on all their land, not just that excluded by the property bond. But he didn't tell them that, so a lot of them lost their land."

The method of posting a property bond has always been available to the public as a way of getting out of jail while awaiting trial. And it's hardly surprising that one person's plight may work to another person's advantage. But, in Colonial County, at least historically, this often meant that the county sheriff (an office that, in Colonial County, was controlled by one family for over fifty years) knew more than anyone about what property had been used for posting bond and also knew if it was forfeited, hence for sale. There was common knowledge in the county that this was one way that some (white) families had accrued wealth. Indeed, much of the recent pricey development at the county's southern end consisted of land that blacks felt had been stolen, first by the federal government (ostensibly to build an airbase during World War II), and subsequently by the sheriff, when the courthouse burned and the deeds to the land (in an area where blacks were the only ones who owned land) were destroyed. Although this event eventually led to various federal inquiries (on civil rights charges) and even to coverage on television, nothing was ever done to provide financial compensation to the black families involved, many of whom still live in the area—albeit across the road from one of the new "plantations."

In a final irony about race and land in Colonial County, some local families are now losing their land, not just to post property bonds (which leave the land secure once the person shows up for trial), but also to raise attorneys' fees. As if to show how hip Colonial County is, despite its rural location, the property bonds and land sales are used by some local black families to get their sons out of jail while facing drug charges. This fact arose by happenstance one day, when I was talking with AC's youngest child, Samuel. As he told me, "Most of the people in Colonial County now have given away a lot of what [land] they had. It's made people living closer and closer together. People have sold their land 'cuz somebody done messed 'em up. Lost land from gambling and crack." I interrupted to ask, "And you didn't see this before crack?" Samuel continued, "No, no. Not like it is now."

In the South, land and race are so interrelated that it is at times difficult to separate them. Land, which would seem to have little to do with race, becomes one more commodity heavily infused with race. The land-race relationship is part and parcel of the local social-historical context. Land is a basic element of life in Colonial County, as fundamental as water and air. But it differs from these because, unlike water and air, land can be owned and, in this way, one's name is attached to it By extension then, the land is *in* and *of* oneself—hence one's identity is tied up in it. How much more personal can it be than to be born on a plot of land; grow up there; die there; and be buried there? This is *roots* in the truest and largest sense. But, as many people told me, those roots are jeopardized and, once lost, they will not be easily replanted or regrown.

As Children See the World—In Black and White

For AC's children and those born after them (including the current generation), race in Colonial County is mostly benign. Indeed, Althea's earlier comment strikes this same tone: whites may live around me but they have little relevance to my everyday experience. Although AC feels that some younger blacks are resentful about whites (for whites' advantages in the past; for the advantages they still have), he too believes that race relations in Colonial County are in general fairly good. The granddaughter he raised with Patrice was, while attending the local schools, and is, as a senior in college, best friends with a local white girl. As Patrice tells me one day, "They party together, even now."

A sense of race relations in the county can be tracked, albeit loosely, by conversations with AC's children. The oldest, Alice, remembers well when the schools were racially segregated but when, ironically, many local children knew one another across racial lines and often played together. It was only as the children got older that they became more aware of their difference.

"Until we got bigger, you didn't know there was a difference. But then you realized that we had to go to the back [especially of restaurants] to order, or there were 'whites only' clubs and things like that. Growing up, you didn't notice the difference. We played together and lived across the street from them. Shoot, Grace [her barely younger sister] is named after one of them; in fact, she's her godmother."

Alice's career in the military furthered her own sense of race, causing her to interact with a diverse population, both men and women, in the military. I wondered what it had been like for a black woman to achieve some success as an enlisted person, and to wind up supervising whites for whom this kind of power relationship might have seemed truly strange. As Alice told me: "When you talk about a woman, and one with a little bit of rank and a black woman on top of that, and a little bit outspoken, well, some people can't accept that. And believe it or not, a lot of people, when they came into the military, had never seen a black person—in this day and age, had never seen a black person!"[8]

But it became clear that, for Alice, twenty years in the military had been affected by race. "Like Tommy, my husband, he got out 'cuz he was tired of bein' a babysitter. One of these guys he supervised told him that he 'don't take no orders from no nigger.' So Tommy decked him. I guess the guy figured that their ranks weren't that different so he didn't have to take orders from him.

"Now in Germany, at least in some places, they look at you funny. It was a hard thing sometimes. And in the military, some people would say, when you didn't get things, that it wasn't race, but the military is about the most racist place because you have cliques. We'd say that's the redneck group over there, and this is the group that would tolerate you a little bit, and this is the group that's alright. With me, I carried some extra protection: I prayed and went about my business. Like my Daddy, I'd say, 'You just got to get on with your business,' and you could still do it the way you wanted to do. All you got to do is go on. They not gonna come on behind you, and you can alleviate a lot of the pressure between blacks and whites.

"Now when I think about it, I went to school with all blacks. And once we stopped living across from Miss Rider [Grace's godmother], I don't know any whites. My brother had some white friends, but I don't know one white person. I don't know very few blacks, unless they are kin to me. I'm a very family-orientated person.

"But since I've been back, now since I been doing volunteer work with the schools, I know some whites [she laughs at this, especially given what she's been telling me]. They're really sweet people. I told 'em one day, 'I'm gonna be your token.' When they were kidding me one day, I knew it wasn't just 'cuz I was black. It was a group of people working toward a common goal, bettering the school for the kids, and it didn't matter what color you were."

Alice's sense of commitment to the schools transcends race;, in fact, race seems to have little or nothing to do with it. But she is aware of how race plays a role in the schools, even thirty years after the start of integration. She sees the kids get on the buses at the end of the day, and it's a reminder of how far there is to go: "It's still segregated, believe it or not. Most of the whites ride on one bus; most of the blacks ride on another bus. When the kids are together in one group, you have mostly white or mostly black. There's no togetherness. Like the Color Guard I'm running—everybody who tried out is black."

Nevertheless, Alice shares her parents' conviction that the best future is an integrated one, one that must be achieved through common purpose. So she continues with her volunteer work in the schools, thinks about running for the school board, is committed to this place.

Rhonda, the youngest family member, like her siblings and many black people I spoke with in Colonial County, thinks that race is more subtle now, not as overt as it once was. "The prejudice is undercover now; it's not out in the open. They do it undercover. If it stayed out on top, you'd know where it is. But now that it's undercover, you still have to be careful, and I'm not talking about just white folks, either, but black folks, too." I stopped Rhonda midstream to ask, "Black folks, too? Why do you mention them?" Mine was almost a knee-jerk sociological response to anything that challenges the common, taken-for-granted, prevailing wisdom. As though black people couldn't harbor their own prejudices, as though that would not be alright for *them* to do, as though brotherly love would be uniquely ingrained in blacks.

Rhonda continues, "You have a lot of black people who will hurt you quicker than a white person. Their priority is money, what they can get. They don't care who they hurt to get where they're going. They'll slap you down to get there. There are black people who will hurt you, but you have to be careful because you don't know who.

"If people would just be people, it would be easier. That's the worse thing. That is the root of all evil—people wantin' to use people to get ahead. If we'd be satisfied with who we are, then things wouldn't be so bad. I mean, if I was happy and you were happy, then why would I try to hurt you to get ahead? Prejudice is just undercover."

Rhonda's feelings caused me to share a remembrance of my own. As I told her, "The first black woman I ever worked with was a woman named Yvonne Ewell. She's about your dad's age. When I first worked with her, twenty-seven years ago, she told me the same thing you've just been talking about. She claimed that when the Dallas school system was racially segregated, you knew exactly who was for you and who wasn't. But once they desegregated, then it was much harder to tell because, for the whites especially, they had to watch themselves more closely around blacks. So their true feelings were more masked, more hidden."

In a sad bit of irony, our conversation was followed shortly by the announcement that Texaco executives had been caught on tape making highly disparaging racial remarks. Whether it is Texaco executives, Denny's restaurant managers, members of the U.S. Congress, Rush Limbaugh, or, no doubt, countless others, Rhonda seems quite accurate in her sense of race prejudice as having gone undercover. To some degree, civility is like a veneer that, scratched even lightly, uncovers the true grain of character. And no matter how one tries to mask this—for example, by media or public reference to "the 'n' word"—the harshness of reality cannot be wished away.

I can tell that this is a sore spot with Terrence. He is from the civil rights generation and had worked hard to expand the rights of blacks, hoping that they could compete more equally with whites, not in a large urban area but at least in this rural place, and had found he was often at odds with his neighbors, even with family members. So when I ask him about his sense of blacks and whites interacting on an everyday basis in integrated ways, he gives me a predictable (and, by my observation, accurate) response "Eating meals? Going to church? All that's still racially segregated."

Race in a Historically Black Place

I wondered what, if anything, local black people thought about their historically black county, a place that had been majority black for most of their lives. As Alice told me, "You always knew there were more of us than them. But to talk about it? No, not that I recall. Like now, I realize: if you want things different, you don't have to have it this way. You've got the majority, the knowledge, you can get together and do things. It's not just white or black, though, you know? You got someone to pull behind, all of us need that. I wasn't old enough to realize that, but I do now. Since I've been back here, I'm tryin' to get back into what's goin' on in the county. It doesn't matter who you're behind. It isn't just white and black anymore. We all need to be more active. A lot of the things I'm into, there's not a lot of black parents in them, even though the schools are majority black."

Alice's feelings are echoed by her sister, Grace. Grace, though—considered by all family members the intellectual of the group—has opinions at odds with many of theirs, both hopeful and realistic about whites and blacks living together.

We were talking one evening about race in Colonial County, and I told Grace that Alice had commented on the tendency for the races to self-segregate, not only in housing but in nearly all ways that would bring them into much social contact. For example, the county's long history of "juke joints" as places where some black people would hang out at night has changed little over the years. But Grace saw both hope for less segregation, and a desire to keep some.

She told me: "People live in separate areas, but here everybody owns property. I think, if someone came in here and built a big subdivision that people could afford, you'd see whites and blacks living next door to one another. You see that in Conaty, where they live in closer proximity. But I think if someone built some nice houses, whites and blacks would live right there together. Like my brother lives in Coastal City, and he has a German [white] wife. He doesn't have any problem in the black community 'cuz his wife isn't related to them here. She might get a little jive 'cuz she married a black guy but, for the most part, it's not a problem.

"My thing is, though, I'm not in favor of interracial marriages. I'm the only one in my family who will say that, the only one. Like I say, I'm a radical. I teach my children, like my son, . . . I tell him: 'You come home with someone, it better be a black girl.' I'm not prejudic' but he's not gonna be accepted in her world, and I have no animosity toward her but I'm not gonna make my world easily accessible to you when your world is not easily accessible to me. And that's my whole opinion based on that. I will not open my arms and welcome your child into my house when my child cannot go into yours. That may be selfish but that's just the way I feel. I love my child just as much as you love yours."

For Grace, then, there is an optimism around how blacks and whites may be able to live together as neighbors in the county, but, based on her experience, she sees little hope for them living together as partners. As she tells me on other occasions, the "cultures" are simply too different to be easily bridged.

And yet, living in the next county, is her youngest brother, who by all accounts has been highly successful. He did well in the local schools and graduated from high school, and completed twenty years of service in the military, retiring at a very high rank after having had considerable responsibility. He married a white woman in Germany who works as a nurse, and they bought a huge, beautiful new house in a fashionable suburb.

Samuel does not mince his words. He speaks his mind, and this occurs no matter the topic. He does not quickly blame race for causing problems, but he sees the ways it comes into play, especially in Colonial County and the Lowcountry region where he grew up. "Well, I never grew up with the color barrier. It never bothered me. I've seen nice white people and nasty white people. I just accept them." This, of course, sounds much like his father, AC.

"The racial stuff here is pretty much what you make out of it," he continues. "If you close your eyes and think it doesn't exist, you're fooling yourself. It doesn't bother me because I expect it. I don't talk to anybody who sees me as a black guy or a pink guy or a blue guy. They need to address me as 'Samuel.' I grew up color blind. My Dad said, 'I don't know about you.' I was sneaking around with a white girl in Conaty, and that wasn't accepted. We were just friends. I picked people for who they were. If I see something beautiful in their personality, then that's what I deal with. If I see ugly, then I stay away from it. I just worry about my environment right here. Now with my wife, I've had stares and long looks. If someone looks too long, I'll say, 'Ma'am, is there a problem?' And you know they're going to move out. All those years we lived in Yvonne [when he was posted at a nearby military installation], they got used to my wife and me." More sociologically, the couple became one more part of people's taken-for-granted everyday lives.

His comments refocus our conversation on life in Colonial County. I wonder, specifically, about his sense of race there in recent years. After all, it is still a very rural place and much about it seems—outwardly, at least—unchanged for decades.

Samuel believes that one of the more quiet and important changes that has occurred has been for the worse—that black families no longer have the strength they once had, and such social forces as drugs and female-headed households have hurt them badly. "We've lost something. When crack moved in, it destroyed us . . . we've lost families and blacks and kids. It's that family-values thing. It's based on pride."[9] Samuel, like some political segments and media commentators laments the loss of "family values." Of course, they have not been lost; they have simply changed. But Samuel, like many social critics and, for that matter, much of the American population, feels that family values have changed for the worse. In an earlier era (always, it seems, within one's lifetime), values reflected greater morality and less instability than today's "values." The family-values axis to social argument seems something that will continue forever and never be resolved to everyone's satisfaction. "This generation" will always be somewhat out of tune with previous ones, and, in the eyes of many elders, the old days will always be remembered as both good and, by implication, better.

As Samuel tells me, "We've lost something." Of course, he's right. But something lost is usually replaced. And in time, it, too, will be remembered as part of its own "good old days"—no doubt days better in some people's minds, but never agreed upon by all. What is lost can only be understood for what it was (in its own historical epoch) and for what it is (now, as a reconstruction, hence changed in form from what it was). "Family values" is a phrase for the times—all times, it would seem.

Color Is Only Skin Deep

Early in my days with AC, we had started talking about how his family had become so prominent. They were not wealthy, and only one family member had been heavily engaged in politics, so they were not a political dynasty. But they had a very strong sense of themselves as a family, and as having to live up to certain standards. For them, this was a normative context learned early and repeatedly. All the children can recall its many lessons, not only from AC, but from Clorice as well. Having a clear sense of high standards was a point of pride but not of vanity, rather an integral strength in their very being. It is precisely having standards that is linked to their sense of independence and their ability always to stand on their own.

As AC told me one time, "We shouldn't a been nothin'. Shouldn't a-been nothin'. But they [his parents] were always poundin' us that we could do whatever anyone else could. Taught us that color wasn't nothin' but skin deep. Color only skin deep. You can make yo'self anything you want. Taught you can be whatever you want to be. Taught us that. Color skin deep. Cut the white man or black man, it bleed red. Sunday school taught us all men created equal. Black people make themself—just like us—the best." He pauses to think about this for a second, then continues, "Some make the best. Some make the worst."

In other words, the burden of doing well is placed primarily on the individual. It is not up to someone else or to some program to make one's life easier. Sociologists often see the social world contrastingly as individual and as structural perspectives—the one emphasizing the individual's role, the other the norms that arise to govern social life. Thus, for the sociologist, abstract concepts like "equality" are always grounded in some larger sociohistorical context. Sophisticated measures are developed to gauge how this works out for any given population. And there is always the conclusion that a concept like equality is a fluid one, subject to change, but has relatively great predictability for its usual manifestation as "inequality." In the case of race in America, gauging equality usually means knowing ahead of time that, as in any running competition, not all start with the same advantages. In a sense, some carry more weight (disadvantages) than others, thus influencing and perhaps predetermining the outcome.

This sociological theory and critical, doubting stance toward the social world is not readily embraced by a family such as AC's. For them, people must grapple with the world as they find it; it does them little good to wring their hands and perhaps feel sorry for themselves. AC's family grew up feeling they were as good as anyone else, and the need to succeed formed inside them.

But they learned early on that they would have to work hard to succeed, that they would have to adhere to the "twice as hard" rule. This rule is something I had heard years before (when I was a very young man working in Dallas) from an older black man. As he explained it, blacks knew they could succeed and compete equally with whites, but they also knew that they would have to work twice as hard to do this. Here, sitting in the living room nearly thirty years later, AC one day told me, "Learned that you'd have to work twice as hard as whites but you could do it. Color only skin deep. Skin deep. Color don't matter. What you do matters."

Rhonda explained this, another day. "I tell the kids all the time: 'Color is only skin deep.' There's no place you can't go. There's nothing you can't do. I believe that real, real strong. I'm a living witness. I never thought I'd go to college. I never thought I was college material. I never thought I could do it. But after I went to school, school is a light bulb. Once it goes on, it doesn't ever go off. It's something I want to do the rest of my life. After my kids are out of here, when I don't have them to worry about, I want to just go to school. There's so much it has to offer—that's why it's the light bulb. I knew I needed education to get a job, and I needed to work and I wasn't sure of myself. But now, there's a hundred jobs out there waiting on me if I want it. It's not what they can do for me. It's what I can do for them."

But in the End . . .

If one spends any time in a place like Colonial County, it is inevitable that one notices racial customs. Of course, this result was part of my reason for being there, so these customs were even higher on my radar screen. For me, it was important to learn how race played out in a *rural* place, a place much different from the large cities and suburbs near where I live (the Baltimore-Washington area). In these urban places, race is a constant force in people's daily lives; too often, it means some people avoiding others, a delicate dance through daily life. And sadly, for most Americans everywhere, the life that Terrence describes as one absent of real interracial socializing is true,. The civil rights revolution led to some changes, but many social patterns are slow to change in any meaningful way. People are told now to celebrate "diversity"; on college campuses, this is a mantra for faculty and administrators.[10] In rural, southern places like Colonial County, "diversity" is just another term for "blacks and whites." I never heard the term "diversity" during my stay in Colonial County; I was never aware of any "diversity initiative," although there may have been such a thing. My impression was that places like Colonial County are more common than not; what I saw there, I could have seen in many other southern rural places, at least those with large black populations.[11]

In these places, flawed though they may seem to outsiders, life is lived one day at a time. Such a place may not be perfect but it is *their* place, that of the people who live there. They must make their own sacrifices and decisions about what is and is not tolerable. What seems indisputable is that these small, mostly isolated, rural, southern places create their own comfort zones. Contemporary weather forecasts on television provide indexes for heat and humidity; perhaps there should be developed a "comfort zone index" for the "degrees" by which people get along in different places, by how much or little they tolerate one another, say mean-spirited things, share a sense of community, have a sense of being in it for the long run—for better or worse, "'til death do them part."

Although no one wants to encounter hostility from others, Clorice's description of her life, and her sense of life for other local black folk, is that—aside from the local political culture becoming more neglectful than ever toward blacks—Colonial County is still a good place to live. In part, this is because its norms are well-known to all residents (except newcomers). Those few white people who are openly hostile to blacks are easily identified, hence easily anticipated, and can, for the most part, be avoided or, in a more Machiavellian way, controlled to some degree precisely because their views and behaviors are so predictable.

The one certainty about race in Colonial County is that blacks will not be going away. Their numbers may continue to become proportionally smaller as more and more whites move into the county, but the old ways are likely to dominate for some time among many county residents, black and white. What is less certain is how the demographic shift in terms of race (to more whites), class (to the better educated and much more affluent), and residence (to nearly entirely new development at one end of the county) will affect life in the county. As AC told me, in reference to racial acceptance, "We get along real good for the most part. Real good." And, for the most part, even if interaction is limited, they do—get along.

Seven

Home Is Where the Heart Is

For AC and his family, there is one thing that, transcending work, gender, school, or church, is always of paramount importance: home. Although this is hardly unique to them, I was very curious about it in light of my initial research questions about why people chose to not migrate away from the area. Other than our individual identities, no referent more strongly indicates one's sense of place than talking about "home." The line from Robert Frost, "Home is the place where, when you have to go there, they have to take you in," has some truth to it. "Home" is more than a physical place, more than a structure with rooms in it, more than a house. Home represents a larger set of things. To be sure, a house may be an important part of *home*, one of the primary places in which the drama of one's life has been played out. But it is the drama itself, and all the lesser acts within it, that collectively adhere to form a sense of a place called home. And, in turn, this place often transcends one bit of geography and a house or two upon it to encompass a community or a town or a county. Or, to use another well-known phrase, "Home is where the heart is."

In Colonial County, the county itself is a common frame of reference for many local people. When asked where they are from, the typical response would be "Colonial" (without the word "County"). People talk easily about the county as a home place, as a community, as a place they would not be anxious to leave and to which, if they did, they would be anxious to return.

It has a hold on their heads and hearts. It is a reverential, spiritual place for them, with a Kantian quality—its essence held not in photographs but in their heads. The late anthropologist and rural sociologist Janet Fitchen captures this quality nicely in discussing the idea of community. She says, "the deeper meaning of community . . . is of the mind, the ideational or symbolic sense of community, of belonging not only *to* a place but *in* its institutions and *with* its people."[1] Thus we live in a place both physically and mentally. In the most dialectical way, the place is in us and we are in it. In the case of home, love is a kind of glue that holds things together.

In my very first meeting with AC, this issue arose. I had wondered why he hadn't migrated to the North, along with two of his sisters. As he told me, "I wasn't goin' no way, no how. Most of my family, goin' didn't excite us. One reason they [his sisters] went was to get a better job, but they all have intentions to come home. We love bein' 'round one another. We have barbeques, even the ones from New Yawk come. And then they take back rice, sauces, bacon with skin on it, steaks, everythin'. My sister moved back from New Yawk to South Carolina so she's four hours away. She wanted my son to bring her some groceries. She called and put in her order [he laughs heartily].

"My father always told us that Colonial County was the best place in the South you could stay. In Colonial County, they had a sense of doin' most of the things you wanted to do. Even at a time when there was lots of discrimination, you could do pretty much what you wanted.

"Now, my children, three in the service. They all left Colonial County but they all comin' back. My oldest daughter, she bought a house on a hill over here [he points behind him, though the daughter's house turns out to be several miles away, almost directly in the middle of the county, on a large piece of land]. She just got out of the army after twenty years, so she's back for good. The other two girls, they ain't neva' left. Lived right down the road there, near where they was bo'n [born]. My two sons both been in the military, but they's about to get out now. Them two boys love each other; want to spend their lives near one another. Plan on goin' into business once they both outta the service."

Very early in my relationship with AC, and in exploring my central research questions, I was reminded about the emotional importance and depth of family ties, and how living locally (thus choosing not to move away) is an assertion about control of one's everyday life. When AC references his family's "love bein' 'round one another," "Them two boys love each other," and the family's getting together, these are very telling statements. They illustrate Fitchen's comments about "belonging not only *to* a place but *in* its institutions and *with* its people,"—in this case, specifically in a family and with its members. This, as I was to learn, was practically synonymous with being a member of AC's family.

But, beyond this, AC identified another key point for why people might have stayed: "you could do pretty much what you wanted." Phrased differently, even during the years of more overt racial discrimination than today's, local black people understood well the norms; more sociologically, they knew well the local white power structure and the well-established normative boundaries. Thus, black people could navigate their way through everyday life and nearly all situations that presented themselves. Indeed, they could, in fact, "do pretty much what they wanted," in that there was a certain kind of freedom with staying put and not moving away. One aspect of this for people of AC's generation was lending a hand at raising the next generation.

I wondered what role AC had played in raising the children of his children. It is well known that many black families in the North often sent their children "home" to spend summers with, or in some cases to be raised by, their grandparents. "Home" was thought of as a more nurturing, loving, and, importantly, safer place to grow up. Too, it was a place where family values could be imparted with less interference from urban distractions.

AC told me that "Janice [then twenty-one] is the only grand [grandchild] I raised. Me and this wife [his second] took her in when she was little. Her older sister died from an epileptic fit or something; she died in the hospital. Her mother figured that might happen to her but that nothin' would happen to her if she was raised by us.

"My sister sent her children here every year when they were out of school. Now they're all gone to college. Every summer, they were sent here to get them off the street. 'Send you to AC,' she'd tell 'em. They like to come. I tell 'em all kinda tales and stories like my father did to me. Fixed candied yams, potatoes and bacon, then rice and eggs. They all 'member stayin' up waitin' fo' me to git off work. Straight shift work, three to twelve. Even now when they come they want me to fix my little ol' special [he laughs, remembering those days]."

It is precisely such personal moments that reinforce and underscore one's sense of home. Moments large and small coalesce to create this unique, warm feeling. For AC and his wife, there is a principle of reciprocity operating: "You give me something; I give you something." The most obvious factor here is that AC and his wife (like millions of other families) did a favor for their relatives. I doubt that they asked or expected much in return. But what did they get, besides an opportunity to provide a loving, caring home for these children? There were two rewards in particular. First, playing the caregiving role for these children was also a way for AC and his wife to keep in close contact with family members who had moved away; it kept them from being isolated and, indeed, made them centrally responsible in a very important task. Second, playing the role allowed them to develop jointly shared memories of family, and crucially of place, with this younger generation. This was especially important for the children; in their formative years, a key part of their memories would be of time spent far from their other home. In short, the mutable, evolutionary nature of what is meant by "home" was not, for these children, fixed to one place on the planet. Indeed, wherever they were sufficiently loved by others (in this case, family members), the possibility of "home" was there. And would their hearts be there, too? It seems likely.

The Nuclear Family and the TV Generation

The historical era during which AC's immediate family housed other family members was a time when the term "nuclear family" was still fairly new in the American vocabulary. Without going into the term's history, it is fair to say that this term arose as a way of capturing how families became much more internalized, less dependent upon family members, and, not coincidentally, much smaller. This stood in sharp contrast to the extended family, rooted in agricultural history with its large families, both immediate and nearby, that were more multigenerational, working collectively toward a common goal—sustaining the farm and the livelihood it produced.

AC's family was a blend of permanent residents and occasional visitors. Given how the family members interacted and spent considerable time together (in both its immediate and its extended forms), I had wondered how their lives were changed when television first appeared. This may seem like an odd, mundane thing to wonder about, but my curiosity was piqued, primarily because the history of television has been one of reinforcing insularity, thus reducing or precluding outside contact. When television first came to Yvonne and AC's house, however, it opened up a new world to his family and others, and—surprisingly—fostered a sense of community, as well.

"I was workin' in Coastal City and we'd cash our checks there. We wasn't makin' 'bout thirty dollars a week, that was it. I was only makin' twenty-five at the creosote plant [where he'd coated pine poles with creosote]. But at the trailer place we were makin' big money—thirty-five to forty dollars. Now at this big appliance place where we cashed our checks, they had a TV and the man told me, 'AC, you ought to buy this television.' Back in them times, it cost three somethin'. And I had to cover everything with what I was makin'. The man tol' me he could set it up for me. We could come by every week. He set it up for me so I could make payments. It was a great big thing. Had a rotor on it so you could hit a button and get better reception. I was gettin' number one reception! I had like a movie in Yvonne; I was the only one. So my house would stay full all the time with everyone watching television."[2]

Knowing that television had further reinforced a sense of family and even community, I wondered about other forms of entertainment in his community. I knew that Conaty had a movie house at one time, but did Yvonne? I saw no sign of one, and southern movie houses were, until court-ordered desegregation, one more place with rigid segregation practices. Indeed, this division yielded a form of southern architecture, with buildings designed in such a way that blacks were removed to balconies and kept away from the white patrons as much as possible. AC told me that, in Yvonne, a local black man filled the need for movies. "There was a fella here, that's all he used to do. He had a picture show—in a buildin' or outside. He charged ten or fifteen cent[s] depending on what kind of movie he got. You'd sit on a chair or a stump or the ground. Outdoors, he'd hang a sheet, and show the movie there. If he had a buildin', he'd tack that sheet to the wall. Sometime he'd have forty to fifty people. He'd go to Liberty County, go all about different places showin' that same movie. But we had the movies at our house, too, with that TV. I guess that's why we always had so much company when the children were little."

Building a House—and a Home

AC told me many times about the family get-togethers at his house, especially about the "block house" that he built. It was built at a time when he could read, but not very well. His first wife, Clorice, helped him reason out what he needed to do. As she remembers it, "I taught AC. I kept pushing him to go back to school. I laid on the bed and read books to him, I really did." I interrupted to say that the children had told me about when their parents built the block house, and had said that AC couldn't read at that time so their mother had read the directions to him.

Clorice continued, "We were about the most prosperous young couple here. We were the only young couple with a TV. There'd be thirty-five to forty people at our house. They knew they'd get a hot meal and look at television. We decided we were going to build a house—a block house, because we wanted something different. We got all the books on how to do it, how to do the concrete, how to mix the mortar. But, see, AC couldn't understand those terms. He could read but he couldn't understand what the term meant. He couldn't read that well, catching a word here and there. And he said, 'Will you explain it to me?' So I'd read and explain it. 'The common blocks go up so high and this is what we do about the foundation and everything' [a kind of joy in telling becomes apparent as her memories of a shared adventure take hold]. We went over books I don't know how many times, laying across the bed, just the two of us. And finally we started building. I remember when we got 'way to the top—I had major surgery, but three weeks later I climbed the ladder to the top of the house to help my husband out. But our family is that kind of family. We go after whatever we want and we succeed in doing it. That's why we work so hard."

AC's recollection is only slightly different. I told him one day that I was under the impression that Clorice read the instructions as he built the house. He responded, "What she was tryin' to do was say how she wanted it built. We didn't have much insight into that, like they do now. I had one fella helped me doin' the electrical stuff. We'd work until nine or ten o'clock, then we'd go back to work [at their regular jobs at a steel mill]. And on the weekends, that's how I did it. And she'd say what she wanted. I laid all them blocks and I'd never done that befo'. That was the first time I tried it. And the curious thing was that, as soon as I got mine built, I had three more to build. Sho' did [and, as he often does, he laughs, remembering how he got started in building houses, his own as well as others']".

Building the house not only provided a place to live; it also provided an opportunity to demonstrate again the virtues to thrift and hard work, the sense that one could succeed if one tried hard enough.

Coming Home

Eventually, Clorice's life with AC soured. Like many marriages, theirs did not survive. AC found another woman and married her. Clorice moved to New York to live near her older sister, who had earned a doctorate at Columbia University and had a successful career in New York. Clorice took Samuel (the youngest son) with her, and he did well in school there. But the "call to home" (as Carol Stack so rightly puts it) drew her back.

"I caught a bus one day from New York to go visit Disney World in Florida. I had the bus driver put me off right on [Interstate] 95, over there [she points to where the interstate passes by, within feet of where the road ends, very near her house]. I walked over to my house and looked at the trees and my yard. I had had the prettiest yard in the community. This was in '76; I had left in '73.

"I hated that Samuel came back, because he was doing so well in school. But he wanted to come home. After I came home, I saw the way the place looked. I couldn't let what I had be destroyed. I left New York, two months later, and just came home. My daddy said that he didn't want me over here [moving back] 'until you get that house squared away.' My daddy was strict, even in my old age; my father was my father and I respected him. My kids respect me, too, today. Whatever I say, they respect. With my daddy, if I came home at nine-thirty or ten, he'd be asking me 'Where you been?' [she laughs at this memory]. I brought my German shepherd dog with me because I knew he'd protect me. I stayed in that one room and cleaned until I got the dishes put back, and I bought me a lawn mower. And I've been here ever since. I came home because I could not stand to see my house go down."

Status, like many aspects of Clorice's life, is important not only as a form of self-identification but also as a form of pride in family. Her behavior represents more than herself; it represents what her family stands for in the community—holding to a higher standard and not succumbing to the temptation to let things slide, even if this means more work for her. At the same time, her behavior evinces her sense of personal responsibility to her family and herself: she came home with no job but quickly found one at a "little place along side of the road" until she obtained a better, more professional job in Coastal City.

Clorice also told me, "Everybody [in this family] is trying to succeed, to have something. I have a little business, too. . . . It's a laundrymat. It's the only thing over there. We're planning for retirement. That's why this house looks like this. This is my fourth time starting over from scratch after the house burned down.[3] My income level was so low I had to use what I had for resources—my hands. I'd make drapes, bedspreads, dresses for weddings, whatever, anything that comes up. I played for four churches. And I do it, so long as it's honest. I thought we need something to help us with retirement. I thought of a laundrymat because there's none in the area and we'll make it nice—with chairs and flowers [in sharp contrast to the laundromat in Conaty, which is barren of charm and industrial-looking]. Then we started a convenience store. Store and a laundrymat, that's mine. My husband and his brother run the store. He works the morning shift and then goes to his regular job. He's always worked two jobs. We're both starting over. We were classmates, of course, but never dated. I never planned to remarry but it just happened, and I'm glad it did, really. I've been through a lot and he's been beside me. The peace within these walls [she gestures], I wouldn't exchange it for anything. I don't have to worry about an argument. It's just so peaceful. And that's why I want to share some of that with other people."

Clorice's assertion of "everybody trying to succeed" certainly supported my own sense of her family. They all worked very hard and, although no one else spoke as openly about social status as she did, by any societal measure of social status, the success she referenced had been achieved or was still in the making.

Although her family was willing to work very hard, its members were also willing to accept good fortune that came their way. Her mentioning the walls in her home made me wonder: had she, too, been the beneficiary of the truck that had tipped over and spilled an enormous amount of sheetrock? This was an incident chronicled wonderfully in Melissa Faye Greene's book *Praying for Sheetrock*; although this book is primarily about the contentious relationship between an older white sheriff and a younger black man, it is, in a larger sense, about social change in a rural, Lowcountry county. I had developed a sense, from speaking with local people, that the sheetrock from the accident had found its way even into homes and buildings far from the accident.

Clorice laughs before answering, then says, "I did, too," and laughs again. "That's when I came from New York and I had a lot of work to do on the house. I was on the side of the road after that truck, and there was some of that stuff fifteen feet long. Come to think of it, there's three sheets of it in this house. Yes, I had tied it over there [she points at the wall beside where we are sitting]. I was hustling for everything I could get." As AC had told me, "Lots of people got sheetrock in their house off that truck."

As Clorice and I came to the end of our conversation, she started to speak about her sister who was about to move back "home," right across the road; this will also put the sister next door to Clorice's brother. As Clorice began to tell me about this, I realized for the first time that I could clearly hear the interstate. I knew it was only a short way down the road; nonetheless, hearing it surprised me, as though it was an unwanted intrusion in this rural, isolated place.

It was a final reminder of the trip Clorice had made, a trip that millions of rural African Americans have made—initially going North, increasingly taking the same roads back South. Back *home*. Without thinking, I suddenly asked her, "Did you ever think about not coming back here?" She quickly responded, "Oh, no! My whole intention was to come back. I love this place. I love being free. If you read [the state's] history, the British colonies moved here because it was the only state where they could serve God freely. I must have been born of that vision, because I love to be free, and I know we have some problems and stuff but it's not bothering me, because I'm not doing it. The atmosphere is free. I can get in my car and go anywhere I want to go."

Staying Home

AC's family members always speak of "love" for Colonial County. Their bond to it is one of deep emotion, as though they have taken an unsworn allegiance. This love of place is evoked with little prompting by me, and it always leads them to talk about how they never wanted to leave and were quick to return if they did.

This attitude used to be common in America, when it was still a mostly rural place, but all that changed with urbanization (and, later, suburbanization). Cities and suburbs are more amorphous locations, as are our places in them.[4] Many urban "migrants" moved again from their urban dwellings, as soon as they could afford to; often this precipitated other moves. This was part of Americans' desire for mobility of all forms, from the mobility of moving "up" (usually through job success) to the mobility of moving "out" (usually to a bigger house in a pricier neighborhood, often in the suburbs, whether older ["inner"] or newer). The essence of this mobility is captured nicely by John Warfield Simpson in his book *Yearning for the Land*.[5] There, he searches for the meaning of "place," of how we come to give significance to where we live, for what it means to us. He says, "I take the land for granted. . . . It's mostly just property to me—a commodity, a thing to which I have little historical connection. . . . I live in a vast sea of suburbia and I like it. Yet I also yearn for a more meaningful connection to my home and a deeper understanding of its past. Have I lost something in my freedom of land ownership and mobility, some psychological benefit from that connection? Can such a connection enrich in the same subtle, subconscious way that knowledge of one's lineage enriches?"

Many Americans, especially those in the suburbs, don't "live" in houses so much as inhabit or occupy them. They are transients, almost assuredly destined to move on to other accommodations. In rural areas, on the other hand, residents are much likelier to occupy the family home or, alternately, to live not far from it. Dorthea, AC's former sister-in-law and now good friend, lives within a stone's throw of where she was born and raised. She has lived in her modest house for forty years. It is a little worn on the outside but neat and tidy within. The carpet is a mosaic of pieces and colors fitted together. Pictures of children and grandchildren are the most common decorative touch, and there are lots of them; it is easy to see family history from them. There are so many smiling happy faces around that it is easy to feel that way yourself.

Dorthea told me about her life in Colonial County, one day as we sat at her dining-room table. "I was born right down there [she pointed, meaning to indicate an area called "the Bluff," a sort of buffer between the wetlands and the mainland]. My mother born in Smithville [the next settlement over]; my father born right over to the old house, in the Bluff [a high point looking

over the marsh]. I have two boys in Alaska, both in the military. One retired, one fixin' to. Oldest one said he's comin' home. One daughter work
in Washington but live in Maryland. She'll be home soon to build. I said,
'Honey, I don't care what you do,' and she said, 'Mama, I'm comin' home.'
Other children in Coastal City. I love all of 'em, I'll tell ya. They be home all
the time, the ones who live nearby. My oldest son said he want to come
back and build.

"I like it home. I'd rather be in the country. I wouldn't want to live in
Coastal City or Conaty. I like it here. It's a quiet place. After I start raisin'
kids, there's a place to play in, playin' ball, havin' a good time.

"People still go to sleep with their windows open. Somebody come in
here, they don't know what's inside [and she laughs heartily at the implication that they would have to deal with her and the gun she keeps]. I'm safe
here. Nice and quiet here. I'd rather be home than anywheres. When I was
in Miama [where she lived for two years, and is spelled as she pronounced],
I told my sister, 'When my mind say "home," home I'm comin'!' When I got
to Miama', first thing I did when I started workin' was save money to go
home. So, when I ready to go home, I did. When I visit my daughter in Maryland, I tell her I'm goin' home on the twelfth of April, and I know I'm goin'
home. I start countin' the days. One day she ax' me, 'Mama, why you so
quiet? You ready to go home, aren't you?' I said, 'Yes.' And when I visit my
son in Washington state, I tell him the day I'm goin' home, and he say, 'When
Mama ready to go home, you can't stop her when that day come.' It's nothin'
but woods, but I'm ready to come home to my chirren. And they happy to
see me. That's my reason for stayin' here. I just love it."

Her former sister-in-law, Althea, told me a similar story. "I was bo'n right
heah, between AC and heah [a distance of a mile or so]. Got married right
heah. Married for 'bout twenty years. I wasn't married but one time. Had
thirteen children [second only to her oldest brother, BW, who had so many
that he had lost track of the number]. Three live in Atlanta and all the rest
live right round heah. Three died but all the rest heah."

When I ask her about the era when so many people left, she recalls it.
"Most peoples went to find jobs. I didn't go because, I guess, I was young
and I had my mother to take care of me. I didn't neva' care bout goin'. Too
far away. Anotha' thing, I don't like to ride a plane. Neva' ride a plane, and
neva' will ride one. Neva' ride a train, neither. I ride the bus. I want to go, I

ride the bus, even if it take me two or three days to get there. I love it; I really do. See some of the country, how pretty it is.

"Colonial County been a good place. We neva' went hungry, always had somethin' to eat. My parents wanted me to go but I neva' would. When I was small, I went to Fort Myers to see my cousin, I must a-been 'bout nine or ten. I cried so they had to bring me home. And I wasn't satisfied 'til I did git back home. And I didn't want to go nowheres else to live where I couldn't just walk back.

"When my husband died, my daughter and my sons in Atlanta said, 'Mama, ain't nobody home butchou [but you]. Why don't you move up heah with us?' And I said, 'Uh-uh. I'd rather stay right heah. I'll visit sometime but I don't want to go and stay.' My daughter said, 'Mama, I could git a big house fo' us and you can stay heah with me.' But I said, 'No.' Now, I'll go to Atlanta and I'll stay awhile but, at a certain time, I'm ready to come home. Put me on the bus and I go home.

"I love this place. I love it. I wouldn't want to be nowheres else but heah. And I been heah so long, all these many years, that I can't remember anywheres else [she laughs]. I don't think I could live anywheres else. I wouldn't be satisfied. When my son retire from the post office, he gonna retire right back heah."

Going home or—more often, with older residents—staying there was a refrain heard often. As Dorthea and Althea both told me, "I love it." You can only "love it" if you put a considerable amount of psychic energy into it. Given this emotional, and not simply sentimental, response and reasoning, it was not surprising to hear Dorthea and Althea comment on people retiring back home. This was something I heard again and again from older people, in reference to either their siblings or their children. For the children, "retiring back home" often involved retirement from the military or some other public sector employment. This is important to note because this group of returnees had some things in common: they had left the area, and, in nearly all cases, they had done quite well financially: they had secured decent jobs that paid fringe benefits, not least a reasonable pension that they could start drawing while still quite young. The current sheriff used to be a police officer in New Jersey. Now he draws his pension from there, and a salary from Colonial County, which in time will also provide a pension. The same is true for some teachers and others who have come back. This is precisely what Stack realized and wrote about in *Call to Home*. Black families never left their sense of "home" even if they moved away for awhile. And many thousands of them have in recent years returned,[6] bringing skills and pensions earned while away, and inheriting or buying a "spot" of land near where they grew up.

AC's oldest living brother, BW, is another family member who never moved away. He has lived in the county his entire seventy years. His only time away was to work in pulpwood in an adjacent county and to work in commercial fishing (always working on boats based out of Colonial County). He was the one person with whom I spoke who had children who did not plan on returning. Two of his sons live in Alaska (and are among those who have used the military to leave the area), but they have no desire to come back to Colonial County. In both cases, they retired from military careers and chose to stay far from "home." BW says that he told them, "Anything happen to you theah, I can't come to see you. I ain't flyin' in no plane, and it take me ova' a week to drive, so . . . " As for BW, "Colonial County is a nice place to live, nice place to live. I didn't know it was a nice place to live 'til I start goin' to different places. People heah, if you got somethin', they ax' you fo' it. Two to one, if you need somethin' and they got it, they give it to ya'. Know what I mean? But you go to Flo'da [Florida] or some of them places, it's dog eat dog. They not friendly. I'm glad I live heah. No place I'd rather live. Can take my gun and git a wild hog, or coon, or squirrel. Can git o'ster [oyster]—one time, could git all the o'ster you want. Got family 'round. Nice place to raise a family. Nice place to live. Glad I stayed right heah. My kids mostly scattered round heah. Got them two in Alaska and my oldest daughter gone [he'd not seen or heard from her in over thirty years], but the rest scattered 'round in them woods, right round heah."

BW's comments about being able to get what he needs locally suggest how powerful the sense of community can be. Although not equally true everywhere, there is considerable truth to the notion that rural folk are much likelier to engage in forms of exchange in which bartering or trades of some kind occur. Some of this activity may be to sustain friendships but, more generally, sharing wealth of the moment (e.g., too many oysters to eat or a hog or deer to share, or too many pieces of sheetrock) is more common than not. And such sharing suggests, usually more implicitly than explicitly, a kind of indebtedness; an exchange between two people that has been uneven, leaving one person with a sense of owing the other. Over a lifetime, this may be kept in balance by a long series of exchanges, giving back in return for what one is given. Thus BW might well have given something to those from whom he had received things. In AC's case, distributing extra fish caught or game killed was a nearly daily experience. (It is precisely such small, daily events that lead to the expression "What goes around comes around.") This sense of mutuality is also reinforced by the cohesiveness of families. AC's, including BW, often made reference to looking out for one another.

Terrence, AC's youngest brother, remembers fondly when they got together for "barbeques, ice cream, all the family be gathered round on the weekends." He also remembers how he, along with other family members, had to help Althea when her husband died and she continued to have children, with no fathers to support them. As Terrence told me, one day, "I don't think there's anything more important than knowing that 'the family that prays together stays together.' Like right here, the Goodman family over there, where AC married [Clorice's family] and the Young family over here, where I married [his former wife]. So instead of having one big family, we had one huge family! [We] be a great big family—we married into different families."

Terrence also agreed that those most likely to leave the county (in the days of the great outmigration) were the women. "When you got a big family like that, who's gonna be the first one shipped off? They never ship off a boy. Them old men in those times would never ship off a boy to go to school or nowhere to look for a job, not as long as he can do something here. That's what you need, to keep your family together. That's what all them families use to do back then. Keep the boy child from goin' off, to further help the family.

"If the girls stayed here, there wasn't nothin' for them. Marriage and babies. That's why you find so many young girls leave and the men stayed. Now Althea, she was married once but all her other kids born out of wedlock. Had eleven kids with no husband. We used to say: 'Instead of sending Sally [now in her early seventies] to New York, we shoulda sent Althea.'" He laughs hard at this memory. "All the kids was born right here and lived with us, and that was more responsibility. Two or three might be by one father but, oh my God! you had a mixture. But Daddy kept 'em all right here. This is all something you have to deal with. That's what families do."

Terrence told me how he had left the area at one time but not for long. "I went North in 1953. My aunt from New Jersey came to pick me up. While there, I got a chance to visit New York. It was like migrant workers. Tomatoes, potatoes—had to do somethin' to get away from here in the summer. Some boys was doin' cotton. I was like, 'Hey, I'm here. Bright lights and big city.' But that wasn't for me. So I came back here and started back to school. I accomplished more at home than I could abroad, you know, in a big city. Everyone has potentials, but it's hard to realize them in a big city. A person can really get lost in the city. So I came back here."

Terrence's recalling his one big trip away as a young man is also a reminder of the days, not so long ago, when migrant workers—many of them black—followed row crops and fruit up the East Coast; disproportionately, it was young men who first left (contrary to what Terrence says about the women from Colonial County).[7] For Terrence, his one trip North was a brief and exciting chance to see a new place and "the big city." But it was also a chance to determine for himself whether this was for him or not. As the writer Dwayne Walls says of the great outmigration period, paraphrasing one migrant: "Gradually it became clear that Baltimore and Hell often were the same place. The word began trickling back to the farms: stay where you are. The city is no place for people like us. . . . You ain't gonna like it. Man, it ain't human up there."[8]

Terrence's recollection of his experience sounds eerily like the main character in Ralph Ellison's book *The Invisible Man*. As Terrence says, "A person can really get lost in the city." That, of course, is what happened to Ellison's main character and to the man Walls cites. Each gets to the big city only to discover that he is "invisible," that "It ain't human up there." Terrence chose to stay at home where (as Jesse Jackson would have crowds chant, especially at civil rights rallies) "I am somebody." In Colonial County, Terrence could more easily find and seize opportunities, even though one eventually led to his political downfall.

As Walls says about blacks returning home, what many sought was "to give in finally to that eternal longing to chuck it all and get back home again—to a place where a man could live in peace and raise his kids the way they ought to be raised. A strange thing for a black man to say of the South" (24).

And the Children after Them

All AC's children live fairly close by. His daughters live a few minutes away (two are up the street from him), and his sons live in Coastal City, about forty-five minutes away. But distance is mostly irrelevant to their collective sense of place and of their place here. They are in and out of one another's homes on a daily basis, and certainly no more than a week goes by before they see one another somewhere. AC's sons make a point of driving over to visit him; in turn, AC is often running to their houses or meeting with them somewhere in between for an evening meal. They have a very strong sense of family. On the one hand, this seems effortless, simply an extension of their love and concern for one another. On the other hand, all social relationships, *especially* those involving love and concern, require care and nurturing; it is precisely when they become too taken-for-granted that they are most likely to deteriorate. For AC's family (like many extended families), there is a commitment to sustaining family ties; such ties are important and the frequent family get-togethers and visits to one another's homes reinforce, in myriad ways, the continuity of "the family."

AC's oldest daughter, like her brothers, had been in the military and traveled extensively, with tours of duty overseas. I wondered if she had ever thought of living somewhere other than Colonial County? After all, this was a worldly, bright woman, who could envision a variety of career opportunities driven in part by where she lived: Europe, the West Coast, . . . These were not for Alice. Her frequent visits home while in the service had kept her not only in touch with family members, but also attuned to the need to find housing when she came back. Unlike her brothers, pioneers in seeking housing outside of the county (although, even there, when the one brother found a lot to buy and told his brother about it, the latter almost immediately bought the lot across the street), Alice did not want to live anywhere but near her parents and the memories that came with such a location.

Her house sits on a large lot, far back from the road. It is a very conventional-looking, brick, ranch-style house. Like many rural residents, including those returning after long absences, she found her house without a real estate agent. "My brother saw this house and told me about it. My daddy knew who built it and he said it was a good house—handmade cabinets and everything. My husband didn't say 'nay' or 'yea,' but I knew I wasn't goin' no place but home so we bought it [she laughs heartily at the memory]." As she further explained, "I knew I would come home. Where else was there to go? Where could you go and be at home? My mother and father was here. My big thing is family. When I was growing up, I knew my grandparents and my great grandparents. Matter of fact, I knew my great grandmother on my mother's side—I mean *knew her*, 'cuz she lived right down the lane from us. . . . you grow up and git up on Saturday mornins and stuff and go help her pump the water—'cuz she still had a pump—and follow her into the woods to get berries and deer tongue [a tobacco-looking leaf that grows directly out of the ground, can be sold, and even smells like tobacco] or dog tongue [a long-stemmed, fairly large, leafy plant similar to deer tongue]. It smells like that [like deer tongue and dog tongue] all the way to the road, out my front door. We'd go to do things like that nearly every day in the summer. We'd follow them into the woods and pick huckleberries, a patch of wild strawberries, with my daddy's mama; it's a swamp back there.

"My daddy and his mother would go out there fishin' with a reed [cane] pole. I took my sister to one of daddy's fishin' holes yesterday to go fishin'. Have to get down to the bank with a rope that's tied up there. I remember when we caught eels and I'm terrified of snakes. I remember turnin' over that bucket when I was eight or so—I had a fit! About the time my mother's house burned down.

"I remember bein' with my mama's grandmother and spendin' time in the field. Pickin' corn, butter beans, okra; diggin' potatoes. My grandmother would always get me some okra even when I was grown, when she knew I was comin' home.

"Everywhere I went I had me a garden.[9] I've met people in the military who never wanted to go home, but I couldn't think of anything but. My daddy's daddy—we called him Granddaddy—when he'd go to the field, when that son of mine was a baby, he'd always bring him something, a yellow watermelon, anything. When we'd catch the bus to school when I was little, my granddaddy would've already been out walkin' and checkin' his gum trees [for turpentine] and he'd been in his field. And that was before we caught the bus. He would've already walked seven–twelve miles. I can remember thinkin', 'Boy, how can you be up that early and do all that?' And he was doin' that, only two or three years before he died.

"A lot of things, my kids don't like it like I do. I can't understand it. We had a field there where Mr. Jack is [where the men hang out each day]. That was PawPaw's field ["PawPaw" being a name used for her grandfather on her mother's side]. On the other side, where Miss Cornelia and Daddy plant today, that was Granddaddy's field. Further down the road, Miss Alma Jackson, on the other side of where Daddy livin'. What else to do? There's water to fish; there's seafood, fish from the ocean and river. I was lucky enough to get five acres, so I don't have to be closed in. I'd like to visit other places, but I wouldn't want to live anywhere but here.

"This county is a good county. People love to come here. People in the army who visit us or other friends . . . bring 'em down and go crabbin' and they meet people and say there's nothin' like it. It doesn't have to be black and white. It can be anybody. My brother [Samuel] has all kinda' friends come down and meet my daddy.

"Daddy, to this day, he'd help anybody. Like hoboes. He'd bring people home to feed 'em. It's always been like that, to this day. He'll do things for anybody. 'Don't worry, Sweets. It'll be alright.' If it came out of his pocket, that was alright. And he'd send 'im on his way.

"I just can't see not bein' here. I think the best thing in the world is to have my kids know my mama and daddy."

Alice's comments evoke a strong sense of how powerful memories are and, in turn, how powerful is the sense that to sustain a family's ties to a place is a responsibility, a form of stewardship, something entrusted even if not by force or contract. It is a moral imperative, albeit chosen without duress. It is not only the choice to live with memories (as in Alice's comments about her relatives), but also the choice to create future memories, to perpetuate the prominence of this place for one's family. As the writer John Warfield Simpson says, "History becomes alive and ever present; it becomes the story of place. And places fill with the ghosts of the past. Past, present, and future fuse to form a seamless whole."

This view is shared strongly by Alice's youngest sister, Rhonda. Rhonda, more than anyone, speaks directly of the role that land plays in one's sense of place, and of how the land is fused with her sense of family: her family, their land, their place.

"Now when I lived with my mother in New York and then stayed on for about another year, I saw a lot of people who lived in apartments, had nothing of their own. Had to pay people to live there. That wasn't for me.

Wherever I live, it has to be mine. That was one thing that made me know how much I wanted to be home. You don't have no family, no friends, you're on your own. There's not a neighbor you know. You're up the creek in the city and that's bad. People valued their cousins because there wasn't anyone else. Here, everybody around you is family and you know everybody. That made me realize, I want to be home. I want to come back."

Later in our conversation, I asked Rhonda what she thought best about living in Colonial County. She so rarely ever said anything critical about the place, and yet this is the sort of thing that most sociologists would look for—that is, given the outsider's sense of the area's poverty, how can someone here be so happy? I wondered out loud, "What's the single best thing about living here in Colonial County?" Her immediate response: "The best thing is the sense of family. I'm comfortable here. I can have anything I can have anywhere else, that I want. If I was after something different, maybe then I'd have to move to someplace else. For what I want, though, this is the best place possible." "But," I asked, "do you think your kids will say that? Will they also feel that way about this place?" Rhonda responded, "I hope not. I hope my kids go out to experience different cultures and varieties. I encourage them to go. My dad always encouraged us to stay, but I encourage mine to go. I hope they do. I really do, but I like it here because of what it has for me. If I need something different, I'll go get it. But this is for me."

As historian McFeely says of the people on Sapelo Island (a barrier island off the Georgia coast, where direct descendants of slaves are the only full-time residents), "Their sense of the place was grown strong with memory." This is true, of somewhere, for each of us—especially for AC's family. All of us have memories of people and places past and present; still, it is difficult to sustain them without fairly regular contact. I told Rhonda, "I have no contact with any of the people I grew up with. I moved away physically and otherwise. In fact, this project has really made me think a lot about my sense of 'home.' My own family is literally scattered from coast to coast, and we almost never see one another. But your family has worked at remaining in contact and staying around here. Everybody I've spoken with remembers growing up here with a strong sense of love, of belonging."

Rhonda, who has inched forward on the couch and is anxious to start talking, responds, "It's home. It's home. Where I am right now, when I was a little girl, we'd walk back here [she points outside], and me and Samuel, we'd climb these trees. This is where [she pauses, clearly reflective, caught up in pondering something usually taken for granted, and then continues slowly; her words measured in a new way]. There's a piece of me on every piece of this land. When we were kids, we didn't have things to do, so we made things to do. And it's like it becomes a part of you. Even though Samuel moved away, something inside of him makes him want to be here. I know that because he and I were the last two children. We shared so much in these woods. Back then, I was a little tomboy. We would climb the pine trees [which are extremely tall, as high as sixty to seventy feet], and he'd get up toward the top and sway back and forth. And we'd play on the limbs. Just the things we did coming up. To leave it, you'd leave a part of you. I wouldn't leave here, not for good. I'd have to come back. I wouldn't leave and not come back. I'd move away if I knew I could maintain my home here. But I would never leave and just say 'goodbye' because I'd be leaving a part of me."

Given where her land is, I wondered if her father had given her a "spot" on the twenty-seven acres of family land that he felt had been entrusted to his care. [10] "Yes; he pays the taxes. From here to the road [she points], that's all ours. I got any place I want in here." Actually, her "spot" is truly beautiful. It is far enough from the road to not be seen. A small bend in her dirt driveway helps with this, giving a sense of isolation. And the house itself (a trailer), a little worse for wear but very livable, sits in a large grove of pine trees, some the same trees she climbed with her brother. It is quite idyllic, fairly high and dry for that part of the country. "It's peaceful [this she drags out, speaking very slowly]. Peaceful [again speaking very slowly]. Like out here, it's so peaceful."

So, this land where her trailer now sits is a place full of memories. She grew up playing on it, and it has been in her family for three generations with every likelihood of a fourth to follow, at least for some of the children. Her grandfather was the original owner, at least in her family. And, again, it is precisely this relationship to the land that helps to foster a sense of stewardship for it. It isn't simply one's own. It is something with a history, having belonged to their family, something they hope to pass on to the next generation. It is "home" in the most rooted sense. As Walter Stegner has stated: "A place is not a place until people have been born into it, have grown up in it, lived in it, known it, and died in it—have both experienced and shaped it, as individuals, families, neighborhoods, and communities, over more than one generation."[11]

Coming and Going and . . .

For Rhonda's sister Grace (the middle sister), Colonial County also has a powerful pull, but in this regard, as with much in her life, she is, as she would say, "the little radical." She is more critical of all things, and this is no exception. She relativizes her relationship to the place, even while acknowledging the good things about it. And, with a response more akin to what many sociologists say arises from social institutions, she feels trapped by many existing social relationships, including her family and this place. her Uncle Terrence felt that he would be denied his real self in the city; Grace feels similarly about Colonial County. Yet, although she had left for brief periods, she had always returned. It was over twenty years since her last extended trip away from the county.

As she tells me, "I will leave again. I'm thinking of moving to Boston. I've got this somethin' in me that makes me want to live someplace else for awhile. My youngest and me are thinkin' of lookin' around this summer. If not there, then maybe somewhere else. . . . I don't care where I go."

"But," I tell her, "you are still here. Your family is here and, well, it just seems to me like it's awfully comfortable for you. Would you really leave? For the rest of your family, there seems to be a powerful pull to this place."

Grace responds, "That's why I come back. But for now, I feel the need to go places and do things. And I have the feeling that I'll never be the person I want to be as long as I stay here. I get the same feeling like I did in my marriage—suffocated. Like his world was too small and he couldn't come into my world, couldn't deal with it, and I felt like I was suffocating. I got up one day and said, 'Today is the day.' And he said, 'What day?' And I said, 'The day I leave.'"

Clearly, for Grace there is a sense that no matter how comforting it is to be surrounded by family, so much love and assurance has a price. What by the others is seen as an asset is seen by her as also a liability. The cost for staying is denial—of what she might become. She has shown herself on numerous occasions to be like a butterfly encased in a cocoon, waiting to emerge as something new, something perhaps even beautiful. No matter what she does locally, she is trapped; the gauge of her success then remains a local one, limited by what is available. For her, "home" gives a sense warm and fuzzy but also chilly and clear—creating for her a mental picture of being capable of more, but not in this place.

Like everyone else in her family, Grace has no question about the role that family plays. Whether in helping to organize a big birthday party for her father, or in keeping an eye on her sister's children, or for whatever else, family is crucial. And nothing is more crucial than the family she has created. Her children are instruments capable of playing the tunes Grace wants to hear—whether the tune comes from Sheila, her teenage daughter, telling me how few children they should have, or comes from one of the children stressing the need to stand on one's own two feet and be successful. Yet for Grace there is a profound sense of being limited as long as she lives locally, and she fears that this may also hold for some of her children's friends. She is torn by serving as a role model, on the one hand, someone who has truly succeeded against all odds, and wanting to leave, on the other hand, and so encourage others to do so—as though such a move will enhance the chances of greater lifetime success and, one may suppose, happiness.

Her brother Samuel is the youngest sibling, and one of the most committed to living locally. Although he has grown frustrated with much about Colonial County, he has (like virtually everyone in his family except Grace) no desire to live elsewhere. His is a "been there and done that" attitude. He readily admits to the flaws of local living, but also realizes that all places are flawed. He believes that nearly every place is, at root, the same.

"You talk to a lot of people, not just blacks but whites, too, we spend all of our lives here. We don't have any idea of what's out there for us. Some families have the opportunity to send their kids away and see that there's more than Colonial County. I disagree, though. Life is no different out there than in Colonial County. You got to go for what you want. The world isn't what somebody wants to give you. I always get what I want. I'm sure there's times where I pay more than the other fellow, but it doesn't bother me. I just believe that I'll get mine. I don't worry about it.

"You asked me why I came back here? To me there's no prettier place. You'd be surprised, there's a love of home here. You take 95 [the interstate], crossing into Colonial County. When I die, if I was trying to find a place to put my ashes, it'd be Colonial County. I just love the oaks."

I tell Samuel that I can understand his sense of the beauty of the place, but that I, as a sociologist and especially as an outsider, am also struck by the amount of poverty that exists. In particular, I am struck by how poor so many houses look—junky, really.

Samuel tells me: "It's not poverty, it's priorities. I don't care if the house is a shack. To clean it up and what not is making it a priority, not poverty. Yvonne wasn't bad, but [he pauses] . . . I get on my dad. We clean up that yard but it gets bad again. That's why I say it's priorities, not poverty. You get to where you accept what you see and it no longer means anything to you. You really don't see it the way other people see it. That's what it is. It's a nice place. It ain't about the material things. Like around here, you won't see abandoned cars, junk in the yard, and doors coming off the hinges. It's just priorities."

Local Values and Valuing Localness

When Samuel and I first met, we talked about our time in the military—mine when the Berlin Wall was being erected, Samuel's as it came down. We both believed that the military can play a positive role for young people, especially in teaching them discipline and a commitment to group goals and norms. Samuel's decision (like that of his brother and oldest sister, as well as of numerous cousins) to have a career in the military is a choice made by a disproportionate number of rural southerners, white and black.[12] But no group is more overrepresented in the armed services than African Americans; they account for about 30 percent of the U.S. Army. Although blacks are far more prevalent among enlisted personnel than among officers, in either case it is in the American military that they are most likely to have supervisory authority over other ethnic groups, including whites, from the U.S. population. The American military has provided what some scholars refer to as a "bridging" experience, an opportunity to be trained and serve in roles that may then be a bridge as they reenter civilian life.[13] And it is African Americans who seem to have benefited most from this "bridging," as opposed to whites, for whom a career in the military may result in a net loss of career earnings.[14]

What Samuel found in the military was an opportunity to develop considerable leadership skill, overseeing a unit of nearly one hundred soldiers. As he sees it, the military (especially for minorities and blacks) "helps to make up what the family fails to provide or doesn't give." Samuel anticipates that his respect at work, and his ability to make his expectations for others clearly understood, mirroring his reciprocally high expectations for himself, will always serve him well, wherever he is. In particular, these capacities will serve him well in a place like Colonial County and in an historical era when the norms seem less clear to many people; he knows that not all families have the sense of strength and perseverance that his does.

One of the greatest lessons he took from growing up in Colonial County—and in particular from his socialization by parents and relatives whom he knew well—was to assume a sense of responsibility for wherever one was, to recognize that one could not default or wait for others to make important decisions. In a somewhat militaristic sense, one simply had to take command of one's life and whatever came with it. As he told me, "You need to get out and do something for yourself so that you can then help others." But I could not help but wonder what that vision would mean for rural areas, and especially for blacks who had migrated out of them to experience—I presumed—the fuller possibilities of life elsewhere, often in urban areas.

"Do you think people will come back to rural areas and have a commitment to them?" I asked.

Samuel told me, "In rural areas, we all know one another. That's the big difference between us and the inner city."

"Well," I responded, "do you have a sense that people come back in part because they'd rather be bitten by the dog they know than the one they don't? Like you said, you've traveled, and could have gone to any number of places to live when you got discharged, but you came back here. Why here? Is it the familiarity of the place, or your family, or what?"

"You've always got to have roots to keep other roots growing," he told me. "There's no other place I'd rather be. Even by my being here, I talk to a lot of the young guys. And they look at me and they say, 'Wow, you've got a nice truck. You've done okay.' And I tell them, 'There's no shortcut.' The only thing for them to do right now is go to school, and they won't do that. So what happens? They fail.

"There will always be a fight within me about this. I'm not through. I just got started. Like here where I live. If I see a sign that says 'For Sale,' if the house is for the right price, I'll buy the whole block! That's the kind of hunger I have. It doesn't matter to me what these other people are doing.

Someone might make a crack, implying that the only reason it's for sale is because I live here, but I can't control them.

"I'll let standards speak. Respect doesn't require money. It's what your hands can do around the yard and your house. You don't have to have lots of money. All you need to do is be conservative. It's priorities. That's what I drive off of. The military didn't make me like this. I went to the military like that.

"Our mom and dad set a standard for us. We had a TV when no one else had one, and we had a block house when no one else did. He [his father, AC] brought in the block house era. It wasn't dirty; it was a clean place. That's the picture I keep. To me, I got to do better than that. That little boy upstairs [his son] and my wife, there's a lot that drives you. Right now, every time I drive in Colonial County, I look at the trailers and the blacks who live there. We fail ourselves. Houses without septic tanks. There will be a nice house here, and then there's a little trailer in front of the house. It's priorities, it's priorities. For too many people, 'If it's quick, I'll take it. If I can have it right now, I will.' They just don't understand that most things worth having require hard work and sacrifice."

To use a horticultural metaphor, Samuel sees that his roots must be nurtured locally to help produce a new crop, a new generation committed to family and responsibility, and to creating a place much as he is trying to do. As he says, "You've always got to have roots to keep other roots growing." Of course, he also believes passionately in personal responsibility and making good decisions—that it's "not poverty, it's priorities." Although this sounds a little glib and too easy, it does highlight his entire family's sense that people are their own keepers. What their family has always practiced is not simply a matter of survival, although that no doubt weighs into the equation, but a kind of philosophical commitment to life itself.

Such values, of course, are well rooted in the larger society of which they are a part. But they are learned locally, in one's family and community. It is there, in all kinds of contexts, that we encounter one another and become the people we are. The places themselves have an important bearing on this. When the social psychologist George Herbert Mead talks about the "generalized other" as influencing a person, he is really saying that the community's norms act upon the person. Individuals in the community reinforce the norms by reminding each individual of them every time the person breaks a rule and gets sanctioned.

For sociologists, it is the family that is the first and most lasting influence on people. It presents a reality that, as Berger and Luckmann say, "cannot be wished away." AC's family is a powerful illustration of this. At a time when many believe that the black family, in particular, is in crisis, it is good to be reminded that this is not true of most families, black or otherwise. Instead, they move along, meeting their obligations, doing the best they can. They work with whatever resources they have, more times than not hoping that their children will do better than they did, and trying their damnedest to see that this happens. There will be no awards for this. They will have to settle for the sense of inner satisfaction that comes with having done one's best, and deriving some pleasure or at least acceptance of having done so.

Getting Together to Stay Together

One way of doing this is through the ownership of land. As Richard Cuoto puts it, "for . . . most African Americans in the rural South, the economic promise of Emancipation was in land ownership"[15] Land is both commodity and cultural artifact. We can never "own" it as such, since at best we can use it for a little while as we are passing through. There may be legal mandates and deeds indicating that it is in our name, but, as the Kwakiutul Indians might say, "Not forever on this earth. Only here for a little while." So, too, for all of us. Thus land is in our hands for safekeeping, to the degree that we have some control over it, to the degree that it "belongs" to us. Samuel's reference to "needing roots to grow them" is an apt way of putting this. So, too, is AC's stewardship of his family's twenty-seven acres, entrusted to him precisely because his father knew he wouldn't break it up. As the writer Marita Golden says, "'That land's got more of our blood in it than theirs . . . some of us got to stay, so y'all have a place to come back to.'"[16]

Family reunions provide such an occasion, a something "to come back to." In AC's family, such gatherings seemed mostly unnecessary, since their history of living in such close proximity and interacting regularly created one long, ongoing family reunion. But family reunions as intended events are a step beyond, not usually impromptu, but requiring some organizing and planning. In AC's family, his sister Althea took on this responsibility. The project grew, really, out of financial difficulty (thus giving testament to the adage, "Necessity is the mother of invention").

Althea found that she could no longer afford to buy everyone a birthday gift and/or Christmas presents. With her eleven children and the myriad "grands," it was simply too much. Too, with some of her family living away, it was no longer so easy to get the entire family together. So she decided that the best thing to do was to organize an annual family get-together. This would allow everyone to celebrate together and assure at least one day when most of them would be present.

As she told me, "I started somethin' a coupla' years ago. I wasn't able to give all of 'em a present for their birthdays. To get all of 'em home, we have a big party once a year, for the last three years. The last Saturday in September. We have a big family get-together. I fix a lot of food and we have drinks. I have it in my yard. We had a tent this year [provided by Samuel and on loan from the army]. All the kids got together and want to keep it up. My kids and all of 'em . . . the whole [extended] family, they scattered out so far. Very rarely you can get everyone to come at the same time."

AC had told me about this when we first started meeting. I had wondered how they kept intact their sense of themselves as a family, since there were so many of them and given that quite a few lived away from Colonial County. Althea's party now provides an opportunity to do this. Of course, for AC's immediate family, this is not necessary; they get together regularly for one thing or another—as he told me one time, "any old excuse." Given how numerous they are, there are many birthdays or anniversaries to celebrate.

But Althea's experience and AC's family's participation in it was also a reminder to me of the fragility of a family; once separated for sufficiently long periods of time, it would be easy to grow apart. Family members once familiar would eventually become blurred images, if not reinforced on an occasional basis.[17]

It is Dorothy Height, former president of the National Council of Negro Women, who first gave organizational emphasis to regularly scheduled black family reunions. Although, as initiated by her, these might embrace folk in and out of one's family and living in urban areas, the themes stressed are those found in abundance in AC's family: self-help, traditional values, family, and community. Precisely these things helped to foster a strong sense of extended family in the black community, and the imperative that families and individuals look out for one another.

Living on the East Coast, I had been aware for some time of black family reunions. Indeed, it is not unusual to visit a hotel on some weekend and encounter large numbers of African Americans, many perhaps sporting T-shirts that say "Johnson Family Reunion, 1998," or something similar. Again, the extent of such reunions underscores the fragile nature of families and the need to, on occasion, recognize them. To put one's family name on a T-shirt is to assert the family's presence. Wearing the T-shirt is to say "I am part of this." And to spend the time and money to attend such a function is a further testimony.

During the days of the "peculiar institution" (as slavery was once called), blacks could be bought and sold, moved hither and yon, with little control over their lives. This provided a sense of rupture and impermanence to black families, a fact that, the historian Steven Ruggles[18] has noted, has consequences to the present day. Against this backdrop, it is easy to understand why family reunions are more than simply friendly get-togethers but may come of a certain necessity not to take for granted the relationships they represent. Such a necessity is true for all family reunions, but is particularly significant for African Americans. In the end, it is family relationships that provide a person's sense of place and celebration of place. It is these relationships that are cultivated and harvested—sometimes bountiful, sometimes not. It is these relationships collectively—to the land, the people, the place—that people reference when they say "I love this place." For the place is theirs in a way that nothing else is or ever can be.[19]

Eight

The Power of Place

When I first visited Colonial County, I went to ask older African American residents about their migration histories, especially about why they might have chosen to stay in Colonial County rather than, as so many others did, to migrate North. My reading of both academic and fictionalized accounts of the black experience in the South had led me to believe that nearly every black person there must have been highly motivated to move away; to get "out of Dixie" as fast as possible, to leave Dixieland for the Promised Land. What I and many other academics had failed to give much thought to was the huge number of African Americans who continued to live in the South, including the rural South. I gave little thought to the possibility of encountering people who might greet with genuine puzzlement my unstated assumption, "Didn't everyone want to leave?"

With similar assumption, and, to some degree, prejudice, I also anticipated finding a place that was very poor. This expectation was based on a careful analysis of U.S. Census data, which did, indeed, lead to such a conclusion. And when I first went to Colonial County, I did see a rural, sparsely settled place with many houses and other buildings that cried out "poverty." This, I thought, is what many outsiders would see on driving through for the first time, especially on the county's main road, U.S. 17. As Dwayne Walls bombastically (but probably with some accuracy) says of such places:

"The tourist sees the barns and then he sees the houses, and he shakes his head and asks of his wife: 'Which is the barn and which is the house, for Christ's sake? Oh yeah. That's the house. See the car out front? See the stove and refrigerator and wringer washing machine on the front porch? See the TV antenna?'

"Now his wife shakes her head and asks of her husband: 'What kind of people would live in a place like that? Why don't they fix the place up a little? You'd think the least they could do is paint it. . . . '

"'Lazy people. Shiftless people. Black people,' the husband says. And then he puts them out of his mind. It is more pleasant to think of Florida and the sun."[1]

It is regrettably easy to imagine this conversation taking place. People are often quick to judge another by the standards most known and comfortable to themselves, a tendency that social scientists call "ethnocentrism." Although my view of Colonial County and the small communities within it was never as bad (or racist) as that described by Walls, nonetheless I, too— ostensibly the enlightened sociologist—had an initially harsh, judgmental, and mostly negative reaction to much of what I saw. What I failed to consider was that "poverty," like similar concepts, is situated in space and time and heavily dependent on whom one asks about it. Phrased differently, "poverty" to one person may be "plenty" to another or, more likely, may be distinguished as more severe or less severe.

My initial view of poverty in Colonial County changed over time; in fact, it changed dramatically. I continued to visit the same place; at least geographically it was the "same," but it also became a quite different place. I came increasingly to see it from the perspective of the people who lived there. If you will, I came to see it as "their place." This change, in turn, appealed to my academic side, so that I began wondering how we construct places and imbue them with meaning. At the outset, they are simply there, inert, offering little, until we render some judgment on them. What especially interested me about Colonial County was how such a seemingly poor place could have such pronounced and profound meaning for its black citizens, who had been treated (I assumed) extremely poorly there. Why would they not just like the place but always speak of their love for it?

Historian William McFeely wrote of a similar thing, when he spent time in another historically black place, Sapelo Island. This is a barrier island off the Georgia coast. In the mid–1800s, it was "home" to over four hundred slaves and the handful of white people who owned them. During the Civil War, the slaves were removed from the island and were marched inland, removing any chance of their being freed by Union troops, who were on the march South. But after the war, instead of staying away from the island, most of these ex-slaves chose to return there. Why? How could we explain this action, this return to a place of enslavement?

As McFeely says, "Why would people who had been forced to work the land as slaves ever want to see that dirt again? They were free now from those who had done that forcing; why did they go back to the scene of the crime? The clue to the mystery lies in the fact that the memory of the scene was as strong as that of the crime. The Sapelo people who went back saw the place as separable from the oppression that had taken place there. . . . They knew no other place as home."[2]

Cornelia Walker Bailey, a native and longtime resident of Sapelo Island, makes a similar observation. After visiting Sierra Leone (the origin of Sapelo's slaves and their descendants, including herself), Bailey reflects on its relationship to Sapelo Island: "Is this part of the reason, after slavery, why people didn't leave the South and go up North? Could it be that there's something familiar about the land, that there's a link to our ancestral homeland that is remembered only by the soul?" When she thought about Sapelo, versus New York or other places in the North, she concluded that "Mama and Papa would never leave. . . . There is something within them that says 'No, this look more like our Mother country. We can't leave.'"[3]

For McFeely and Bailey (and, I should note, for many others writing about "place"), one thing is essentially axiomatic (viz., its truth so widely assumed that it is usually untested): the power that place can have on a person. Even though any given place may appear highly flawed, to outsiders, to those who live there, it is—flaws and all—*theirs*. Thus place is not so much geography as how people come to use it and define it into existence for themselves. In this way, it is purely a social construction, established and maintained by a history of social relationships, thus given meaning by residents. That a place may not look very good to some is irrelevant, or less relevant (as an evaluative criterion), to others, especially those who live there. The way in which one is related to the place is what matters. Thus, for a supposedly "poor" place like Colonial County, the real testament of faith for local people is:

This is where I live. This is where my history is grounded. My biography is here. I know everyone here, at least everyone who matters most to me. Here, me and mine are left to ourselves. I may not know much that matters to some people, but I know well this place and my place in it. It is a place consisting of memories good and bad, but all of them are mine, things that cannot be bought or taken away from me. I am quite literally grounded in this place. It is in me; I am in it. As the sociologist Thomas Gieryn says about the role that place can have on our identity, "To be without a place of one's own—*persona non locata*—is to be almost non-existent."[4]

It is the important southern author Eudora Welty who is usually credited with first using the expression "a sense of place" to describe not only southerners' commitment to their homes and lives but also, in a much larger sense, to the region of which they are a part. The sense of place is something that finds support in the social science literature. Tony Hiss, in his book *The Experience of Place*, discusses in depth the relationship between people and nature-made environments, a dialectical relationship, with each influencing the other, often in ways not easily seen or fully understood. As Hiss says, "Walking through a landscape, we have the sense that the plants and animals around us have purposes of their own. At the same time, our sense of ourselves now has more to do with noticing how we are connected to the people and things around us—as part of a family, a crowd, a community, a species, the biosphere."[5] Historian McFeely, in discussing the history of African Americans on Sapelo Island, makes a similar point. He says, "the land comes to possess us, to give us grounding, to allow us to know who we are, where we belong, . . . [and] we gain something of our identity, our sense of being a part of the whole, from some almost innate loyalty to whatever is a space called home. . . . By working the island's land, by laughing, weeping, praying on it, being born and dying on it, the former slaves traded possessor and became the island's, and it became theirs."[6]

Sociologist John Shelton Reed, is no doubt correct when he says, "The theme of place and community . . . has special meaning for most southerners . . . [they] are more likely than non-southerners . . . to be anchored in their homeplace."[7] Such anchoring seems especially likely to happen to African Americans. After all, it was for them that place had special significance, since they were the most likely to have had families who were legally tied to the South, as slaves—as chattel, "owned" by others no matter where they worked and lived. Even in more contemporary times, these ties to the land and to one's ancestors are not easily forgotten, and nothing is more powerful in this equation than the family. As political economist Stanley Greenberg notes, "Ties of language, color, religion, or culture, unlike other identities, are established at the beginning—with the family." Harold Isaacs writes, "These legacies come to the child bearing the immense weight of the whole past as his family has received it. They shape the only reality in his existence and are made part of him before he has barely any consciousness at all. This 'beginning' gives race and ethnicity a special tenacity and emotional force."[8]

This relationship posited between residents and the land is immensely important not just in a place like Colonial County but in all rural counties. Reed sees the importance of land and "homeplace" as particularly powerful among all southerners (and, I think he would agree, for none more than for rural southerners, who are far more likely than their urban counterparts to remain in their homeplace and hence must have much greater emotional attachment to it). Of course, what Reed and others have argued for southerners, white and black, is no less true for other rural folk, wherever they live and probably whatever their ethnicity. Rural people in New England or Appalachia (almost all of whom are white), planters and sharecroppers across the South, farmers in the Midwest, Mexican Americans in the Rio Grande Valley of Texas or the Imperial Valley of California or elsewhere, Native Americans in the Southwest, ranchers in the West, all no doubt believe strongly in their connection to their own homeplaces and to the land forming a part of them.

For me, however, there is a unique side to this for African Americans. Although slavery is now over a century in the past, its vestiges continue in ways large and small. Inequalities have not disappeared, nor are they likely to, soon. African Americans, most of whose roots in America are in the South, were the only racial or ethnic group in this country bought and sold. Others, especially white sharecroppers, had fates not unlike those for poor blacks, since they too were often tethered legally to the land, by virtue of their contracts with the landowner. But unlike poor rural blacks, white sharecroppers endured forms of peasantry from which escape was at least somewhat likely.[9] For blacks, working the land, especially owning it (as was much more common in the Lowcountry, including Colonial County), was a reflection of self-determination and freedom. The anthropologist Hortense Powdermaker recognized and analytically described this in her book *After Freedom*, focusing primarily on rural blacks but also taking note of poor rural whites and more affluent whites.[10]

Regardless of racial or ethnic group, but cognizant of a group's poverty and tie to the land, the larger point remains: why would people who had experienced so much difficulty have so much sentiment for their homeplaces? To me, there is more than a little wisdom in McFeely's comments quoted above. Here, I paraphrase them and try to broaden their application: by working the land, by living on it for a sufficiently long time, by sustaining a lifetime of relationships tied to it—and in the process constructing a shared family history on it—by laughing, weeping, praying on it, and by being born and dying on it, residents become the land's and it becomes theirs. In this way, people construct a sense of place. In turn, (again extending and paraphrasing McFeely): as the land comes to possess us, to give us grounding, to allow us to know who we are, where we belong, we gain something of our identity, our sense of being part of the whole, of being connected not only to our families but to a larger constellation of things, called *place*.

Discovering "Poor" People

When I first came into Colonial County and began to talk to people there, they quickly disavowed me of any sociological notions I had about "poor people" and the difficult conditions under which they lived their lives. Instead, they may have thought that my questions about their daily lives and my never-ending pursuit of "Why did you continue to live here?" were both simpleminded and silly (although people were too kind to ever say this to me). After all, as a sociologist with a longstanding interest in African Americans in the rural South, I was mostly interested in the residual part of the "Great Migration"; that is, I wanted to focus my attention on the people who did not leave, who stayed behind. Given that there was a great sense of optimism and opportunity on the part of those who left, what could the residuals have, I wondered, other than a sense of fatalism and destiny—or of, as the sociologist Max Weber might have put it, an "other worldly" religious orientation, in the hope that life in the hereafter would be better.[11]

Dwayne Walls, writing about the great outmigration, describes those who left versus those who stayed, in a succinct (and somewhat sarcastic) way : "The people who left, and who continue to leave, are commonly regarded as the best ones—the strongest, the healthiest, the most industrious, the cream of the crop. The people left behind are the crippled, the very young, and the very old—and by debatable inference, the weakest. They have been described at times as 'the damned scrubs' (by rural white farmers), and as the end result of the weak breeding the weak (by learned doctors of philosophy)."[12]

Like (I suspect) many social scientists and, for that matter, many in the general population, my presumption was that life for blacks in the rural South had been more hardship than not, and that life there until the present day was one of difficulty. What I failed to consider was that, for millions of blacks in the rural South: they had always lived there. Their roots were deep and not easily severed. And a life of "difficulty" had to be understood in relative and relational terms—relative to other folk (especially local ones), and related to where people lived and the opportunities to be found there.

As Walls says dismissively, "Professors know facts, and they come up with a lot of theories. Even anthropologists are like that . . . but they don't tell people who read their books what goes on inside people—in their souls, I mean, not in their minds."[13] Charles Joyner makes a similar assessment and challenge, urging researchers to focus on "this exciting totality of the verbal, spiritual, and material aspects of a culture."[14] It was precisely such a soulful inquiry that I eventually tried to engage in, seeking to get at the roots of people who had lived their entire lives in one place or, if they had left at all, carried mental pictures of the place, always wanting to return there. As sociologist Elizabeth Bethel says of a similar southern rural black community, "It is still the land . . . which binds the generations together in a timelessness that defies the changes of a century."[15]

Mitchell Duneier chastises sociologists for their failure to understand the complexity of much social life among African Americans. As he says, "Sociologists fail to acknowledge the historical strength of the black working and lower working classes. . . . Thus social theory about urban poverty fails to recognize that the working poor are moral beings that can provide their own role models, at least on moral grounds."[16]

It is my belief that the same thing can be said about rural poverty—and, for that matter, about poverty generally. Social theory (and, for me, sociological theory in particular) is very much a product of those who produce it; rare in sociology has been the social theory that is grounded in the everyday experiences of those who live in "poor" places. Indeed, one of my most profound lessons—a kind of epiphany, really—was that we may not know nearly so much about "poverty" as we think; more kindly, we know some things well (how to conceptualize and measure "poverty") from a certain methodological point of view, but our view is a much more limited one than we would wish to believe.[17] Our view is almost always from a distance, from the vantage point of what social scientists call "secondary data" (i.e., data not collected by the analysts or, for that matter, intended necessarily for the use that they envision; good examples are census data or polling data such as the General Social Survey). These data are excellent when the emphasis is on "structure" (patterned behaviors) but, as a rule, tell us little about people's motivations and nothing about their subjectively experienced everyday lives, where virtually all "social action" (to use another long-standing, well-known social science concept) occurs.

This was driven home to me when I first met Grace. She asked about my impressions of Colonial County. I tried to hedge, at first, wanting to be asking questions rather than answering them, and I said that the county struck me as a very "poor" place, that I had noticed many houses with old, abandoned vehicles and boats, and refuse of one kind or another. Before I could say anything else, Grace pointedly asked me, "What do you know about these so-called 'poor' people? How many of them have you talked to? What do you really know about their poverty?" This was a brutal reminder about what we assume versus what we know; or alternately that what we know, we "know" from a certain perspective and so inevitably it is limited in many ways. I had to admit to Grace that I had talked to few people other than her family. And, although several lived in houses that looked worn and had the very kinds of refuse I credited to "poor" people, I did not think of any of her relatives as poor.

My wonderment about what we even mean by the term "the poor" was further challenged one day when I was at AC's. It was late and I was leaving for my house. AC asked if I liked crabmeat. When I said, "Yes, very much," he said, "I got somethin' for you." It was a pound of freshly picked crabmeat. He had been given several pounds and he wanted me to have one. When I said I thought he should keep it, he insisted; I took it.

As I drove home, I was reminded of a story told me by one of my professors in graduate school.[18] He had interviewed African Americans in the Mississippi Delta in the 1960s as part of his dissertation research. One of his interviews had been with an old man, seated on the porch of the sharecropper's shack where he lived with his wife. When my friend asked the man what he would do if he had five hundred dollars, the man paused and said, "Well, I would give two-hundred fifty to my daughter, 'cuz she's having hard times. And I would give the rest to my church." My friend was flabbergasted. Here was a man who seemed so economically disadvantaged and yet, if given a relatively large sum of money, he would give it to those less fortunate. No doubt, there are countless stories similar to this, but it was one more reminder about the kinds of assumptions we sometimes make instead of empirically ascertaining with greater certainty what people are actually like.

Diverse Cultures

Many outsiders presume a homogeneity about life for rural black folk, as if to say: rural, black, and southern form a seamless piece of cloth, with little in it that varies. But, as I said at the outset of this book, nothing is more incorrect than this view. As one of the founders of regional sociology, Rupert Vance, noted over sixty years ago, "the South is not one region but many."[19] This point has also been made by well-known rural historian Jack Kirby, especially in his characterization of the South as it goes through modernization.[20]

This sort of diversity of place is true for all southerners, black ones included. The experience for rural, black southerners is by no means homogeneous. Indeed, they vary considerably by life experiences on and off plantations, by whether they have been "croppers" or tenants or not, owned land or not, and, perhaps most importantly, by the degree to which they have been dependent on others, especially on a planter class that controlled much about their lives. On this latter item, where they lived is essential.

The people I spent time with in Colonial County were descendents of slaves who most likely grew up on plantations where they engaged in "task," not "gang," labor.[21] Thus, they were assigned tasks at the day's beginning and, once done, were free to pursue other things. This helped to foster a sense of independence among them, even while technically someone else's

property. For them, then, the move from slavery to freedom was comparatively less than for blacks in the Mississippi Delta and other places where
gang labor dominated. There, all worked as one, a kind of human-mechanical
precursor to mechanized agriculture. This arrangement was dictated by the
dominance of cotton in their lives. Much of their time was spent harvesting or in some way cultivating this one crop, not in the more diversified agriculture slaves experienced in the Lowcountry, in places like Colonial County.
Freedom for most slaves guaranteed little more than an opportunity to continue what they already knew: growing cotton and working on someone
else's land. Historian Jack Kirby reports one older black man telling a white
interviewer in Arkansas during the 1930s, "De landlord is landlord [i.e.,
white], de politician is landlord, de judge is landlord, de shurf [sheriff] is
landlord, everbody is landlord, and we ain't got nothin'."[22]

But in the Lowcountry, unlike in much of the cotton South, a task labor
system had encouraged the development of a range of individual skills, thus
allowing more bartering and an opportunity to establish social relations with
others based on something other than race. Lowcountry historian Eric
Foner describes this well: "Only in coastal Georgia and South Carolina,
where the task system allowed slaves considerable time to cultivate their
own crops and the planters were absent much of the year, did an extensive
system of marketing and property accumulation emerge under American
slavery."[23] And, he notes later, unlike most of the rest of the South after
the Civil War (where blacks were adversely affected by statutes limiting their
rights), the majority of counties in the Lowcountry were majority-black
places well into the late 1800s; thus "African culture retained its vitality here
to a greater degree than elsewhere in the South."[24] As one planter noted,
"The Negroes there will not work for wages, as they can live almost without work on fish, crawfish, and oysters; a little patch of cotton furnishing
them the means for tobacco and clothing. The result of all this, one newspaper complained, was that Lowcountry blacks had become perfectly independent of the white man."[25]

Charles Joyner, another well-known Lowcountry historian, says of these
people: "it should come as no surprise . . . that certain African work patterns in rice culture survived with little change among second and third
generations of Afro-Americans under favorable circumstances. After all, West
Africa—the true 'homeplace' for most of these slaves—had highly developed

technologies in metalwork, woodwork, leatherwork, ivorywork, pottery, and weaving. [Thus was developed] a protopeasant internal economy."[26]

Nothing may have been more important for Lowcountry blacks than the opportunity to own land. Ownership of land is perhaps the sharpest contrast between blacks in the Lowcountry and those in much of the area from central Georgia west into the Delta. Blacks throughout that geographic space were far more likely to be sharecroppers or tenant farmers; this helped to make them a class heavily, and essentially permanently, dependent on the white landowners (as Kirby notes, "de landlord") for everything from the use of land to credit at the plantation store. In the Lowcountry, however, sharecropping was almost absent.[27]

In sum, where people lived had a huge effect on their everyday life situations. Having always lived with comparatively great independence, blacks in the Lowcountry were also far more likely to have had employment outside of agriculture and to have owned land. Blacks in the Mississippi Delta, by contrast, were more likely to have been dependent upon white planters and to have had employment dependent upon production agriculture, and were less likely to have owned land. Although this is something of an oversimplification, it underscores my larger thesis: place, as found and as subjectively experienced, varies considerably for African Americans depending upon where in the South they live and what political, economic, and social history pertains to that place.[28]

Personal Responsibility

As I experienced the local scene and the people who lived in Colonial County, I also heard—in different ways but with a thematic sameness—that local people had a strong sense of having to do for themselves. I never met anyone born into the lap of luxury. All were born with little; few older people had graduated from high school; all had worked their entire adult lives or until they were too disabled to work; all owned their homes; nearly all had families much smaller than the families they had been born into. Over and over, people—especially the older ones—would talk to me about their sense of personal responsibility, in a sort of testament to "God helps those who help themselves." Indeed, their lives often personified the Protestant ethic: hard work would lead to salvation; worldly goods and economic success mattered little but a life lived well counted considerably.[29]

The notion of personal responsibility to self and others is a theme running through other sociological accounts of everyday life among African Americans, as though personal responsibility is a trait that cannot be taken for granted. This point is often found in discussions of the need for families to be "resilient," for individuals to band together to create family cohesion and solidarity. African American writer Harriet Pipe McAdoo has said recently that "patterns of resiliency have continued to provide protective cover for entire families and communities."[30] Sociologist Michael Thornton echoes this assessment when he discusses "a family's ability to change itself, to adapt to a situation, and the ability to change its circumstances and environment. In all cases, the family is resilient by virtue of its proactive responses to circumstances."[31] Although family resiliency may be notable, concern about the African American family remains,[32] and nowhere does this concern focus more than upon men.

Sociologists William Julius Wilson and Elijah Anderson worry openly about the loss of appropriate role models in inner-city areas, especially for young black males.[33] Duneier, in his book *Slim's Table*, cites Anderson to buttress his own findings. As he says, in citing Anderson, "Traditionally the 'old head' was a man of stable means who believed in hard work, family life, and the church. He was an aggressive agent of the wider society whose acknowledged role was to teach, support, encourage, and in effect socialize young men to meet their responsibilities regarding work, family, the law, and common decency."[34] This, of course, sounds eerily like AC and many of his friends. It is also an apt description of many rural men, as well as of urban ones. It is a portrait of a generation of men with a strong sense of community.

Foremost in the calculus of personal responsibility was the premise that family matters most. It was to be revered and maintained no matter what. For AC's family, the expression "blood is thicker than water" had real meaning. Family, like people's sense of self, was solidly grounded in place, in their collective memory and perpetuation of it.

As Carol Stack poetically says, "Speak of the South as you will, but you still have to speak of it. There was no forgetting a southern upbringing. The intensities and contradictions have nurtured African American song and story from the beginning. . . . [For them] home is a hard fact, not just a souvenir of restless memory; . . . home is in a hard land—hard to explain, hard to make a living in, hard to swallow."[35]

Yet virtually everyone I spoke with "loved" their homeplace. Yes, it was southern. Yes, some terrible things had happened to them there. But, on balance, it was not merely liked but loved. It seemed less something "hard to swallow" than (as acknowledged by Stack throughout her book, though not stated in quite this way) something hard to forget. Thus, no matter in what way this region was "hard," it was clearly embraced. Such collective memory helps to situate and perpetuate the sense of one's family, specifically, and the sense of place, more generally; it also helps in fostering a shared sense of commitment that continuity be assured. As the generations come and go, some events (for example, family reunions) may need to be organized as a form of intergenerational integration. As Samuel had once told me, "You've got to have roots to keep roots going."

Dwayne Walls says, in a related way: "Why would he [a black person] come back to the South? I was born and raised here. It's like I just can't get out of place here. . . . This love of home, of place, is every bit as strong among whites and blacks as it has been portrayed in song and drama, and strong enough at times to border on chauvinism. . . . It is in his love of land, of place, that the Southern black most readily shows his Southernness. . . . But how can this Southern sense of belonging held by native blacks be accounted for? Perhaps it is that . . . some of the toughest times of one's life—and the places where one has suffered these times—are rich because one survived and came through. . . . Whatever the reason, the attachment exists widely and deeply, and it is far more than simple nostalgia."[36] Or as Willie Morris says, with reference to one of the South's most famous writers, William Faulkner, "one loves a place not just because but despite."[37]

Small Places, Big Lessons

Colonial County is a small place. Numbering a little more than ten thousand residents, it is hardly representative of contemporary America, rural or urban. It is southern, in the Lowcountry, has relatively little productive agriculture, and hosts a population that has until recently been majority black. And yet, it has important lessons to teach all of us.

It was in the most serendipitous way that I, a sociologist, stumbled onto this place and onto the issues I eventually pursued. Like most social scientists, especially ones of some years experience, I had what I would call a certain amount of "academic arrogance": we may not know much, but what we do know, we know with certainty! My father used to say that "the problem with a radio is that it's always broadcasting." That was his way of saying that if you are talking all the time, you can't ever hear what the other person says. His lesson? Spend more time listening, less time talking. I had to learn to do precisely that. I had to bite my tongue many times, so that I could listen with care to what the black people of Colonial County had to tell me. As I hope is clear by now, they had a lot to say. I felt, as time went on, that they had entrusted me to be their storyteller. And what I have told is a story—mostly of AC's family but in a wider way about many families, rural black especially but also every other family.[38]

Perhaps nothing was more important for me, both as sociologist and as fellow traveler with AC and his family, than a lesson learned from the sociologist C. Wright Mills. It was Mills who coined the term "the sociological imagination."[39] This, for me, is a kind of mantra, the closest I come to a profession of faith in my discipline. Mills argued that what was needed for sociology was a quality of mind to understand what was going on around one, so that one could understand what was going on inside oneself—alternately, to understand "the intersections of biography with history": around us and inside us, biography and history.[40] The idea is to grapple with social change so that we can better understand it—as analyst but also as participant, as one with a vested interest, as one to whom it is happening.

For me, time spent in Colonial County was a reminder of my own rural roots, my parents having grown up in rural New York, my mother on a farm, my father in a small town—and of my own growing-up experience, with almost exactly the first half of my youth in the city and the latter half in a rural area of Michigan. When Alice told me one time about being in the military and meeting people who had never before met a black person, it was easy for me to imagine this; I, too, had spent much of my youth in a place that was virtually all-white and it had only been on occasional ventures out of there, as a teenager, that I had seen (but never really known) black people. Rural Michigan was my "place," a place that, much as the one Grace worried about, could delimit considerably one's horizons even while one embraced the familial warmth and certainty that may come with it.

The political scientist Andrew Hacker stated his concern about race in America in his book *Two Nations: Black and White, Separate, Hostile, Unequal.*[41] This title gives the sense of worlds apart, the sense that, no matter how much good may have come from the civil rights revolution, blacks and whites still live most often apart, not together. We don't live near each other; go to church together; eat together; or marry one another—at least not in the proportions that many had hoped for and assumed would happen. Nor does each group get similar forms of justice, or react to judicial outcomes as the other group might expect, or have their votes counted equally. In recent history, it took only the Simi Valley jury in the Rodney King case, the two verdicts in the O. J. Simpson cases, and the 2000 U.S. presidential election to remind Americans of these things.

During my time in Colonial County, and especially with AC's family, nothing affected me more than being in so many people's homes. I became very aware of Hacker's 'separate' racial worlds. I had the opportunity to speak candidly with these people about things they thought little about but felt strongly about once asked. This was my opportunity for dialogue; it is what all ethnographers get to do. I was given a wonderful opportunity to see worlds previously unknown to me, even if only briefly and in a limited way. But, without doubt, it was a unique experience, one not experienced by most white people and certainly not by those of my generation.

For AC and his family, life in Colonial County had been ongoing for three generations, with a fourth enrolled in the local schools. In a way reminiscent of Alex Haley's book *Roots*,[42] they have "roots" in this place, roots that have been cultivated and nurtured, and that have helped to produce a crop of their own, with new people and new relationships but helping to perpetuate important older values and ties to local institutions. Andrew Billingsley comments, on this very point, about roots and the intergenerational "stories" that perpetuate them: "Robert Bellah, in *Habits of the Heart*, has given voice to the concept that a rural community is one that does not forget its past. In order not to forget that past, a community is involved in retelling its story, its constructive narrative, and in so doing, it offers examples of the men and women who have embodied and exemplified the meaning of community. These stories of collective history and exemplary individuals are an important part of the tradition that is so central to a community of memory."[43] As I have tried to make clear, for me such a memory of community is essential to fostering a sense of place.

I had come to Colonial County, knowing it from afar, knowing it as most social scientists know what they write about: from long distance. From such a perspective, the people in a place have disappeared, replaced by statistics and other abstractions. This is an excellent way to proceed on many topics, including ones covered in this book. But in so doing, a place like Colonial County might be labeled neatly as "poor" or perhaps, even more harshly, "persistently poor." What is often ignored is that it takes little to leap from such a characterization to inferring similar characterizations about the people in these places. As I learned, this is wrong or, more conservatively, may be a gross overgeneralization; Mitchell Duneier worried in *Slim's Table* about this very possibility, cautioning social scientists to avoid this type of inference.

For me, prior to my visit, Colonial County was differentiated little from other historically black counties in which I had been interested. But, once there and involved in the area's daily life, I came to understand it on its own grounds: Yes, it is an historically black place, but sociological concepts such as "poverty" cannot be understood apart from the people to whom they ostensibly apply, and, as Grace had been quick to ask me one time, "What do you know about these so-called 'poor people'?" Had I been totally candid, I suspect, my answer would have been "not much."

What do I now know about Colonial County? Well, quite a bit about one family but little about the others. Does this worry me? Yes and no. Yes, because as researchers we would always like to know more than we can, but no, because our knowledge is always limited in one way or another. Is AC's family representative of all rural black families or, more restrictively, of rural black families in the Lowcountry? I didn't choose the family because it would allow me to do a sophisticated statistical analysis requiring principles of randomization. So "validity" might, for some scholars, be an issue. For me, AC's family members provided a window into a world that (usually white) sociologists don't often get to see. I leave it for others to determine how accurately the family represents other similarly situated families. For me, it was enough that these people had lived in the area for several generations and, demographically, in all ways were (intergenerationally) much like the larger African American population, certainly in the Lowcountry, of which they were a part. To be sure, the black populations elsewhere in the rural South will each have its own sense(s) of place and stories to tell about this. How different the experience has been for blacks in the Low-country than for those in the Mississippi Delta would be a wonderful point of departure for other researchers.

Are there more questions to ask, not only about life in Colonial County but about life in other historically black counties throughout the South? Yes. Indeed, asking such questions is the sine qua non of social science. It is precisely the quality of mind that Mills envisioned with his "sociological imagination." For all of us, whether academics or simply inquisitive citizens, wondering about how our lives are affected by what goes on around us seems a timelessly important question. In the "story" told here, it has been possible to see how I have pursued this question in one place, for one fairly restricted period of time—to see how, in a Millsian way, I have asked about the intersection of biography with history, about how people's everyday lives were affected by, and responded to, their circumstances. As I discovered, their sense of place was heavily grounded in their sense of family; their love for family basically trumped all other issues.

The largest lesson I got from this small place was like one learned by Warfield Simpson. Like Simpson, I went in search of people's stories about their lives "on the land," or, more specifically in my case, in a historically black place, and what it had meant to them. Like him, I wound up learning and concluding some surprising things, not least the following: "Somehow the visit wasn't what I expected and I hadn't worked out in my mind how or why . . . I expected [or, in my case, did *not* expect] them to talk at length about the land and their deep emotional attachment to it . . . instead they talked more about family . . . they talked about the practical, workaday world. . . . Their linkage to the land and feeling for place can't be separated from their family ties. . . . Family ties and feeling for place *are* inextricably linked, enriched by the length of residency. Each complements and enhances the other."[44] And, extending this point a little, each nurtures and reinforces a sense of belonging, a sense of this land as "their" place.

A Magic Moment

Toward the end of my stay in Colonial County, I was visiting one day with AC's brother, Terrence. He had to leave me alone for a little while to speak with another visitor. I was suddenly overcome with a powerful sense of melancholy and self-reflection, thinking about what my time in Yvonne had been about but, especially, what it meant for me as a person.

I sat back on Terrence's couch. Here I was in this man's living room, which also had to serve as his kitchen. His bedroom had been made out of what used to be the carport. One of his sons slept in what had been a storage room off the carport. Terrence had returned from prison to see the burned-out remains of his house, a house he had built himself nearly thirty years before. During his time in prison, his former wife had lived in the house. Only a year or so prior to his release, the house had mysteriously caught fire, and the damage was extensive. About half the house bore the telltale signs of fire, including a charred roof and one section of the house totally destroyed. Terrence, with some help from his family, tried to make the house habitable, and had tacked up large sheets of clear plastic to separate the livable parts of the house from those that weren't.

It was midmorning when Terrence had left me sitting alone. As he visited with his friend, he also grabbed another beer out of the refrigerator, a pattern that would continue throughout the day, perhaps enhanced by harder liquor if money could be found. He smoked a filtered cigarette, asking me first if I minded. As I continued to sit by myself, I looked around at how he had tried to make order out of the ruin of his life. I gazed at the old but useable couches, chairs, and tables—at the microwave oven—set on what used to be a counter in the living room but was now a cooking area—and at the box of eggs sitting nearby and the pan and plates drying on a towel, at the family pictures in one corner, at the wood-burning stove that heated the entire house, at the decorative false fireplace (at one time meant to make the room more fashionable).

When he rejoined me, we talked about both what his life had been and what it had become. He was trying to help me understand the mystery of this place and his role in it. In a great bit of irony, the program *Columbo* seemed to run forever on the television, turned down but not off. So here, in person, was a man talking in a very composed, articulate way about this place where he had lived all his life; and there, on television, was the stumbling but always clever Columbo engaged in as much mystery-solving as he could fit between commercials. Me and Columbo, two detectives.

There I sat, a fifty-plus-year-old white man in an older black man's home.

I was a stranger. This black man had let me into his life. He was sharing some powerful memories with me, at the same time glad for the opportunity to talk about them. He seemed not terribly bitter but, rather, resigned to his lot in life. We chatted away like a couple of old friends, laughing heartily at times, pensive and reflective at others. We were focused intently on what we were saying to one another, yet relaxed, as though we had done this together many times. All I could think was: in our huge society, with millions of us, black and white, how often do people of different races and circumstances ever have occasion to speak as we were? I was reminded of William McFeely saying that "After thirty years of scholarly cogitation and more than fifty of head scratching, I still don't quite know what race is. But it is."[45] For me, too. And you?

Some Notes on Methods, the Study Site, and Emergent Theory

Methods

In this book's introduction and at other places throughout, I have commented on the methods used in this project. At the risk of some repetition, I provide here a bit more detailed, chronological reconstruction of my methodology. I do this primarily (1) to provide a record of how I did what I did, (2) for the sake of those who may wish to follow in my footsteps, and (3) with a sense that, for some people (primarily students, I expect), this appendix, coupled with much of the introduction, may be read as a freestanding explanation of how I did my work.

I did not start out to do an ethnography that would become a book. Instead, I sought to extend my earlier work on and interest in historically black southern counties (the Black Belt). Initially, I envisioned writing a kind of demographic social history of these places, focusing on a century of change (from 1900 to 2000). But I also thought that it would make the book more interesting if I could integrate some stories from older African Americans living in counties throughout the Black Belt. I envisioned a very simple form of oral history.

When I stepped down as the chair of the Department of Sociology at the University of Maryland, I had a research leave. Aware of what the census data from 1880 to 1990 showed for the Black Belt, I planned on using some of my time to visit selected counties throughout the region—diverse counties in the Lowcountry, Alabama, and the Mississippi Delta. Instead, I never left the Lowcountry.

I arrived there in January 1996. My visit was facilitated greatly by a colleague at a Lowcountry university. This colleague had an African American student who was from the Lowcountry. I visited with the student at the university and she was confident that her grandparents, especially her grandfather (whom I have here called AC) would be interested in what I wanted to do—talk to older African Americans who had never left the South for any long period. She arranged for me to meet her grandparents, and my initial visit lasted for a couple of hours, because it was so easy to speak with them—and because her grandfather, as she had predicted, seemed so willing to help me meet other older African Americans. This led to three months of regular visits, in the grandparents' home but also in the homes of others, most introduced to me by AC.

Although my initial questions were about choosing to stay in the county, eventually and inevitably other questions arose, often in the most serendipitous ways. Thus questions about religion and school and work arose as by-products of my "main" questions. They came up in conversations as little surprises. Carol Stack had told me that one technique I might employ was to ask local people what kinds of questions *they* would ask. I did, but with limited success; the key thing was that, as I spent time locally, I became more and more curious about many aspects of the local scene, far beyond my original, quite limited focus on migration.

I taped all interviews except two, and even those two people were glad to talk to me. I began each meeting with a rather standard script about who I was and what I was doing in the county. I assured people that my questions were not about personal matters and that they were free to not answer any given questions. Since I was not talking to them about personal issues or attitudes or behaviors that might have made them uncomfortable, no one ever said "I would prefer to not discuss that." I told each person, especially after I had met with several, that people in this place seemed to enjoy talking about their lives. They did.

In general, my data were collected via interviews conducted in people's homes. In one case, I interviewed a man in a house, in his car, and at a local restaurant. For AC, interviews occurred whenever we were together but, for the most part, the more focused interviews were in his house. I did my own transcribing for every interview. Many contemporary ethnographers seem to use transcribing services but I drew a lesson from the old school of social research that essentially argues, "the closer to the data, the more that can be learned." And this was definitely true for me. I did in fact identify many items to pursue by virtue of this close contact with processing the data. As my wife listened to one interview, she remarked, "I honestly did not know that you could keep from talking for that long." Indeed, for an academic, this took considerable self-restraint.

Besides conducting in-home visits, I spent considerable time in a regional library that had a good Lowcountry book collection, as well as local newspapers on microfiche. I read every local history book and all other related material that I could find. Especially important was access to the newspapers. Colonial County's newspaper is weekly—and has been since it began. I read through its one hundred years of copy, looking mostly for coverage of issues related to race—e.g., elections, legal issues, the schools, stories about "our colored neighbors," cartoons that depicted black people, and so on. This helped me to form a stronger sense of how Colonial County was depicted and written about in the local media, especially by local people who wrote letters to the editor or commentaries of one kind or another.

Beyond doing my visits with individuals and my library work, I also traveled every road in the county. The main roads were all paved but many secondary ones were not. Their surfaces included gravel, crushed oyster shells and, most often, dirt. As one example of what one finds, I was exploring the western part of the county one day on a very good paved road. It was marked with standard signs indicating the speed limit and the road's identifier (state name followed by a number). Suddenly, with no advance warning, the pavement ended and a dirt lane extended ahead as far as I could see. With considerable caution, I drove slowly forward. Sure enough, this was still the same road, but in a part of the county that seemed to have few houses. In time, the road connected to another main road.

It is precisely such trips that allow one, as a researcher, to form a lasting impression of a place. I occasionally had to stop and ask directions, and often these encounters became occasions to ask a few general questions about the county: What was it like to live there? What did people do for a living? In other words, nothing personal, mostly just making conversation or, as southerners might say, "visiting." I always told people that I was a sociologist working on a project in which this county was one of several places I anticipated visiting.

By the time I left Colonial County in 1996, I had immersed myself in the place. I had talked mostly to AC's family, and it is important to note that, in my three months of regular visits, I spoke mostly to them and other African Americans. Rarely did I speak at length to any white residents of the county. I did not avoid them; it was simply that my focus was on the migration experience of older black people. Nonetheless, I did eat in local restaurants and frequent local businesses, so I had many opportunities to observe white people in everyday situations, including their interactions with black people. But I had few real conversations with white residents.

The Study Site

Since my initial visit in 1996, I have visited the county at least once a year. One visit was for a month, but the others have generally been for a week or a few days. Each time, I have spoken with AC and also revisited the library to review the previous year's Colonial County newspaper. The newspaper has been very helpful for identifying new social forces. Especially noteworthy is the very recent and impressive amount of capital flowing into the county in the form of large-scale, expensive housing developments, all situated on the water. These are often accompanied by the one recreational activity found in abundance in the Lowcountry, golf courses, which are wonderful sociodemographic predictors—of affluent white people. Golf courses, which are almost always coupled with expensive housing, are testament to the adage "Build it and they will come." Colonial County for decades had about nine thousand people, a majority of whom were black. With the first large development in the 1980s, the demography began to change. By the late 1980s, the county was, for the first time in memory (and, historically, for the first time since about 1840), majority white. By the 2000 census, the demographic profile of the county had continued to change, with the shift fueled by continual development that was bringing in, disproportionately and almost entirely, white people—people who, as a group, are better educated, far more affluent, far more mobile, and, on average, much older than either local whites or local blacks. Today, the proportion of blacks in the county has fallen to about one-third of the total population.

This demographic change has dramatized a growing black-white divide. Blacks, always the disproportionate share of the county's poor, will seem even poorer with the continuing influx of more affluent whites. But interestingly, many whites will also seem this way. The county historically has had a very small proportion of people with college degrees and professional careers; nearly all local workers have had blue collar jobs, often in neighboring counties that had more industry of any type. The resultant relatively small economic gap between local whites and blacks has, until now, helped to minimize the sense of "haves" and "have-nots." In the most rural parts of the county—again, until the new developments came in—it was nearly impossible to drive by a house and tell whether blacks or whites lived in it. This is still true for most of the county. For example, a new "double-wide" (two trailers spliced together to form one larger house) or a single trailer is just as likely to have white occupants as black. The same is true of what is outside; pickup trucks, older cars or newer but inexpensive ones, boats and trailers, farm-type tractors—none indicate much about the race of the house's occupants.

This is the antithesis of what one finds in the newer developments, all called "plantations." There, one is most likely to find large SUVs and/or newer, expensive domestic and foreign cars, boats on lifts at piers in front of the house or along community marinas, and newer yard-type tractors for mowing the expansive lawns. At least in the short run, the relatively affluent white newcomers will stand in sharp contrast to most of the indigenous, local population. And it is a certainty that they will live largely ghettoized lives within their gated communities. This, it should be noted, is always a key part of "plantation" living; gates open and close to control who belongs and who doesn't. Among other ironies to this development is that, much like Native Americans, older local Colonial County residents have little memory of lacking access to vast tracts of land and water, of being fenced out or, with the gated communities, locked out. Instead, people used to move around freely to hunt and fish, with historical precedent and longstanding agreement the guiding principle. When I would drive around with AC, he would often say "Used to go hunting in there" or "There was good shrimpin' on that river" or some similar thing.

The divide between newcomers and locals is likely, I believe, to be registered by not only what work one does but where one does it. At the end of the county that has considerable development (all, at present, new housing), there is a regular outflow in the morning, not to jobs in the county but almost entirely to jobs outside it. Equally, children in these new developments are as likely as not to attend private schools outside the county—a self-induced form of busing with carpools being common. In sum, the world of many—admittedly, not all—newcomers is apart from that of most local residents from the indigenous population.

The one thing unlikely to change much, I suspect, is the local schools. Even though blacks now represent only about one in three local residents, they represent the vast majority of school students. Even without knowing the exact proportion, this conclusion is easily noted by viewing the smiling faces of each year's graduating class when its picture is shown in the local paper, or by looking at the schools' athletic teams or driving by the school buildings: blacks outnumber whites by about three to one. Given that many of those white newcomers not "out-busing" their children are retirees or people who no longer have school-age children, it seems clear that these new residents will have no affect on school population proportions.

Where the newcomers will, I suspect, have a more pronounced effect is on local politics. To the newcomers, most of whom have migrated from larger, ostensibly more sophisticated places, local politics probably appears a vestige from some bygone era, definitely small town and small time. On that front, change is coming. Newcomers, better educated and more used to arguing openly for what they want, have increasingly attended county board of supervisor meetings and argued for increasing services for their part of the county. To date, none have held elected office, but this is sure to happen, probably in the near future. Politics, however, is one place where the old norms will be slow to change (since the board of supervisors has always been in the hands of the older, well-entrenched white power structure). Its meetings are definitely a place where you can openly hear people say, usually in very measured tones, "The way we do things here" or, more often, and usually in response to someone's comparatively impassioned pleading, "That's not how we do things here."

I have tried my best to be vague about descriptions of the county and its residents. Virtually all rural counties in the coastal Lowcountry look much like Colonial County. So, too, are there many "Yvonnes," small, crossroads communities that are historically and presently majority black. So, too, are many of these Lowcountry counties experiencing massive new developments that are altering forever local people's "sense of place." In all cases, these developments are characterized by the same economic and demographic dynamics found in Colonial County and, as far as I have been able to tell (by driving the Lowcountry multiple times, top to bottom), "plantation" or "country club" are the operative terms to describe these places. So, too, have these Lowcountry counties (most of which were majority black for about one hundred fifty years) experienced some return migration of African Americans who migrated out and have now "come home." It remains to be seen how these comparatively better educated, more affluent, pension-supported, disproportionately single and female returnees will be embraced by kith and kin, to say nothing of white residents, old or new.

For AC's family and the small community of Yvonne, the years since my initial visit have, as one would expect, brought further changes. Some of AC's siblings have died. Grace moved away for awhile, only to return fairly recently, with a new husband. She no longer lives in the "big old white house"; instead, she bought a lot and a trailer closer to her older sister. Her children continue to live in her old house. Both Alice and Rhonda work outside the county. Their brothers did start their own construction company, but Samuel is supplementing his income by also working at a nearby airport. Yvonne today looks very much as it did when I first went there. Even with new development bringing so much money into the county, it is hard to imagine that Yvonne will change dramatically any time soon.

Emergent Theory—and Theorist

It is well to remember that, like all social researchers, I could not divorce who I am from what I did. I am an older white man, a sociologist who had no ties to Colonial County. I came to the place in search of information on processes related to migration. Along the way, serendipitously, I pursued not only my main focus but secondary issues that seemed to merit attention. I was always careful to let people speak openly, with little response from me that would bias what they might say, but, to be sure, my "bias" was reflected in what I chose to ask about and, no doubt, in how I asked it. Others researchers—younger, of color, of a different gender, from a different social class, from a different part of the country or from abroad, from different disciplines—would, almost assuredly, pursue totally different stories than the ones I have reported here. Regardless, they would all, I believe, do well to be guided by something Charles Colson has said: "Men are born with two eyes, but with a single tongue in order that they should see twice as much as they say."

There is a lot to see in the social world. What you report and how you do it are your choices to make. I made mine. I was never "in the lion's mouth" as AC usually used the term, but to some degree we all often make choices in which we try to minimize risk, in which we struggle to avoid the lion's mouth. My main risk here has lain in trying to report on a place and a family that I came to value greatly. I encourage others, especially sociologists, to undertake similar ventures or, more accurately, adventures. Not only did I find myself challenged methodologically, but I also found myself pondering the utility of various sociological concepts. There are so many that I chose to use only a few, most of which are well known and require little explanation.

For me, Berger and Luckmann's classic book on "the social construction of reality" is one way of conceptualizing the individual-structure relationship. I was—as Berger and Luckmann might say—"in it" and "of it." I tried to be mindful of this as I did the fieldwork and also as I reported what I found. I have provided my own reconstruction of the ongoing social constructions I observed. I make no apologies for my methods or, to the degree discernible, conceptual argument.

"Place" was something onto which I stumbled. I knew nothing about its literature until my time in Colonial County forced me to make sense out of my experience. It was in this way, again serendipitously, that I floundered around in a new, interdisciplinary literature. In so doing, I saw "place" as a historically situated social construction, as something constructed that acts back on us. Thus, for me, place was a sort of Durkheimian "social fact." It was external and coercive; it could not be wished away. It helped to set the limits on what people knew and on the ways they experienced the world (as primarily a socially constructed thing). I could have asserted a more well-articulated theoretical argument from the outset; in that case, I would have been "testing theory" in the most normal scientific way. I opted instead for an inductive and almost creatively intuitive form of investigation, more akin to grounded theory or what I have called emergent theory. That is, without strict adherence to phenomenological principles, I let the "essence" of the story arise from the actors. I listened with care to what they told me. And from what they said, I tried to string together individual stories to create a larger, synthetic sense of what had been most meaningful. At this point, it is up to readers—from whatever your vantage point—to determine how much to agree or disagree with what I did and what I concluded.

Notes

Introduction   A Brief Autobiographical Note

1. Charles Horton Cooley, *Human Nature and the Social Order* (New York: Charles Scribner's Sons, 1930).

2. C. Wright Mills, *The Sociological Imagination* (New York: Grove Press, 1959).

3. William W. Falk and Thomas A. Lyson, *High Tech, Low Tech, No Tech: Industrial and Occupational Change in the South* (Albany: State University of New York Press, 1988).

4. Among the better books, see Neil Fligstein, *Going North: Migration of Blacks and Whites from the South, 1900–1950* (New York: Academic Press, 1981); James R. Grossman, *Land of Hope: Chicago, Black Southerners, and the Great Migration* (Chicago: University of Chicago Press, 1989); Nicholas Lehmann, *The Promised Land: The Great Black Migration and How It Changed America* (New York: Alfred A. Knopf, 1991); Joe William Trotter Jr., *The Great Migration in Historical Perspective* (Bloomington: Indiana University Press, 1991); Carole Marks, *Farewell—We're Good and Gone: The Great Black Migration* (Bloomington: Indiana University Press, 1993).

5. The "badness" of the South relative to the rest of the United States is so widely assumed that even social scientists treat it in a mostly taken-for-granted, almost axiomatic, way. "The South" is often used as a "dummy variable" in statistical analyses precisely because it is the category against which other regions are compared. For a good social science book on the complexity of the contemporary South, and by implication the possible error in the usual assumption, see Larry J. Griffin and Don H. Doyle, eds., *The South as an American Problem* (Athens: University of Georgia Press, 1995). See Jimmie Lewis Franklin, "Black Southerners, Shared Experience, and Place: A Reflection," in *The South as an American Problem,* ed. Griffin and Doyle, 210–233.

6. Carol Stack, *Call to Home: African Americans Reclaim the South* (New York: Basic Books, 1996).

7. Melissa Fay Greene, *Praying for Sheetrock* (New York: Fawcett Columbine, 1991).

8. My experience was much like that of John Egerton, who also did an inter-generational study of one family (see John Egerton, *Generations: An American Family* [Lexington: University of Kentucky Press, 1983]). As he has said, "The story of any large family, I thought, would give those who read it a glimpse of their own history, a better vision of themselves. One family could be a prism through which the shape and texture and resonance of American Life could be transmitted—and the more carefully the family was chosen for its typicality, the more universally recognizable the resulting portrait would be" (15). AC, an older black man with little formal education, from a large family, divorced and remarried, highly religious, and with considerable wisdom was, I believe, not unlike many men of his generation with whom I might have spent time. But admittedly, he was also a special person; someone I was very lucky to meet.

9. Theodore Rosengarten, *All God's Dangers: The Life of Nate Shaw* (New York: Alfred A. Knopf, 1975).

10. Common on most sociologists lists, I suspect, would be these books: Oscar Lewis, *Five Families: Mexican Case Studies in the Culture of Poverty* (New York: New American Library, 1959); W. H. Whyte, *Street Corner Society: The Social Structure of an Italian Slum* (Chicago: University of Chicago Press, 1993); Elliot Liebow, *Tally's Corner: A Study of Negro Streetcorner Men* (Boston: Little Brown, 1967); Erving Goffman, *Interaction Ritual and Stigma*: *Essays on Face-to-Face Behavior* (Garden City, NY: Anchor Books, 1967); Mitchell Duneier, *Slim's Table: Race, Respectability, and Masculinity* (Chicago: University of Chicago Press, 1992); Kathryn Edin and Laura Lein, *Making Ends Meet: How Single Mothers Survive Welfare and Low-Wage Work* (New York: Russell Sage Foundation, 1997); Kathryn Edin, *There's a Lot of Month Left at the End of the Money: How Welfare Recipients Make Ends Meet in Chicago* (New York: Garland, 1993); Howard Becker, *Boys in White: Student Culture in Medical School* (Chicago: University of Chicago Press, 1961).

11. Duneier, *Slim's Table*.

12. Especially good on dialect in the sea islands is Jacquiline P. Jones-Jackson's ethnography of St. John's Island, *When Roots Die: Endangered Traditions on the Sea Islands* (Athens: University of Georgia Press, 1987).

13. John Shelton Reed, *One South: An Ethnic Approach to Regional Culture* (Baton Rouge: Louisiana State University Press, 1982).

14. Egerton, *Generations,* 20.

15. William Least Heat-Moon, *Blue Highways: A Journey into America* (New York: Ballantine Books, 1983).

One   A Region, a Place, a Man

1. Most omnipresent and indicative of this are Cracker Barrel stores. Although these stores are present now in more than forty states, their southern roots (they

started in Tennessee) and the fare on their menus are vivid testament to their rural *and* southern tone.

2. This is a term that has at least four common spellings: Lowcountry, as I have spelled it; Low Country; lowcountry; and low-country. As far as I can determine, there is no absolutely preferred way to spell the term.

3. Arthur Raper, *Preface to Peasantry: A Tale of Two Black Belt Counties* (Chapel Hill: University of North Carolina Press, 1936), 3.

4. Jim Auchmutey and Priscella Painton, "Black Belt: The Abandoned South," a series published in the *Atlanta Journal Constitution,* beginning 16 November 1986, 1A. As the well-known African American scholar Cornel West has said, "The basic claim is that African Americans constitute or once constituted an oppressed nation in the Southern Black Belt, and, much like Puerto Ricans, form an oppressed national minority." (*The Cornel West Reader* [New York: Basic Civitas Books, 1999].) A similar point had been made nearly sixty years earlier in the famous sociological study by Charles S. Johnson, *Growing Up in the Black Belt* (Washington, DC: American Council on Education, 1941).

5. Robert Hoppe, *Economic Structure and Change in Persistently Low-Income Nonmetro Counties,* Rural Development Research Report No. 50 (Washington, DC: Economic Research Service. U.S. Department of Agriculture). Similar facts have been noted by sociologists writing about contemporary urban places (see William Julius Wilson, *The Truly Disadvantaged: The Inner City, the Underclass, and Public Policy* [Chicago: University of Chicago Press, 1987]), as well as when writing about contemporary rural areas (see Cynthia M. Duncan, *Worlds Apart: Why Poverty Persists in Rural America* [New Haven, CT: Yale University Press, 1999]).

6. Dwight B. Billings Jr., *Planters and the Making of a "New South"* (Chapel Hill: University of North Carolina Press, 1979).

7. Pete Daniel, *The Shadow of Slavery: Peonage in the South* (Urbana: University of Illinois Press, 1972), 898.

8. Carole Marks, *Farewell—We're Good and Gone*, 1.

9. Clifton Taulbert, *When We Were Colored* (New York: Penguin Books, 1995), 134.

10. Alice Walker, *The Color Purple* (Cambridge: Cambridge University Press, 1990).

11. John B. Cromartie and Carole B. Stack, "Reinterpretation of Black Return and Nonreturn Migration to the South, 1975–1980," *Geographical Review* 79 (1989):297–310.

12. Peter Uhlenberg, "Noneconomic Determinants of Nonmigration: Sociological Considerations of Migration Theory," *Rural Sociology* 38 (1987):296–311.

13. Emile Durkheim, *The Rules of Sociological Method* (London: Macmillan, 1982).

14. Peter Berger and Thomas Luckmann, *The Social Construction of Reality: A Treatise in the Sociology of Knowledge* (Garden City, NY: Anchor Books, 1966).

15. See *Perceptions of Rural America* (Battle Creek, MI: The Kellogg Foundation, 2001).

16. For a very good history of black migration, and of the Black Belt in particular, see George A. Davis and O. Fred Donaldson, *Blacks in the United States: A Geographic Perspective* (Boston: Houghton Mifflin, 1975).

17. In the 2000 U.S. census, ninety-five counties were still majority black. A nearly

equal number were 40–49 percent black. Virtually all were rural. For an excellent set of maps showing this distribution, see Ronald Wimberly and Libby Morris, *The Southern Black Belt: A National Perspective* (Lexington, KY: TVA Rural Studies, 1995).

18. Thomas Krech, *Praise the Bridge that Carries You Over: The Life of Joseph L. Sutton* (Cambridge, MA: Schenkman, 1981).

19. Indeed, in a true bit of civil rights irony, the South is home to most of the nation's black elected officials, with Mississippi having more black elected officials than any other state. According to the most recent data on this, southern states and the District of Columbia account for two-thirds of all elected African American officials in the U.S. A mere seven states—Alabama, Arkansas, Georgia, Louisiana, Mississippi, North Carolina, and South Carolina—account for half African American politicians.

20. This, like all other person and place names used in this book, is fictitious. Only when names of people or places do not jeopardize the anonymity of the study site are real names used.

21. Tony Dunbar, *Delta Time: A Journey Through Mississippi* (New York: Pantheon Books, 1990).

Two   The World of Work—as Experienced and Interpreted by Older Men

1. See J. William Harris, *Deep Souths: Delta, Piedmont, and Sea Island Society in the Age of Segregation* (Baltimore: Johns Hopkins University Press, 2001), 143. Also see Thomas F. Armstrong, "The Transformation of Work: Turpentine Workers in Coastal Georgia, 1865–1901," *Labor History* 25 (1984):518–532.

2. Something also true at one time in such industries as tobacco and resorts, which much like some agricultural labor were seasonal.

3. All of the workers received a small settlement, but nothing compared to what they expected for the time they had spent working at the plant. And did the company quit making steel? No, it simply did what many other companies do: sought even cheaper land, taxes, and workers in another southern state. As AC told me on another occasion, "Only one got any money outta' that deal was the attorney."

4. For sociologists, of course, all "gifts" are open to question in a variety of ways, not the least being the social psychological notion of "reciprocity." Thus, although AC is "giving" something, he may also be "getting" something other than just good will. As a longtime, aging resident, AC is aware that he too may, at some point in his life, need looking after. His lifetime of good deeds with family and friends will, no doubt, lead to a sense of indebtedness that may yield people coming to his aid as he has done for others.

5. Peter Mayle, *A Year in Provence* (London: F. A. Thorpe, 1991).

6. In Colonial County, about 28 percent of all persons between 21 and 64 are disabled (50 percent of these are still employed, compared to 67 percent of those who are not disabled); among persons 65 and older, 50 percent are disabled.

7. Duneier, *Slim's Table*.

8. Elijah Anderson, *Streetwise: Race, Class, and Change in an Urban Community* (Chicago: University of Chicago Press, 1990).

9. Indeed, on a return visit nearly five years after my first trip to Colonial County, I saw that the local paper's lead article was about a murder in a place called "the Patch." The victim was a member of a local posse (gang) killed by a rival group competing for control of local drug sales.

10. On my last visit, in the winter of 2003, AC told me that the drug activity had moved to a new location but remained well known and, for the most part, operated in the open—despite the occasional arrests about which I found stories in the local paper.

11. Anderson, *Streetwise*, 242.

12. Duneier, *Slim's Table*, 35.

13. Ibid., 70.

14. Ibid., 45.

15. Ibid., 66.

16. Alex Kotlowitz, *There Are No Children Here: The Story of Two Boys Growing Up in the Other America* (New York: Random House Children's Books, 1992).

17. A review of articles in the local weekly newspaper for the past few years reveals the never-ending arrests of young black males from the Homewood area of the county. When I recently visited the county, I saw that a major story in the paper was about a "roundup" of those selling drugs.

18. Wilson, *The Truly Disadvantaged*.

19. For good overviews on the military, as written by sociologists, see Charles Moskos and John Sibley Butler, *All We Can Be: Black Leadership and Racial Integration the Army Way* (New York: Basic Books, 1996). Also see David Segal, *Life in the Rank and File: Enlisted Men and Women in the Armed Forces of the U.S., Australia, Canada, and the United Kingdom* (London: Brassey's, 1986).

Three   Strong Women

1. Such traits are widely cited in the social sciences. See Andrew Billingsley, *Climbing Jacob's Ladder: The Enduring Legacy of African-American Families* (New York: Touchstone, 1992); Robert Staples and Leanor Boulin Johnson, *Black Families at the Crossroads: Challenges and Prospects* (San Francisco: Jossey-Bass, 1993); Linda Burton and Vernon L. Bengston, "Black Grandmothers: Issues of Timing and Continuity in Roles," in *Grandparenthood: Research and Policy,* ed. Vernon L. Bengston and J. F. Robertson (Beverly Hills, CA: Sage, 1985), 61–77. Especially good on this topic are: Barbara Barer, "The 'Grands and Greats' of Very Old Black Grandmothers," *Journal of Aging Studies* 15 (1) (2001):1–11; Bonnie T. Dill, "A Better Life for Me and My Children: Low-Income Single Mothers' Struggle for Self-Sufficiency in the Rural South," *Journal of Comparative Family Studies* 29 (1998):419–428; Susan Garrett, *Miles to Go: Aging in Rural Virginia* (Charlottesville: University Press of Virginia, 1998). Although late-in-life poverty has fallen mostly on women, men have not escaped it. This is easily documented in the literature; see, for instance: Maxine Baca Zinn, "Race and the Family

Values Debate," in *Challenges for Work and Family in the Twenty-first Century*, ed. Dana Vannoy and Paula J. Dubeck (New York: Aldine de Gruyter, 1989), 49–62; Joe Feagin, *Racial and Ethnic Relations*, 2d ed. (Englewood Cliff, NJ: Prentice Hall, 1984); Andrew Cherlin and Frank F. Furstenberg, *The New American Grandparent: A Place in the Family, a Life Apart* (New York: Basic Books, 1986).

2. Andrew Billingsley makes a similar point, citing a Howard University study that "found that among strong achieving black families of both single-parent and two-parent structures, the values they rely on to facilitate their achievement includes strong kinship bonds, strong achievement orientation, positive parent-child relationship, strong religious orientation, intellectual-actual orientation, and strong work orientation. In other words, the family, the church, the schools, and the work place" (*Climbing Jacob's Ladder,* 332).

3. See, among others, M. Gutentag and P. F. Secord, *Too Many Women: The Sex Ratio Question* (Beverly Hills, CA: Sage, 1983); also see M. B. Tucker and C. Mitchell-Kernan, eds., *The Decline of Marriage among African Americans* (New York: Russell Sage, 1995). Besides this academic literature, there is considerable folklore on the subject, not least as a staple in blues music, begun by rural black people, and country music, begun by rural white people. In both music forms, the man running around on his woman is a common theme. Almost unheard of is the woman running around on her man. Indeed, the highly gendered and highly biased normativeness to this idea, "running around on," was never made clearer than by the famous line "stand by your man."

4. For an interesting discussion of "spiritual narratives" and a good sense of the literature on the effect of this for African American women, see Helen K. Black, "Poverty and Prayer: Spiritual Narratives of Elderly African American Women," *Review of Religious Research* 40 (4) (1999):359–374.

5. This is a classic notion of the caring white person. No matter how the white is described or how paternalistic he/she may sound, stories like this are commonplace—parables of those more fortunate (almost always white) looking after those less fortunate (almost always black). Dorthea's story also illustrates the prevailing sentiment that southerners are, independent of race, more oriented toward community and, despite personal antipathies, willing to help those less fortunate. This stands in sharp opposition to the even more common stories about blacks (especially women) who looked after and cared for white families, even at the expense of their own.

6. In Robert Hill's book, *The Strengths of African American Families: Twenty-five Years Later* (Lanham, MD: Rowman and Littlefield, 2001), Hill says, citing Joyce Archenbrenner's work on the importance of kinship bonds and family/cultural values: "Among these are (1) a high value placed on children; (2) the approval of strong protective mothers; (3) the emphasis on strict discipline and respect for elders; (4) the strength of family bonds; and (5) the ideal of the independent spirit" (122).

7. Susan Webb describes the lengths that many black women in the South Carolina Lowcountry go not only to remain in their communities, but also to find work. For these women, the trial entails a ninety-minute bus ride (each way)

for low-paying jobs in the tourist hotels. See Susan Webb, "The Bus to Hell Hole Swamp," in *Communities of Work: Rural Restructuring in Local and Global Contexts,* ed. William W. Falk, Michael Schulman, and Ann Tickamyer (Athens: Ohio University Press, 2003). What Webb describes is similar to the work available for many African American women in Colonial County.

8. The idea of the extended family has long been common among African Americans. Citing a few of the many studies, Robert Hill (cited in Billingsley, *Climbing Jacob's Ladder*) says: "Undoubtedly, the most enduring cultural strength that black Americans brought with them from the African continent was the extended family and its strong kinship networks" (122). For more recent citations, see Robert Hill, *The Strengths of African American Families* (Lanham, MD: University Press of America, 1999). Robert Joseph Taylor and Waldo E. Johnson Jr., in comparing northern and southern blacks, state that "(a) older black southerners receive support from extended families more frequently and (b) black southern adults are more likely to use family members" ("Family Roles and Family Satisfaction among Black Men," in *Family Life in Black America,* ed. Robert Joseph Taylor, James S. Jackson, and Linda S. Chatters [Thousand Oaks, CA: Sage Publications, 1997], 260).

9. No one, I believe, does a better job of trying to sort out fact from fiction and demythologize much of what passes as "common sense" on this subject than does Kathryn Edin. In talking about the "month left at the end of the money" or "making ends meet," her writings lucidly tell the story of being welfare-"dependent" and the struggle for survival among persons on welfare, especially single women. See Kathryn Edin and Laura Lein, *Making Ends Meet*; see also Edin's *There's a Lot of Month Left at the End of the Money.*

10. My conversation with Grace about this made me wonder what the welfare picture did look like for Colonial County. Without giving the exact figures (and thereby making the identity of the county more likely), it is worth noting that Grace's impression is more accurate than not. According to the 2000 U.S. Census, about 11 percent of all households in the entire county are in poverty.

11. Particularly good on this are edited collections, such as Taylor, Jackson, and Chatters, eds., *Family Life in Black America*; Hamilton I. McCubbin, Jo A. Futrell, Elizabeth A. Thompson, and Anne I. Thompson, eds., *Resiliency in African American Families* (Thousand Oaks, CA: Sage Publications, 1998); Harriet Pipes McAdoo, ed., *Family Ethnicity: Strength in Diversity* (Thousand Oaks, CA: Sage Publications, 1999); Manning Marable and Leith Mullings, eds., *Let Nobody Turn Us Around: Voices of Resistance, Reform, and Renewal* (Lanham, MD: Rowman and Littlefield, 2000); especially see Billingsley's *Climbing Jacob's Ladder.* For the most recent work in this area, see Charles Vert Willie and Richard J. Reddick, *A New Look at Black Families,* 5th ed. (Lanham, MD: Rowan and Littlefield, 2003).

12. Bonnie Dill is especially good on this with regard to rural black women, albeit ones who labor under tremendous difficulties (see Dill, "A Better Life for Me and My Children"). Like the members of AC's family, the people Dill studies found that it took considerable work to sustain their relationships. Their love for one another, although usually taken for granted, was definitely something

that ebbed and flowed, not always at high tide but never entirely out to sea either. It was and is important, and the women seem to have disproportionately been the ones to value it, to such degree that they nurtured relationships when needed and valued them always. (I should note, this sort of response is also very apparent in Carol Stack's book, *All Our Kin*.)

Four   What Did You Learn in School Today?

1. James S. Coleman et al., *Equality of Educational Opportunity* (Washington, DC: U.S. Government Printing Office, 1966).
2. See Jerry Himelstein, *Segregation Academies in Mississippi: A Case Study of Interest Group Formation.* (Ph.D. diss., Louisiana State University, 1983). David Nevin and Robert E. Bills, *The Schools That Fear Built: Segregationist Academies in the South.* (New York: Acropolis Books, 1976). Christine Rossell, "Desegregation Plans, Racial Isolation, White Flight, and Community Response," in *The Consequences of School Desegregation*, ed. Christine Rossell and Willis Hawley (Philadelphia: Temple University Press, 1983), 13–57. Kenneth T. Andrews, "Movement-Countermovement Dynamics and the Emergence of New Institutions: The Case of 'White Flight' Schools in Mississippi," *Social Forces* 80(3) (2002):911–936.
3. It is axiomatic to state that the greater the proportion black of any given school district, the greater the proportion of white children in private school. For the magnitude of this relationship see the National Center for Education Statistics, *Private School Universe*, 1999/2000.
4. For a good summary of Coleman's major points, and one response to them, see Robert L. Green and Thomas F. Pettigrew, "Urban Desegregation and White Flight: A Response to Coleman," *Phi Delta Kappan* (February 1976):399–402.
5. Throughout their book, *The Price They Paid: Desegregation in an African American Community* (New York: Teachers College Press, 2002), Vivian Gunn Morris and Curtis L. Morris quote people who make similar points. To cite one: "It was not 'their school' as Trenhom was. They felt as if they were in an alien environment. They did not find the family atmosphere that was quite evident to them at Trenholm" (98).
6. As reported in Duneier, *Slim's Table,* 73.
7. William Freudenberg, "The Density of Acquaintanceship: An Overlooked Variable in Community Research," *American Journal of Sociology* 92 (1) (1986):27–63.
8. After I completed most of the fieldwork for this project, the superintendent discussed here was fired. According to the local paper, the reasons were never made clear but her contract was bought out for over one hundred thousand dollars. Her replacement? A white man.
9. The writer Peter Applebome makes a very similar point in discussing the impressions he has gleaned from conversations with older African Americans who had attended a segregated high school in North Carolina: "more often than not, the message, offered with a combination of pride, anger, and regret is this: no school has educated blacks in an integrated world as well as Williston [the all-

black NC school] did in a segregated one" (Peter Applebome, *Dixie Rising* [New York: Times Books, 1996], 212). And he quotes one alumnus who says "I just don't feel like the teachers in the schools today feel as close to those kids as we did in a segregated school" (224).

10. This, of course, is a rather widespread lament of educators today in response to a president's mandate that "no child be left behind." For local educators, the response seems to have been "Fine. But where is the money going to come from to make this possible?"

11. Tom Paxton, "What Did You Learn in School Today?"

Five   In the Lord's House

1. John Shelton Reed, *The Enduring South* (Chapel Hill: University of North Carolina Press, 1971).

2. Billingsley, *Climbing Jacob's Ladder,* 73.

3. C. Eric Lincoln and Lawrence H. Mamiya, *The Black Church in the African American Experience* (Durham, NC: Duke University Press, 1990), 92.

4. Ibid., 93.

5. William McFeely, *Sapelo's People: A Long Walk to Freedom* (Athens: University of Georgia Press, 1994).

6. Jones-Jackson, *When Roots Die.*

7. Georgia Writers Project, *Drums and Shadows: Survival Studies among the Georgia Coastal Negroes* (Athens: University of Georgia Press, 1940).

8. I reference Sunday here because, in America in general and in rural areas in particular (historically black areas included), Sunday is the quintessential Christian day *of* and *for* religion.

9. By way of contrast, think of James Baldwin's description of life as a young man in Harlem, growing up in a storefront church. (See Baldwin, *Another Country* [New York: Dell Publishing, 1985].) At the other extreme, suburban churches offer testimony to "bigger is better." As I was once told, "If you want to significantly raise a church's wealth, build a bigger parking lot."

10. On page 607 in Larry L. Hunt and Matthew O. Hunt, "Race, Region, and Religious Involvement: A Comparative Study of Whites and African Americans," *Social Forces* 80 (2001):605–631.

11. David Hummon, *Commonplaces: Community Ideology and Identity in American Culture* (Albany: State University of New York Press, 1990), 34–35.

12. Peter Berger, *The Sacred Canopy: Elements of a Sociological Theory of Religion* (Garden City, NY: Anchor Books, 1967).

13. Max Weber, *The Protestant Ethic and the Spirit of Capitalism* (New York: Scribner. 1958).

14. Susan Webb, a sociologist in South Carolina, tells me that when she lived in a small town in coastal South Carolina, she had many occasions to witness this same thing with older white and black residents. In the grocery store, clerks sometimes wrote these residents' checks. In the post office, the post mistress read their mail to them.

15. Greene, *Praying for Sheetrock.*

16. Page 55 of Michael C. Thornton, "Indigenous Resources and Strategies of Resistance: Informal Caregiving and Racial Socialization in Black Communities," in McCubbin et al., *Resiliency in African American Families* (49–66).
17. McCubbin et al., 335.
18. McAdoo, *Family Ethnicity*, 22.
19. To reiterate a point made earlier, Helen Black's (1999) article on "spiritual narratives" among older African American women is particularly good on this. It vividly illustrates the ways in which spiritual matters are used to explain and empower. Clorice could easily have found her way into Black's text.
20. This is, in some ways, the penultimate existential point. A person's name was determined by virtue of an experience heavily laden with religious significance. Names, of course, are symbols, in this case with clear religious overtones. And here, with Grace, we find someone who is well aware of its importance in one's own life.
21. For Berger, the "sacred canopy" is clearly a metaphor under which those things most important and most tinged with religious reverence are kept. In a Durkheimian way, this stands in sharp contrast to the more mundane and "profane" world of everyday life. See Emile Durkheim, *The Elementary Forms of the Religious Life* (New York: Free Press, 1915).
22. I had a glimmer into the etiology of the term when I was reading a book written in the 1930s called *Drums and Shadows* (Georgia Writers Project). This was a project during the New Deal in which interviewers were sent out to catalogue the presence of African religious practices, especially those using drums, and also documenting old customs and practices found in religious ceremonies. They actually found one place, very near Yvonne, where the local people had rarely seen white people. This area was remote and part of the barrier islands culture, thus still preserved quite well from more modern influences in the 1930s. Also see Cornelia Bailey's book for more on the long-lasting effects of African-based religious practices in the sea islands. Cornelia Walker Bailey, *God, Dr. Buzzard, and the Bolito Man: A Saltwater Geechee Talks about Life on Sapelo Island, Georgia* (New York: Random House Children's Books, 2001).
23. Lincoln and Mamiya, *The Black Church in the African American Experience,* make a very similar point. "One of the unintended consequences of the civil rights movement and the desegregation of public accommodations is the decreased use of black churches as meeting places for community groups and events" (11).
24. It is hard to determine the accuracy of AC's assessment on this. Although national data indicate that blacks indeed may attend church less than they once did, the same is true for whites. The larger point seems to be: Blacks may feel less need, and, for that matter, may hope that the church will lead them to a "promised land" in the here and now. Although the church (in many forms, from store front to enormous [as in some large urban areas]) is still a bedrock of most black communities, it has increasingly, since the 1960s, been government action, not church activism, that has been instrumental in expanding civil liberties.
25. Or, as he told me another time, "a dipper put in my lo'n [lung]."
26. See Anderson, *Streetwise*.

27. See Carol Stack, *Call to Home*. For a classic older book on the black family more generally, see Herbert Gutman, *The Black Family in Slavery and Freedom* (New York: Pantheon, 1976).
28. Andrew Billingsley, *Climbing Jacob's Ladder*. And as I completed writing the present volume, a new book came to my attention that should help to clarify the role of the black church in contemporary urban life: Omar M. McRoberts, *Streets of Glory: Church and Community in a Black Urban Neighborhood* (Chicago: University of Chicago Press, 2003).
29. Christopher G. Ellison, "Religious Involvement and the Subjective Quality of Family Life among African Americans," 130. In Taylor et al., *Black America* (117–131).
30. Lincoln and Mamiya, *The Black Church in the African American Experience*.
31. Berger and Luckmann, *Social Construction of Reality*.
32. Reed, *The Enduring South*.
33. John Egerton, *Generations*, 15.

Six   Race and Everyday Life

1. The notable exception has been the migration of Hispanics (and Asians, to a lesser degree) into some rural areas, mostly to work in food processing, in particular the processing of swine and poultry. This has also occurred in the Midwest. There, according to the 2000 U.S. Census, for example, Omaha, Nebraska, saw its Hispanic population triple between 1990 and 2000.
2. Langston Hughes, *The Collected Poems of Langston Hughes,* ed. Arnold Rampersad and David Roessel (New York: Alfred A. Knopf, 1994).
3. It is the antithesis of the equal society that sociologists have investigated via "segregation indices." These are measures of how many whites and blacks would have to move within some geographic area to achieve racial balance. The rhetoric used to reflect how dramatic the racial separation may be is captured well by Massey and Denton, who refer to some places as "hyper-segregated." See Douglas S. Massey and Nancy Denton, *American Apartheid: Segregation and the Making of the Underclass* (Cambridge, MA: Harvard University Press, 1993).
4. One need only think of the debates around social and ethnic categories in the 2000 U.S. Census, or around certain elections or Supreme Court appointments or the Trent Lott episode. As this book was completed, the 2003 U.S. Supreme Court decision in the University of Michigan "affirmative action" case is providing still another example.
5. The "big ol' fires" references here are not and should not be interpreted as something overtly racial like a cross burning. Instead, such fires sometimes occur on winter evenings when men (usually men) gather to discuss whatever issues are on their minds. Terrence's comment about this is akin to Freud's comment about paranoia: "sometimes they really are talking about you." Terrence's suggestion, mostly by implication, that they may be discussing race as one issue is no doubt at times correct.
6. Pat Conroy, *The Water Is Wide* (New York: Houghton Mifflin, 1976).

7. Although I did not try to determine precisely what proportion of all land trans-actions involved whites buying and blacks either selling or defaulting, I did speak with the local tax assessor. She told me that all land transactions along the wa-terfront were with white people and, further, that two new, quite large develop-ments along the water were initiated and owned by white developers. This has been true at virtually every island development in the Lowcountry, from Hilton Head to St. Simons. Indeed, the Penn Center's prominence near Beaufort, South Carolina, has been driven in part by its attempt to keep land owned historically by blacks in their families.

8. I interrupted her, because her remark had taken me back nearly forty years to my own youth, in a rural area of Michigan where blacks were a rare sight. And I also recalled going in the military where, like the persons in Alice's descrip-tion, I had the experience of being around black people for the first time. In fact, in the military I had the novel experience of being around a cross-section of the American population, people from all regions, religions, and ethnic groups. As I told her, "Even today, there are states in this country, especially in the Midwest and West, where there just aren't any black people—or at least there are very few of them. So it's easy to imagine some of these people you met who had never seen a black person."

9. Peter Applebome (in *Dixie Rising*), quoting a black woman, makes a similar point: "Black people used to live all together, shacks and nice houses . . . now they're divided . . . drugs have succeeded in doing what slavery and all the white people in the world could not—destroy the black family" (132).

10. Although to what degree it is embraced by the students is open to question. In-deed, the University of Maryland student paper, *The Diamondback*, had an ar-ticle on this very matter (4 December 2002).

11. A news story from central Georgia during the spring of 2003 bears witness to this. The story was about rural high school students who had chosen, on their own, to have separate proms, one for blacks, one for whites. To use a phrase used earlier, "history repeating itself."

Seven   Home Is Where the Heart Is

1. Janet M. Fitchen, *Enduring Spaces, Enduring Places: Change, Identity, and Sur-vival in Rural America*, (Boulder, CO: Westview Press, 1991), 252.

2. Knowing that AC had obtained a television in the late 1950s made me remem-ber my own youth and seeing television for the first time. As AC described this, "It was a great big thing." Younger people have no recollection of those days, of course. The television, I recall, dominated our living room—with a huge cabi-net with a tiny screen, and an antenna on the roof, occasionally needing adjust-ing. Even today, one can date houses and neighborhoods by looking at the roofs to see if there are antennas. As AC describes it (and as his children remember it), their TV did not, initially at least, keep people from visiting; to the contrary, it encouraged them. The truly nuclear, isolated family of late twentieth-century America was foreign to AC's world at that time, since his TV brought the family together.

3. Having a house burn down seemed a common fate in Colonial County. Two of Clorice's daughters had houses burn down, as had her brother-in-law. And these were merely the incidents I knew about without asking explicitly. As in most rural counties, people can build nearly anything they want if they own some land. It is only in the newer developments that restrictions are placed on what is built. It is not unusual to see burned-out houses in any rural county, no matter where located. This is, I believe, easily explained by several factors. First, there is often no oversight by county inspectors; thus one may build nearly anything, and houses built by many property owners may, in ways large and small, be in technical violation of local building codes—*if* (a large *IF*) there are any. Second, and directly related, violating the codes may involve both materials and the use of them; thus flammable materials may be used near sources of electricity or heat, which would enhance the likelihood of fire. Third, and perhaps most important, fireplaces or wood stoves may have been installed improperly (another possible violation of building codes); this would increase significantly the likelihood of sparks or excessive heat starting a fire. Fourth, space heaters are widely used and, if left plugged in and unattended, may overheat. Fifth, in rural areas a fire department is often a long distance away.

4. The growth of cities and subsequently of the suburbs spawned an enormous literature in the social sciences. Indeed, the famous Chicago School of sociology was founded partly in response to that explosive growth of cities associated with the industrial revolution and migration. Much of the literature, from within the social sciences, that focused on these events emphasized such outcomes as the rise of the nuclear family and alienation (from one's job but also from one's neighbors). At the same time, the school of human ecology was born, as was its derivative, community sociology—both being attempts to better understand not only how population dynamics affected where people lived but also the internal processes and outcomes associated with newer, higher-density living arrangements.

5. John Warfield Simpson, *Yearning for the Land: A Search for the Importance of Place* (New York: Alfred A. Knopf, 2002).

6. But the "return" has been decidedly urban, with about 90 percent of return migrants locating in cities or suburbs. The scale has been huge; nearly a million more African Americans migrated to the South in the 1990s than migrated from it. Cromartie (a geographer) and Stack (an anthropologist) were among the first to catalog this return, especially to rural areas. See John Cromartie and Carol Stack, "Reinterpretation of Black Return and Nonreturn Migration to the South, 1975–80," *Geographical Review* 79 (1989):297–310. More recently, see Glenn V. Fuguitt, John A. Fulton, and Calvin L. Beale, *The Shifting Patterns of Black Migration from and into the Nonmetropolitan South*, 1965–95, Rural Development Research Report No. 93 (Washington, DC: Economic Research Service, U.S. Department of Agriculture, 2001).

7. Until the present day, places like New Jersey (which many outsiders mistakenly think of as one huge urban area) employ thousands of seasonal workers, but increasingly, these workers are Hispanic or Asian. They are often recruited from inner cities and bused out to nearby farms to help with the harvest.

8. Dwayne Walls, *The Chickenbone Special* (New York: Harcourt Brace Jovanovich, 1971), 45–46, 23.

9. The role of gardens in rural peoples' lives is not trivial. Indeed, I asked AC one time how much food he and his family actually bought and he had to think about it. This was because seafood and wild game were staples of their diet; his chickens produced eggs and occasionally were themselves the main course; and he still kept a garden which provided considerable produce. However, the younger generation have less and less use for game and gardens and prefer instead to eat often from local fast-food restaurants. For a wonderful book on blacks and gardens, see Richard N. Westmacott, *African American Gardens and Yards in the Rural South* (Knoxville: University of Tennessee Press, 1992).

10. The same occurrence was common in Carol Stack's book, *Call to Home.*

11. Walter Stegner, *Where the Bluebird Sings in the Lemonade Springs* (New York: Random House, 1992).

12. See Charles C. Moskos and John Sibley Butler, *All That You Can Be* (New York, Basic Books, 1993).

13. Harley L. Browning, Sally C. Lopreato, and Dudley L. Poston Jr., "Income and Veteran Status: Variations among Mexican Americans, Blacks, and Anglos," *American Sociological Review* 38 (1973):74–85

14. See Richard Cooney, Mady W. Segal, David R. Segal, and William W. Falk, "Racial Differences in the Impact of Military Service on the Socioeconomic Status of Women Veterans," *Armed Forces and Society* [forthcoming].

15. Richard Cuoto, *Ain't Gonna Let Nobody Turn Me Round: The Pursuit of Racial Justice in the Rural South* (Philadelphia: Temple University Press, 1991).

16. Marita Golden, *Long Distance Life* (New York: Doubleday, 1989).

17. This has certainly been true in my family, and I suspect it is true for millions of others. It is our very success in society's eyes that has taken us so far apart and torn the fabric of what was once our family. In my family, we always joked about my aunt's family in Buffalo—none of her children ever left home longer than to go to college. In my family, only as we got older did we begin to wonder what price we paid for our mobility. Althea's attempt to keep the family intact (with considerable help from other family members) is a reminder of the need for such effort if family connection is truly valued. Absent that, we are left with little that can show love and concern for one another. The occasional picture and short note hardly suffice, nor, I suspect, will e-mail be fully satisfactory.

18. Steven Ruggles, "The Origins of African-American Family Structure," *American Sociological Review* 59 (1) (1994):136–151

19. Chalmers Archer makes a similar point in his autobiography about growing up in Mississippi. As cited by historian Jimmie Franklin, "His family had lived in rural Holmes County, Mississippi, for more than a hundred years; when he returned to the family's old farm, appropriately called 'The Place,' he still had a deep affection for the land he had left behind. Something about the old Archer place—thoughts of family, remembered friendships, memories of special times, change of seasons, and the open spaces kept calling him back" (222). See Jimmie Lewis Franklin, "Black Southerners, Shared Experience, and Place: A Reflec-

tion," in *The South as an American Problem,* ed. Larry J. Griffin and Don H. Doyle (Athens: University of Georgia Press, 1995), 210–233.

Eight The Power of Place

1. Walls, *The Chickenbone Special,* 45–46.
2. McFeely, *Sapelo's People,* 82–83.
3. Bailey, *God, Dr. Buzzard, and the Bolito Man,* 304.
4. Thomas Gieryn, "A Space for Place in Sociology," *Annual Review of Sociology* 26 (2000):482.
5. Tony Hiss, *The Experience of Place* (New York: Alfred A. Knopf, 1990), 22.
6. McFeely, *Sapelo's People,* 93–94.
7. Reed, *The Enduring South,* 313.
8. Stanley B. Greenberg, *Race and State in Capitalist Development* (New Haven, CT: Yale University Press, 1980), 13–14.
9. Daniel, *The Shadow of Slavery.*
10. Hortense Powdermaker, *After Freedom: A Cultural Study in the Deep South* (New York: Russell and Russell, 1936).
11. Max Weber, *The Sociology of Religion* (Boston: Beacon Press, 1963).
12. Walls, *The Chickenbone Special,* 26–27
13. Ibid, p. xix.
14. Charles Joyner, *Down by the Riverside: A South Carolina Slave Community* (Urbana: University of Illinois Press, 1984). Joyner's observation is much like Thomas Gieryn's reference to place as "an unwindable spiral" (Gieryn, "A Space for Place in Sociology," 471): a view of place as something that can only be fully understood in its totality.
15. Elizabeth Bethel, *Promisedland: A Century of Life in a Negro Community* (Philadelphia: Temple University Press, 1981*),* 271.
16. Duneier, *Slim's Table,* 130.
17. There are notable exceptions, but they are definitely few. See, among others, Duncan, *Worlds Apart*; Edin, *Making Ends Meet*; Duneier, *Slim's Table*; Wilson, *The Truly Disadvantaged*; Anderson, *Streetwise.* Although Carol Stack was not trained as a sociologist, no contemporary anthropologist seems to have found greater favor among sociologists than she has. Among her other books, see *All Our Kin, Call to Home,* and her newest book, *Coming of Age at Minimum Wage.*
18. My long indebted thanks to Art Cosby for this story and for many other lessons about the South.
19. Rupert Vance, *Human Geography of the South: A Study of Regional Resources and Human Adequacy* (Chapel Hill: University of North Carolina Press, 1932), 39.
20. Jack Kirby, *Rural Worlds Lost: The American South, 1920–1960* (Baton Rouge: Louisiana State University Press, 1987).
21. See, among other writings about this: Lewis Cecil Gray, *History of Agriculture in the Southern United States to 1860* (Washington, DC: U.S. Department of Agriculture, 1933); Julia Floyd Smith, *Slavery and Rice Culture in Low Country Georgia, 1750–1860* (Knoxville: University of Tennessee Press, 1985); J. William

Harris, *Deep Souths: Delta, Piedmont, and Sea Island Society in the Age of Segregation* (Baltimore, MD: Johns Hopkins University Press, 2001); Eric Foner, *Nothing but Freedom: Emancipation and Its Legacy* (Baton Rouge: Louisiana State University Press, 1983); and Charles Joyner, *Down by the Riverside.*

22. Kirby, *Rural Worlds Lost.*
23. Foner, *Nothing but Freedom,* 55
24. Ibid., 78.
25. Ibid., 108–109.
26. Joyner, *Down by the Riverside,* 129.
27. See Harris, *Deep South*; also see Peggy G. Hargis and Patrick M. Horan, "The 'Low Country Advantage' for African Americans in Georgia, 1880–1930," *Journal of Interdisciplinary History* 28 (1997):27–46.
28. For a very good source on this geographical variance, see Harris, *Deep Souths.*
29. I realize that this is an ethos rooted in American culture—thus the yeoman farmer and Horatio Alger. Here, however, my focus is on how this was internalized and acted upon by rural African Americans.
30. McAdoo, *Family Ethnicity,* 22.
31. Thornton, cited in McCubbin et al., "Resilient Families in an Ethnic and Cultural Context," 345–346.
32. Taylor et al., *Family Life in Black America.*
33. Wilson, *The Truly Disadvantaged*; Anderson, *Streetwise.*
34. Duneier, *Slim's Table,* 128 (cited from Anderson's *Streetwise,* 248).
35. Stack, *Call to Home,* 16–17.
36. Walls, *Chicken Bone Special,* 113–114.
37. Willie Morris, *Yazoo: Integration in a Deep South Town* (New York: Harper Magazine Press, 1971), 11. In other sources, cited throughout this book, it is easy to find statements similar to those attributed to Morris and Walls. How can we explain the attachment that people have to a place that seems to have treated them so badly? Precisely this puzzlement initially drove my curiosity about the black migration experience.
38. It is important that, although AC's family constitutes an "n" of one, it is in many ways remarkably like other families. I have cited literature throughout, especially in footnotes, that illustrates that the themes about family and community I found with AC's family are widely cited elsewhere. Indeed, Peter Egerton's book on "generations" is a wonderful story making this point for a white, Appalachian family.
39. Mills, *The Sociological Imagination.*
40. Ibid., 7.
41. Andrew Hacker, *Two Nations: Black and White, Separate, Hostile, Unequal* (New York: Ballantine Books, 1995).
42. Alex Haley, *Roots* (New York: Doubleday, 1976).
43. Billingsley, *Climbing Jacob's Ladder,* 74–75.
44. Simpson, *Yearning for the Land,* 119–120.
45. McFeely, *Sapelo's People,* 170–171.

Index

Alice (pseud. AC's daughter), 52, 58, 59, 80–85, 98, 134, 135, 137, 159, 161
Althea (pseud. AC's sister), 85, 96, 123–124, 133, 154, 155, 170
Anderson, Elijah, 40, 42, 183

Bailey, Cornelia Walker, 174
Berger, Peter, 18, 104–105, 113, 115, 117, 169, 198, 210n21
Billingsley, Andrew, 101, 116, 206n2
Black Belt (historically black counties), 12–14, 18–19, 191
black community, 54, 81, 91
black politicians, 124–125, 204n19
block houses, 25, 149–150, 168
burials, 109

children "sent home," 79–80
Christian academies/segregation academies, 14, 75, 99
church, 53, 79, 100, 101, 107, 108, 110, 114, 117. *See also* religion
Clorice (pseud. AC's first wife), 44, 52–57, 71–72, 87–88, 98, 110–112, 120–121, 140, 142, 149, 150–152
Coleman, James, 74–76

Colonial County Academy (CCA), 84, 87, 89
Conroy, Pat, 128
crime, 44, 132. *See also* drugs

deer tongue/dog tongue, 160
"dippin gum," 28
divorce, 8, 26, 150, 157
Dorothea (pseud. AC's former sister-in-law), 58, 86, 124, 128, 129, 153–154
drugs, 24, 26, 41–43, 46–47, 49, 67, 205nn 9, 10, 17, 212n9. *See also* crime
Duneier, Mitchell, 40, 42, 46, 109, 178, 183
Durkheim, Emile, 17, 116, 198

Egerton, John, 117, 202n8
equal contact hypothesis, 40, 96
equal opportunity, 75, 100

family: extended, 207n8; "grands" (grandchildren), 169–171, 206nn2, 6; and place, 23; values, 42, 64–66, 68, 71, 79–80, 205–206n1. *See also* father role; marriage; mother role

father role, 41, 44, 53, 54, 56, 75
fishing, 24, 32
"fooling around," 206n3
Franklin, Jimmy, 5

gardens/gardening, 214n9
Golden, Marita, 169
Grace (pseud. AC's daughter), 54–61,
    64–68, 71–72, 80–83, 111–112, 137–
    138, 164–165, 179, 207n10, 210n20
Great Migration, 4, 177, 201n4
Green, Melissa Faye, 5, 6, 8, 108, 151

"hand in the lion's mouth" metaphor,
    43, 198
home, 2, 5, 15–16, 144–171. *See also*
    place
Hummons, David, 104

Interstate 95, 11, 21, 150
islands, 20, 21, 28, 127–128, 210n22

Jones-Jackson, Jacqueline, 102, 202n12
Joyner, Charles, 178, 181, 215n14

Kirby, Jack, 181–182
Kolkowitz, Alex, 47
Ku Klux Klan, 2, 77

land, land ownership, 13–15, 23, 25,
    127–133, 176–177, 212n7
language, Gullah-Geechee, 8–9, 102,
    202n12
Lincoln, C. Eric, 101, 116
Lowcountry, 5, 8, 9, 12, 14, 19, 20, 128,
    180–182, 197, 203n2

marriage, 29, 157
McAdoo, Harriet Piper, 183
McFeely, William, 101, 162, 173–175,
    190
Mead, George Herbert, 168
migration, moving away, out-migration,
    return-migration, 6, 9, 15, 16, 49,
    158, 201, 203, 213

military, 1–2, 26, 44, 50, 166–167,
    205n19
Mills, C. Wright, 3, 185, 188
Mississippi Delta, 5, 12, 13, 19–20, 118,
    180–181
morality/moral standards, 13, 28, 41,
    43, 44, 53, 114–115
mother role, 57

New South, 3, 4

older black men, 27, 40, 41, 42, 46, 48, 91

Penn Center, 128
personal responsibility, 41–44, 58, 151–
    168, 182–183
place, love of place, 35, 39, 40–42, 47,
    55, 57–59, 68, 71, 74, 76, 162, 163,
    172–177, 183–184, 186, 198, 214n19.
    See also home; land, land ownership
plantations, 12, 14, 19, 29, 50, 132, 195
police, 41, 46
politics/political power, 36, 39, 45, 73,
    98. *See also* black politicians
poverty, 11, 13, 14, 18, 67, 166, 173, 177–
    180, 187, 203n5, 205n1
Promised Land, the, 15, 210n24
protest, against school integration, 76,
    77

race and everyday life, 35–40, 41, 79,
    118–143
race and place, 17–19
racial integration/segregation, 2, 36,
    73–74, 77–80, 211n3, 212n8, 216n37
Raper, Arthur, 12
Reed, John Shelton, 10, 101, 175
religion, 87, 100–117, 155, 116, 176, 182,
    192, 209n8, 210nn20–24. *See also*
    church
restaurants and eating, 29, 37, 29, 40,
    53, 60, 67, 186, 192, 194
Rhonda (pseud. AC's daughter), 54, 59,
    60, 64, 68–70, 72, 86–87, 95–96, 98,
    112–114, 135–136, 141, 161–163

Samuel (pseud. AC's son), 43, 84, 85, 96, 133, 138–139, 150, 165–168
schools, 27, 39, 73–88, 98–99, 196, 208nn2–9, 209n10, 212n11; teachers, 91–97; trade schools, 88–91
seafood processing, 34, 61–63
sense of responsibility, 28, 55
"service" work, 48, 50, 61, 63
Simpson, John Warfield, 153, 161, 188
single parents, 51, 58, 66–69
social fact, 18, 198
sociological imagination, 3, 140, 185, 188
South, the, 103, 108, 113, 117, 118, 201n5
Stack, Carol, 5–7, 16, 48, 183, 184, 192, 215n17

Taulbert, Clifton, 15
television, 59, 67, 68, 103, 148, 168, 212n2
Terrence (pseud. AC's brother), 88–90, 97, 124–127, 137, 157–158
Thornton, Michael, 109, 183

timber cutting, pulpwood, 28–32, 52, 93
trailers, 23, 32, 34, 67
turpentine industry, 28–30
"twice as good," 36, 141

U.S. 17, 20, 21, 23, 27

Vance, Rupert, 180

Walls, Dwayne, 158, 172–173, 178, 184
Weber, Max, 177
welfare, welfare queens, 45, 46, 49, 66–68, 207n9
"whole freedom," 113–115
Wilson, William Julius, 49, 183
women, 8, 22, 28, 33, 34, 44, 51–72, 206n4, 206–207n7, 207–208n12
work, 27–39, 45–51, 53, 56, 61–64

young black men, 40–44, 46, 49, 55, 183, 205n17
young black females, 44–46, 68
younger workers, 39, 40, 42

About the Author

William W. Falk is a professor and chair of the Department of Sociology at the University of Maryland. He is coauthor of *High Tech, Low Tech, No Tech: Recent Industrial and Occupational Change in the South,* coeditor of *Forgotten Places: Uneven Development in Rural America,* and coeditor of *Communities of Work: Rural Restructuring in Local and Global Contexts.* In 2001, he received the Distinguished Rural Sociologist Award from the Rural Sociology Society. His current research focuses on black return migration to the South and on the continuing social changes in the Lowcountry.